Irwin Shaw

Twayne's United States Authors Series

Warren French, Editor
Indiana University, Indianapolis

TUSAS 443

IRWIN SHAW
(1913-)
Photograph reprinted by permission of Irwin Shaw.

Irwin Shaw

By James R. Giles

Northern Illinois University

Twayne Publishers • Boston

Irwin Shaw

James R. Giles

Published by Twayne Publishers
A Division of G. K. Hall & Company
70 Lincoln Street
Boston, Massachusetts 02111

Book Production by Marne B. Sultz
Book Design by Barbara Anderson

Printed on permanent/durable acid-free paper and bound in the United States of America.

Library of Congress Cataloging in Publication Data

Giles, James Richard, 1937-
Irwin Shaw.

(Twayne's United States authors series; TUSAS 443)
Bibliography: p. 188
Includes index.
1. Shaw, Irwin, 1913- —Criticism and interpretation. I. Title. II. Series.
PS3537.H384Z67 1983 818'.5209 82-20009
ISBN 0-8057-7382-7

To Eva Giles,
To Knofel and Georgia Hancock,
And to the Memory of Roger Giles,
Gentle people

Contents

About the Author

James R. Giles, a graduate of Texas Christian University and the University of Texas, is a member of the Department of English at Northern Illinois University. His main scholarly interests are American literary realism and naturalism and black American literature. He has published critical essays on Frank Norris, Jack London, Richard Wright, Zora Neale Hurston, John Rechy, James Baldwin, Willard Motley, William Melvin Kelley, Ernest J. Gaines, and Joyce Carol Oates in such journals as *Western American Literature, Phylon, Negro* (now *Black*)*American Literature Forum, Studies in Black Literature, Minority Voices, Chicago Review, College English, Forum, Southern Humanities Review, Arizona Quarterly, Canadian Literature,* and the *Dalhousie Review*. He is also the author of the Twayne United States Authors series volumes *Claude McKay* and *James Jones*. In 1973 and 1977, Giles presented papers at the Joyce Carol Oates seminars at the Modern Language Association conventions.

He views Irwin Shaw as a major American practitioner of literary realism and believes that Shaw's work in the genres of the short story, the novel, and drama has been seriously underrated by academic critics.

A native of Texas, Giles has published essays about his experience of Texas in the *Texas Observer*, an Austin-based journal of national reputation. He has published fiction in *Western Review, Story Quarterly, Quartet, Descant, Seems, Confrontation*, and other journals; and two of his stories have been anthologized in the Dell paperback collections *Innovative Fiction* and *No Signs from Heaven*.

He plans further work on contemporary American realistic writers such as Shaw, Oates, Norman Mailer, William Styron, and James Jones. He also hopes to publish more short stories.

Preface

Irwin Shaw has been a presence in American literature for over forty-five years. During this long career, he has been critically acclaimed as a major force in a revolutionary new American theater, as a master of the modern short story, and as the author of *The Young Lions*, one of the major American World War II novels. He has also been critically condemned—initially as a polemical writer who sacrificed art to politics and, more recently, as a writer of superficial best-selling fiction. Obviously, there is no critical consensus concerning the value of his work. Moreover, academic critics have increasingly tended to ignore his work entirely.

Yet it seems also obvious that a writer who helped revolutionize the American theater in the 1930s and has produced one of the most important American World War II novels, as well as a significant body of brilliant short fiction, should not be ignored. Thus, a central aim of this study is a careful examination of the various stages of Irwin Shaw's long and diverse career. I hope it will then begin to answer the most persistent critical objection to his work—the charge that it is brittle, at once sophisticated and superficial.

After an introductory chapter focusing on Shaw's life and aesthetic credo, I have devoted individual chapters to analysis of his plays, his short stories, and *The Young Lions*. Two subsequent chapters examine the nine novels he has published since *The Young Lions*. This organization is roughly chronological; Shaw did not publish *The Young Lions* until 1948, more than a decade after he had first achieved recognition as a dramatist and then as a writer of short stories. While he has never stopped writing short fiction, it seemed useful to break with strict chronology in order to devote an entire chapter to the stories since they constitute the most important part of his literary canon. A brief concluding chapter offers some speculations concerning Shaw's total achievement and his place in American literary history.

Periodically throughout this study, the reader will find references to "the 1980 Shaw interview." In July of 1980, Irwin Shaw allowed me a week of daily interviews, during which he talked freely about the central vision underlying all his writing, the concepts of realism and romanticism as they pertain to his work, the major influences—literary and nonliterary—upon his career, and the curiously mixed critical reaction to his work. The interviews took place at Shaw's home in Southampton, New York.

This experience provided me with several examples of the generosity of Irwin Shaw, two of which I must mention here. During this same week, he was working diligently upon a new novel, the first draft of which he had determined to finish before leaving for Switzerland in less than a month. Despite this time pressure, he consistently devoted at least two hours a day to our interview. And it was a devotion, for Irwin Shaw is the most willing and entertaining of conversationalists. Later, he sent me the original Prologue to *The Young Lions*, which he discarded in the final version of the novel and has never subsequently published. This Prologue sheds invaluable light upon the ways in which the novel evolved from Shaw's original conception of it.

These interviews have been the most valuable secondary source for the preparation of my study. I am fully aware of the potential dangers of letting a writer be a primary judge of his own work, but when the writer is as open and honest—and as intelligent—as Irwin Shaw, such a concern becomes merely academic.

James R. Giles

Northern Illinois University

Acknowledgments

I wish to thank several people who made this book possible. Professor James M. Mellard and Dean James Norris of Northern Illinois University helped me obtain financial support for the project. Karen Hipps valiantly typed the manuscript from my handwriting. The secretarial staff of the Northern Illinois University English department (Karen DeVault, Jane Kosek, Sheri Miller, and Pat Francis) gave generously of their time and assistance. Gloria Jones helped in scheduling my interviews with Irwin Shaw and, as she had done once before, in making me feel at home on Long Island. Two excellent editors, Warren French and Wanda Giles, made this book better than it otherwise would have been. In many ways, Wanda Giles contributed generously to *Irwin Shaw*. Finally, I must express appreciation to Irwin. He provided me with much time, insight, and hospitality during the summer of 1980 and asked for nothing in return. That is, I am told, his way.

Expressions of my gratitude are also due to *Commentary* and to Leslie A. Fiedler for granting permission to quote from "Irwin Shaw: Adultery, the Last Politics," which appeared in the July 1956 issue of *Commentary*.

To Viking Penguin Inc. for granting permission to quote from "Interview with Irwin Shaw" in *Writers at Work: The Paris Review Interviews*, Fifth Series, edited by George Plimpton. Copyright © 1981 by The Paris Review, Inc.

To Crown Publishers, Inc., for granting permission to quote from *Twenty Best Plays of the Modern American Theatre 1930-1939,* edited by John Gassner.

To Random House, Inc., for granting permission to quote from

IRWIN SHAW

The Young Lions, The Gentle People, The Assassin, and *Two Weeks in Another Town.*

To Delacorte Press for granting permission to quote from *Rich Man, Poor Man* © 1970; *Voices of a Summer Day* © 1965; *Evening in Byzantium* © 1973; and *Short Stories: Five Decades* © 1937, 1938, 1939, 1940, 1941, 1942, 1943, 1944, 1945, 1946, 1947, 1949, 1950, 1952, 1953, 1954, 1955, 1956, 1957, 1958, 1961, 1963, 1964, 1967, 1968, 1969, 1971, 1973, 1977, 1978.

Chronology

1913 Born 27 February in New York City, son of William and Rose (Tompkins) Shaw.

1934 Graduates from Brooklyn College with B.A. degree. Ends career as Brooklyn College varsity quarterback.

1936 Play, *Bury the Dead*, produced in New York.

1939 Marries Marian Edwards, 13 October.
Play, *The Gentle People*, produced in New York.
Sailor off the Bremen (short-story collection).

1942–1945 In United States Army. Serves in North Africa and Europe. Present at liberation of Paris. Attains rank of warrant officer.

1942 *Welcome to the City* (short-story collection).

1944 Play, *Sons and Soldiers*, produced in New York. O. Henry Memorial Award First Prize for short story, "Walking Wounded."

1945 Play, *The Assassin*, produced in New York. Book version, with different third act and with preface denouncing cowardice and mediocrity of the Broadway theater, published following year. O. Henry Memorial Award Second Prize for short story, "Gunners' Passage."

1946 *Act of Faith and Other Stories* (short-story collection).

1948 *The Young Lions* (novel).

1950 *Mixed Company* (short-story collection). *Report from Israel* (nonfiction book with camera studies by Robert Capa). Son, Adam, born.

1951 Moves to Paris, beginning his expatriate years. *The Troubled Air* (novel).

1956 *Lucy Crown* (novel).

1957 *Tip on a Dead Jockey* (short-story collection).

1958 Film version of *The Young Lions*.

1960 *Two Weeks in Another Town* (novel).

1963 Play, *Children from Their Games*, produced in New York. Film, *In the French Style*, written and produced by Shaw; based on two stories, "A Year to Learn the Language" and "In the French Style."

1964 *In the Company of Dolphins* (travel book).

1965 *Voices of a Summer Day* (novel). *Love on a Dark Street* (short-story collection).

1970 *Rich Man, Poor Man* (novel).

1973 *Evening in Byzantium* (novel). *God Was Here But He Left Early* (short-story collection).

1975 *Nightwork* (novel).

1976 Leaves Paris after stay of twenty-five years. Begins dual residence on Long Island and in Klosters, Switzerland.

1976–1977 *Paris! Paris!* (memoir with Ronald Searle).

1977 *Beggerman, Thief* (novel).

1979 *The Top of the Hill* (novel).

1981 *Bread Upon the Waters* (novel).

1982 *Acceptable Losses* (novel).

Chapter One
A Romantic Realist

Today, Irwin Shaw commands a wide popularity with the American reading public. This mass acceptance is due in no small part to his two novels about the Jordache family, *Rich Man, Poor Man* (1970) and *Beggarman, Thief* (1977), as well as to the ABC television dramatizations of them. It should be pointed out, however, that Shaw had been a generally successful novelist for over twenty years before the appearance of *Rich Man, Poor Man*. In fact, his current popularity has resulted in several of his earlier novels, previously out of print, being reissued. Thus, while never really dropping out of sight, he has benefitted from a unique kind of rediscovery; as he told this writer: "I'm sixty-seven years old now, and the kids are reading me. And they feel they found a new writer. Because they haven't read my books yet."[1]

Shaw is understandably quite pleased about this rediscovery; and, in the 1980 interview, as well as in a 1979 interview in the *Paris Review*, he argues convincingly that it is primarily the result of "luck" and in no way represents a lowering of his artistic standards. His rediscovery has resulted, nevertheless, in some misconceptions and oversimplifications concerning his total career. It is important to remember that Irwin Shaw has been a professional writer for more than forty-five years. During that time, he has lived and supported families exclusively by his writing. Moreover, he did not turn to the novel until 1948 and, in his own words, was known initially as "a kind of cult figure."[2] A brief review of Shaw's life details his career.

Life and Career

Irwin Shaw was born in 1913 in New York City and attended public schools in that city. He entered Brooklyn College, but was expelled in his freshman year "for failure in calculus." Determined to complete his education, Shaw worked at a fascinating variety of odd jobs in New York City until he had earned enough money to return to college—he was employed in a cosmetics factory, an installment furniture house, and a department store. He graduated from Brooklyn College in 1934 with a B.A. and with recognition as the quarterback for the football team; he played in the style of that time, primarily as a running back and blocker.[3]

Since childhood, Shaw had been determined to become a writer, but he grew up in an extremely close family which he felt obligated to support. Thus, he could not retreat to Greenwich Village or to Europe as did so many other American writers of the time. Briefly, he played semiprofessional football, but he soon turned to writing radio serials, primarily "Dick Tracy" and "The Gumps." Shaw looks back at these early years of struggle with some amusement and no little pride: "Even when I was writing the junk, I knew it was junk; but I did it the best way I could. . . . and I make no excuses for eating. Or feeding a family. Or fighting . . . for the freedom to write all these short stories, all these plays, and all these novels."[4]

He was, between 1930s radio scripts, already doing some writing which was anything but junk. "Main Currents of American Thought," a short story which Shaw has described as being "very autobiographical indeed,"[5] describes the desperate struggle of a young writer to find time to work on his play. Between scripts for "Dick Tracy" and "The Gumps," Shaw was, in fact, working on a play, a one-act antiwar fantasy called *Bury the Dead*. In 1936, the leftist-oriented New Theatre League sponsored a contest for new playwrights. Shaw did not complete *Bury the Dead* in time for the contest. Nevertheless, he took it to the League offices, where it was received enthusiastically and given two off-Broadway performances. Several critics saw these performances and were at least as enthusiastic about the play as the New Theatre League had been. Consequently, a commercial Broadway producer, Alex Yokel, moved the play to Times Square, where it became "an immediate sensation."[6]

For the critics, one of the most sensational aspects of *Bury the Dead* was that its author was a previously unknown twenty-three-year-old. Irwin Shaw was no longer unknown. The *Literary Digest* described him as "a new magician in the contemporary theater";[7] and even *Time*'s reviewer, while obviously bothered by the political implications of the play, wrote that "second sight of *Bury the Dead* confirmed critical opinion that Irwin Shaw is a comer."[8] Although *Bury the Dead* brought him critical recognition and his first taste of fame as a "cult figure" in the new radical theater, it did not make Shaw a great deal of money. But a more profitable avenue than radio serials, writing for Hollywood, was opened for him.

Shaw never regarded writing filmscripts as a major outlet for his art even though he enjoys "the movie form":

> I didn't like writing for those studios.... If it weren't such big business, I would write more.... The one time I enjoyed writing for movies, really ... was when I produced the picture myself. It came from two stories of my own, so it was my own material. (*In the French Style*, 1962)

Still, he had no choice during much of his career but to turn occasionally to Hollywood as a means of economic survival.[9] The filmscripts may have delayed the serious work, but they did not prevent it. In 1939, the Group Theatre produced Shaw's three-act "Brooklyn Fable," *The Gentle People*. The play was only "a modest success," but it solidified Shaw's reputation as a leading light in the new radical theater; and it presents the vision underlying much of his work as powerfully as anything Shaw has ever written. In 1980 Shaw described his plans for the play's production:

> I wanted to have a curtain designed, before the play, with a big painting of the Brooklyn Bridge on it, the river; and I wanted to write across it "Once upon a Time" ... and in the program note and as a foreword to the book, I'd say this is a fairy tale in which the meek and humble emerge victorious....
>
> And I said the author does not pretend this happens in real life.... It's a fairy tale with a moral. The moral is that if somebody uses violence against you, finally you have to use violence in return.[10]

Shaw's concept of "the gentle people" is crucial not only to his plays but to much of his fiction as well. It is, essentially, a concept of men and women usually, but not always, of the lower economic classes who simply want to live their lives without external interference. When threatened by the brutality and chaos of the twentieth century, they realize reluctantly the necessity of acting to save themselves.

Shaw's position in the theater became increasingly complex. Despite the critical acclaim for *Bury the Dead* and, to a lesser degree, for *The Gentle People* and a subsequent play, *The Assassin*, his plays did not succeed commercially. Finally, after the early closing of *The Assassin*, he published an angry denunciation of the theater and came close to abandoning drama.

Before graduating from college, Shaw had begun working in another literary genre, which he has never abandoned and in which his greatest achievement lies. While they disagree about other aspects of his career, most critics concede that Irwin Shaw is a master of the modern short story. Several of his stories rank with the most distinguished American short fiction—"The Girls in Their Summer Dresses," "The Eighty-Yard Run," "Main Currents of American Thought," "Second Mortgage," "Gunners' Passage," "Act of Faith," "Then We Were Three," and "Where All Things Wise and Fair Descend," among others. While Shaw's short fiction has appeared throughout his career, several of the best of these stories were published early. In the *Paris Review* interview, Shaw recounts having written "The Girls in Their Summer Dresses" and "Sailor off the Bremen" in one week when he was twenty-five years old.[11]

A somewhat amusing aspect of Shaw's early career was that, while recognized in the theater as a revolutionary young playwright (his name was often linked with that of Clifford Odets), he published many of his early stories in the *New Yorker*, certainly an establishment journal. There was no hypocrisy, however. As will be discussed in Chapter 2, the view of Shaw as a *politically* revolutionary playwright was always an oversimplification. Moreover, the *New Yorker*, in the late 1930s, was run by a group of editors receptive to Shaw's work. In the *Paris Review* interview Shaw remembers Harold Ross with special gratitude and affection:

He could learn to change, which is why the *New Yorker* is still going strong after its dilletantish beginnings. When you think its first cover was

> the fop with the monocle looking at a butterfly, and they wound up publishing *In Cold Blood* by Truman Capote and *Hiroshima* by John Hersey, you can see the ability to grow that made Ross and made the magazine.

He and the interviewers agree that the *New Yorker*'s decision to publish Shaw's "Sailor off the Bremen," perhaps the most overly angry and violent story he has written, had much to do with the beginning of the magazine's movement toward artistic maturity.[12]

Finally, the stories Shaw published in these early years did not depart drastically from the vision underlying *The Gentle People*. They focus primarily on inherently decent individuals, forced by either external or internal circumstances to confront the reality of their lives and the necessity of taking a stand to save their personal integrity. As in the case of Christian Darling in "The Eighty-Yard Run," they sometimes lack the requisite strength for such a stand; but they nearly always come to realize that it is necessary for their salvation.

Early on, Shaw recognized the threat posed to the United States and to the world by the rise of European fascism. He admired Franklin D. Roosevelt's efforts to awaken the American people to the danger of Hitler and Mussolini before a world war became inevitable, and he contributed money to the Loyalists during the Spanish Civil War. Still, when the United States did enter the war, Shaw was faced with more than one difficult choice. He did not have to enlist in the army at all, since his connections with Hollywood could have kept him out; he was eligible for classification as a worker essential to the war effort. This was never really an option for Shaw, however. In fact, only family responsibilities kept him from enlisting as early as he would have preferred.[13]

He did enlist some six months later, in June 1942, and served until his discharge in October 1945. He was assigned to a camera crew; and while he never did any actual fighting, he was quite often under fire. He arrived at Normandy two weeks after the Allied invasion and helped photograph battles for the liberation of towns throughout France. In the 1980 interview, Shaw remembered one incident quite graphically: "A bullet went between me, right behind my neck, and under the chin of the guy sitting in the jeep behind me."[14] In addition, he was present at the liberation of Paris and recounts in *Paris! Paris!* photographing a battle over the Chamber of Deputies from the top of the Comédie Française.

Three years after his discharge from the army, he published his panoramic World War II novel, *The Young Lions*. Since Shaw had been a prominent figure in both the theater and the short story for more than a decade, *The Young Lions* was a much-anticipated novel. Although attacked by John W. Aldridge and a few other critics, it was generally well received. Perhaps more than any other American World War II novel, it attempted a sweeping overview of the major historical incidents associated with the war. Shaw attempted to unify this panoramic sweep through a comprehensive pattern of allegory; while the novel has structural flaws, it stands as one of the most important American World War II novels.

Shaw's second novel, *The Troubled Air* (1951), resulted from his concern over the rise of McCarthyism and especially over the right-wing hysteria that threatened the radio industry. Shaw was himself a victim of industry blacklisting; in *Paris! Paris!* he describes himself as having been "only glancingly... bruised" by McCarthyism.[15] In the 1980 interview, Shaw described with wry amusement how he got off the blacklist:

> David Selznick, the producer, was asked to produce a [television] show—the seventy-fifth anniversary of the invention of the electric light, a great big spectacular.... And President Eisenhower gave the opening address in it.... And Selznick wanted to do... "The Girls in Their Summer Dresses." The powers that be said, "You can't have Shaw; he's blacklisted." And... he said, "If he's a Communist, then I'm a Communist too.... If I can't have this story, get somebody else to do the program." In ten minutes, I was no longer blacklisted.[16]

The fact that Shaw was ever blacklisted is indicative of the insanity of that period. He had never belonged to the Communist party; in fact, *The Troubled Air* is overtly anti-Communist. A liberal humanitarian, he had believed in Franklin D. Roosevelt, written about the intrinsic strength of the common people of America, and had contributed money to fight Franco in Spain. Such was the extent of his leftist activities.

Yet even though Shaw had been "only glancingly bruised" by McCarthyism, he began in 1951 a twenty-five-year residence in Europe. His exile began by "accident" and was never intended as a repudiation of his native country.[17] Inevitably, his writing was affected by living abroad; such exotic settings as Cannes, Paris, and Rome increasingly dominate his post-1951 novels and stories. Several critics, most notably John W. Aldridge, have charged that the change in his fiction was a disastrous one. The fact that Shaw became an international celebrity during his stay in Europe has also been attacked by Aldridge and similar critics. But the underlying morality in the fiction Shaw has written since 1951 has not changed as drastically as Aldridge and others claim. He is still concerned with the American struggling to be faithful to an inner strength and decency.

In what Shaw himself referred to as "high literary circles,"[18] his reputation is a source of considerable controversy. Since much of this controversy seems to arise from the fact that his literary code and goals have never been fully understood, it might be of use to examine more closely the basic tenets of Shaw's artistic credo.

Reputation and Credo

Beyond the fact that he is a master of the craft of short fiction, critics in "high literary circles" agree about very little concerning Shaw's work. The most serious critical charge against Shaw is that he has been content to be a merely superficial observer of national and international society. Two critics, John W. Aldridge and Leslie A. Fiedler, have been most influential in establishing this negative view of Shaw. In a 1956 essay, Fiedler labeled Shaw's work as "half-art" and, in a highly personal fashion, attacked the sincerity of his aesthetics. Describing his own excitement upon seeing *Bury the Dead*, Fiedler charges that Shaw subsequently chose to write in the name of whatever liberal cause was fashionable: "to be just right always—not a Communist a month past the time when being a Communist seems (to the most enlightened) a creditable excuse.... able to read the right books in the morning but play a good game of tennis in the afternoon."[19]

In fact, Shaw was never a Communist. Fiedler's denunciation reads as a highly personal expression of disappointment in Shaw for not being the writer Fiedler once mistakenly believed him to be. Nevertheless, his dismissal of Shaw's work as a superficial "half-art," especially since the same view had already been expressed in less personal language by Aldridge, became widely accepted in academic critical circles, which increasingly tended to ignore his work.

Still, the absence of any critical consensus concerning Shaw's work can be easily shown. Especially when one remembers that Fiedler's charge is a lack of sincerity, it is fascinating to read Lionel Trilling's 1951 review of *The Troubled Air*. Trilling felt that Shaw's second novel failed for various reasons, but added: "I am inclined to believe that nothing Mr. Shaw might write could be wholly lacking in interest of one kind or another. For one thing, he always *does* observe and always *does* feel, and even when he is facile in observation and sentiment, he is not insincere."[20] It would be difficult to name anyone who personified the highest literary circles more completely than Lionel Trilling.

William Peden, in reviewing Shaw's 1950 collection of stories entitled *Mixed Company*, wrote that "Mr. Shaw is probably the most artistic and articulate exponent of the socially-conscious short story writing today" and concluded his review by comparing Shaw to Charles Dickens in their ability to create "a crowded gallery of memorable people" and to handle a wide variety of scenes "superbly."[21]

In both the 1980 interview with this writer and the 1979 *Paris Review* interview, Shaw discussed the charge of lack of sincerity or serious intent in his writing. He believes that his present popularity with the reading public is a crucial factor in the continuing attack, but he rejects the assumption that public acceptance implies "venality and deliberate debasement of artistic standards."[22] In addition, Shaw asserts that Americans do not understand, as Europeans do, that an artist's career will rarely be a steadily progressing upward movement; it will instead almost inevitably include moments when the artist simply fails to fully realize personal aesthetic intentions:

[The failure to achieve one's "highest standard"] is the failure of every artist.... You look at one Cézanne that he did one week and one that he did the next week, and they may be at the opposite ends of the spectrum. One is good, and one is not so good. But the intention when he started was always the same: to do as well as he could.[23]

The argument over Shaw's sincerity of intent would seem a pointless one if the Fiedler-Aldridge attack were not taken as seriously as it is. Thus, it is significant that, of the critics just discussed, Trilling alone demonstrates a grasp of Shaw's basic aesthetic principles. Trilling observes that, by becoming the spokesman for "the gentle people," Shaw has secured "at least the historical or sociological or cultural interest of whatever he writes":

To these people as his audience and by means of these people as his characters he has tried to represent the social and political activities of our time, setting forth in terms of the private life what economic depression, commercial corruption, fascism, xenophobia, and war really mean, and to suggest the right responses of feeling and action to these grim commonplaces of danger.[24]

As the beginning of an analysis of Shaw's total aesthetic, this evaluation is extremely perceptive. In the 1980 interview, Shaw described himself as a "romantic realist" and then explained this self-definition, which grows out of two fundamental perceptions—one pessimistic and one optimistic.

He asserted that "accidents... are a major cause in... my books" because "that's actually my philosophy of life. Our lives are guided by accident." Such a view inevitably leads to a belief that the world is "chaos" and that

if you organize chaos, you organize as much as you can to show that it's chaos. It's the way *I* do it. To pretend that it's not chaotic is a lie.

Accidents, physical and moral, increasingly become the structural principle in Shaw's post-World War II fiction. Whereas the characters in an early story like "Second Mortgage" are threatened primarily by awesome economic forces, Jack Andrus in *Two Weeks in Another Town* is the victim of internal and external chaos. One cannot help but remember Shaw's account of the German sniper's bullet passing just behind his neck.

The hopeful side of Shaw's aesthetic is his faith in the inherent decency of humanity, and especially of Americans. He believes that our frontier legacy and our democratic institutions have produced a human being capable of resisting the chaos of the universe. He asserted in 1980 that while in many ways he admires books and films like *Saturday Night and Sunday Morning* and *The Last Picture Show*, he resents one thing about them: "[they] never show anybody rising from that class . . . above the level of dumb brutality and resignation. The truth is that the men who wrote them . . . rose right above it." Thus, he admires the American democratic system: "while there are many things in the system that I've denounced, I haven't come across a better system. And people do get a chance to rise in it, and people can be decent here." Thus, while the characters of "Second Mortgage" are poor and Jack Andrus is not, they are decent Americans struggling to maintain their inherent dignity. Shaw effectively summarized both the negative and the positive aspects of this aesthetic: "Believe in man, and take the accidents as they come."[25]

Shaw's faith in the individual, especially the American, can be described as romantic; his vision of the world as a chaotic, accident-ridden place is decidedly pessimistic. In the 1980 interview, Shaw also agreed with the description of him as a "moral," but not a "didactic," writer: "indirectly," he said, his works present a vision of his "opinion of how things should be." Fundamentally, this moral vision is what Trilling touched on: Shaw has spoken for and to the decent "gentle people," rich, middle-class, and poor, about the necessity of struggling to maintain individual integrity in the face of past mistakes and accidents, as well as awesome external forces. His vision is of a steadily increasing difficulty in the struggle to maintain personal integrity as the world becomes more chaotic—but of the absolute moral necessity of making such a struggle.

Shaw believes that, both as an artist and as a man, he has himself accepted the difficult moral challenges he has prescribed for "the gentle people":

> I believe I've led a moral life. I haven't hurt anybody much, not purposely; and I should be rewarded in heaven for the way I've lived. But I don't think I [will be]. Because I don't believe, I don't think there's a heaven.[26]

As he has said, the reward Irwin Shaw really hopes for is lasting life on the library shelves. He can be confident about having achieved that form of immortality.

Chapter Two

The Plays: Fantasy and Protest

In his 1980 interview, Shaw commented on the irony, considering his present status as a best-selling novelist, that he first achieved recognition as a "cult figure" and, moreover, as a theatrical one. He discussed further ironies in his career as a dramatist. By 1945 he had had seven plays produced in New York; and only the first, *Bury the Dead* (1936), had received widespread critical acclaim, and only *The Gentle People* (1939) had been even a "modest" commercial success.[1] When his seventh play, *The Assassin* (1945), closed after ten days, he introduced the published play with a stinging attack on the cowardice of the New York theater and the power of its three most influential critics. Not surprisingly, Shaw's attack inspired responses, and a controversy was underway. In part because of this episode, Shaw has increasingly since 1945 turned away from drama toward the novel as his preferred genre.

Shaw now seems to view himself as a failed playwright, a feeling not without pain, especially when one considers the deep love of the theater that originated in his childhood. In listing his collected works, he now includes only five plays: *Bury the Dead, The Gentle People, The Assassin, Sons and Soldiers* (1943), and *Children from Their Games* (1963). When asked if he had abandoned the theater, he answered, after some hesitation, that it was more accurately a case of the theater abandoning him.[2] The irony of Shaw's theatrical career is intensified when one reads the initial, largely rhapsodic, reviews of *Bury the Dead*, several of which hailed the playwright as a vital new force with the potential to revolutionize American drama.

It would be a serious mistake simply to dismiss Shaw's plays. Two of them, *Bury the Dead* and *The Gentle People*, convey unmistakable force and originality in printed form. *The Assassin* reads like anything but a bad play; its power makes one take seriously Shaw's charge that the state of the New York theater contributed to its Broadway failure. *Sons and Soldiers* and *Children from Their Games* are undeniably flawed plays, but they do have moments of real conviction. Moreover, Shaw is an innovative, experimental playwright. *Bury the Dead, The Gentle People*, and *Sons and Soldiers* utilize fantasy in striking ways; and the form of *Children from Their Games* is that of a French farce used to make a serious point. Only in *The Assassin* does Shaw maintain the formal realism which largely dominates his novels and short stories.

Perhaps nothing Shaw has written is more crucial to an understanding of the central vision of all his work than *The Gentle People*. Finally, as the following detailed discussion of his three most important plays shows, he has a place in the history of the American theater as one of the young men who introduced a uniquely lyrical social protest into American drama in the 1930s.

Bury the Dead

In 1936 Irwin Shaw was an unknown twenty-three-year-old aspiring writer who had just sold a one-act play, *Bury the Dead*, to *New Theatre* magazine. Two benefit performances of the play were given, attracting the attention of Alex Yokel, a commercial producer, who decided to stage it. The results were electrifying. The *Literary Digest* began its review this way:

> For fifteen years the New York theater has not lacked for plays about and mostly against—war. . . .
>
> None of these, seen in retrospect, weighed to the last ounce of its propagandist value, compares with a play little more than one act long, the work of a twenty-three-year-old Brooklyn boy. The play is "Bury the Dead."[3]

Gilbert Gabriel in the *New York American*, Robert Garland in the *New York World-Telegram*, and John Mason Brown in the *New York Post* were equally impressed. *Theatre Arts* reported that

"Irwin Shaw, catapulted into the forefront of young playwrights by this one-act tragedy—his first produced play—has written . . . a shrewd theatre piece and fiery protest against war. . . . "[4] While the bulk of his review is more reserved, Stark Young, writing for the *New Republic*, largely admired *Bury the Dead* and perceptively analyzed the source of its originality:

> "Bury the Dead" . . . presents the finest image that has appeared in our theater this year. A great theater image is when there is discovered something seen and done in which the central idea is completely expressed, and is revealed without effort, as if creation had fully taken place already and were all exhibited. Not often in drama anywhere do we find so powerful an image as dominates the whole of "Bury the Dead." A myth is created, a veritable fable is established.[5]

Joseph Wood Krutch in the *Nation* had serious reservations about much of the writing in the play, but still praised its "central conceit."[6] Even *Time* magazine, which one would not expect to appreciate Shaw's politics, hailed him as "a comer."[7]

Perhaps the most lasting tribute to *Bury the Dead* came from John Gassner, who included it in his collection *20 Best Plays of the Modern American Theatre, 1930–1939*. Gassner's introduction to this volume is an important discussion of Shaw's place in the history of the American theater. Discussing the Group Theatre, Gassner writes that it was formed by "a group of actors and young directors" who "became inspired with the ideal of a collective theatre that would perfect ensemble playing and would give itself to the badly shattered world beyond the footlights." The Group's success was assured, he writes, when Clifford Odets emerged from its ranks; "then . . . the Group gave another new writer, Irwin Shaw, his first Broadway success with *The Gentle People*."[8]

About the appearance of *Bury the Dead,* Gassner comments: "thus another powerful playwright was added to the lists."[9] Throughout his introduction, Gassner links Shaw with Odets and the other young politically radical playwrights of the 1930s: "Indisputably these younger men were firebrands, and their work suffered from violence and one-sidedness. But out of their fire (and smoke) sometimes comes theatrical excitement."[10]

As mentioned, *Bury the Dead* was one of the most acclaimed such excitements. In it, Shaw takes an earlier play, Hans Chlumberg's *Miracle at Verdun,* and transforms it into his own unique vision. As Stark Young saw, the play is a fable, at once simple and shocking. Six American soldiers, killed in "the second year of the war that is to begin tomorrow night"[11] rise up and refuse to be buried. The action of the play consists of the desperate attempts of the military to get the men to lie down peacefully and accept burial. Shaw also utilizes a form of montage to illustrate the effects of the rebellion of the dead on American society.

One of the play's most impressive aspects is its ability to walk a linguistic tightrope of powerful, macabre satire without falling into excess. Shaw's opening line points up the challenge he set himself; a grave detail comes to bury the men, one member of the detail opening the play abruptly and brutally: "'Say, Sergeant, they stink.... Let's bury them in a hurry ...'"(740). For the rest of the play, Shaw never lets the audience forget the stench of the corpses. He further gets a considerable amount of grim satiric comedy out of the dead soldiers' refusal to be buried. The company captain complains at one point: "I was expectng it to happen—some day. So many men each day. It's too bad it had to happen in my company"(744). A general later echoes this concern:

> God only knows what would happen if people began to suspect we couldn't even get our dead to lie down and be buried! ... They never said anything about this sort of thing at West Point. (747)

Another general later exhorts the men:

> You're dead, officially, all of you! I won't mince words! You heard! We're a civilized race, we bury our dead! Lie down! (749)

But *Bury the Dead* is much more than a satire of the military. *Time*'s reviewer argued that "What young Mr. Shaw really hates is not War but Death."[12] That, of course, is an oversimplification—the "young Mr. Shaw" hated both. War, in *Bury the Dead,* is condemned as a means by which corrupt societies rob young men of life. While this vision is hardly original, Shaw's presentation of it is.

In addition to the central conceit, a unique lyricism, often reading like a form of folk poetry, contributes much to the play's originality. One of the dead men, Private Schelling, speculates that

> Maybe there's too many of us under the ground now. Maybe the earth can't stand it no more. You got to change crops sometime. (753)

Another asserts that the grave is no place for him:

> . . . the eyes of women to look at and the bright color of their hair and the soft way they swing their hips when they walk before young men. These are the things that mean life and the earth to me, the joy and the pain. . . . Joy and pain—to each man in his own way, a full seventy years, to be ended by an unhurried fate, not by a colored pin on a General's map. (755)

In the character of Tom Driscoll, the First Corpse, Shaw also utilizes the concept of a secular holy man, a motif which is to appear in much of his later writing. It is he who first stands up in his grave and then forces the others to rise as well. Perhaps the play's key thematic moment is a debate between Driscoll and the Third Corpse on one side and the Captain on the other:

> [Captain:] The earth, I assure you, is a mean place, insignificantly miserable. . . .
> [Driscoll:] We must find out for ourselves. That is our right.
> [Captain:] Man has no rights. . . .
> [Driscoll:] Man can make rights for himself. It requires only determination and the good-will of ordinary men. We have made ourselves the right to walk this earth, seeing it and judging it for ourselves.
> [Captain:] There is peace in the grave. . . .
> [Third Corpse:] Peace and the worms and the roots of grass. There is a deeper peace than that which comes with feeding the roots of the grass. (751; ellipses in text)

Driscoll's assertion of the right of "ordinary men" to control their destiny leads naturally into the thematic concept underlying *The Gentle People*.

Shaw's use of montage to demonstrate the opposition of society as a whole to the dead men's rebellion is less effective; it is the only aspect of the play which now seems somewhat dated and predictable. In contrast, the ending is as fresh and stunning as it must have seemed in 1936. After resisting all arguments and tricks to get them back underground, the dead walk off the stage past a general who is frantically firing a machinegun at them, "like men who have leisurely business that must be attended to in the not too pressing future" (762–63).

Original and daring in conception, largely effective in execution, *Bury the Dead* will live as a fable which helped revolutionize the American theater. In addition, it contains the seeds of thematic concerns central to Shaw's later works in drama and fiction.

The Gentle People

Still, *Bury the Dead* is limited by the very originality of its central concept and by its scope as a one-act play. Shaw's most impressive dramatic work is *The Gentle People*, a three-act "fable," which was produced by the Group Theatre in 1939. Ironically, its reviews did not approach the enthusiasm which greeted Shaw's first play. A brief mention by George Jean Nathan in *Newsweek* did recommend it as "a peculiarly evocative and hintful parable of humble and beset humanity seeking vengeful alms from the great and little fates. . . . "[13] The *New Republic* condemned it, but uneasily, suggesting that perhaps the production, and not the play, was at fault. *Theatre Arts Monthly* gave grudging praise: "Harold Clurman's direction and Boris Aronson's settings conspire to clothe an imaginative if somewhat uneven text with an atmosphere peculiar to its fantastic realism."[14] Reflecting an apparent inability to comprehend innovation in the theater, *Time* was almost hysterical in its denunciation.[15]

It seems that none of these reviewers, except Nathan, even those who liked the play, quite comprehended what they were viewing.

John Gassner does not include *The Gentle People* in *20 Best Plays of the Modern American Theater, 1930–1939,* but still devotes more space to it than to *Bury the Dead* in his introduction. Gassner's comments reveal a much deeper understanding of the play than that shown by the original reviewers:

> Finally, "honey" began to come from the "strong" when the lions of the left stopped pawing the ground and roaring. Irwin Shaw's whimsical *The Gentle People* was quiescent by comparison with his *Bury the Dead*. Although his viewpoint was unaltered, and he still defended the common man and proclaimed his revolt, the treatment was leisurely, unhortatory, and oblique.[16]

This analysis is correct. Neither Shaw's artistic nor his political philosophy had significantly changed since *Bury the Dead. The Gentle People* simply clarified and expanded the central thematic concepts of the earlier play. In addition, *The Gentle People* is as ambitious and innovative as *Bury the Dead,* but in quite different ways.

The subtitle of *The Gentle People* is "A Brooklyn Fable," and Shaw remarks on that concept in a prefatory note: "This play is a fairy tale with a moral. In it justice triumphs and the meek prove victorious over arrogant and violent men. The author does not pretend that this is the case in real life."[17] This brief introductory statement partially explains much of the confusion on the part of several of the play's reviewers. As in *Bury the Dead,* Shaw utilizes a unique folk lyricism in much of the dialogue; but throughout the play, one also senses an angry realism. This combination and the introductory statement explain, in part, a confusion among the reviewers. The *New Republic* man, for instance, seems not to have known whether to respond more strongly to the surface lyricism and comedy or the underlying anger. As Gassner realizes, it is essential for a full understanding of the play to respond to both.

It is a fable "with a moral." The essential conflict is between representatives of totalitarianism and decent ordinary men. It is hardly difficult to understand why Shaw, in 1939, viewed such a conflict as central to world events or why he was pessimistic about the common man's ultimate victory. Still, if he had felt hopeless, rather than merely pessimistic, the play's moral would have been an exercise in superfluous nostalgia.

The fable's plot is simple. Two men in their fifties, Jonah Goodman, a Jew, and Philip Anagnos, a Greek, dream of buying a boat, the *Leif Ericson*, and sailing from Brooklyn to Cuba to fish in the Gulf Stream. The dream is largely a fantasy of escape from the drabness of their lives (Goodman has a chronically ill, nagging wife and Anagnos is being pressured to marry a tyrannical Italian woman for whom he works). The Great Depression is the seemingly inescapable reality of their lives, and dreams seem the only escape from its economic hardships. It is impossible to miss the allegorical intent of such names as Jonah Goodman and *Leif Ericson* or Shaw's emphasis upon the Jewish and Greek ancestry of his two heroes. *The Gentle People* is Shaw's first sustained statement of faith in the United States, the historic "melting pot," as the world's last, best hope—a nation of essentially good men and women of diverse national origins whose spirit of adventure and romance has not been totally crushed. The same vision underlies *The Young Lions, Voices of a Summer Day*, and many of his best short stories.

Still, as illustrated by such short stories as "The City Was in Total Darkness" and "Weep in Years to Come," Shaw, in the years just prior to America's entrance into World War II, became increasingly concerned that the nation's inherent decency might not awaken in time to save itself and the world from the threat of fascism. The play's allegorical representative of American and international fascism is Harold Goff, a petty hoodlum who makes Jonah and Philip's dream even more distant by demanding "protection money" from them. Goff also sets out to seduce Jonah's daughter, Stella. Some of the play's best moments come when Jonah, who fully understands Goff's appeal to Stella as the source of escape from the economic and spiritual drabness of her life, attempts to explain the threat to her ultimate welfare embodied in Goff's lack of basic human decency. The counterpart to Goff is Stella's persistent suitor, Eli Lieber: "Eli is a man of twenty-seven, the ordinary man. He is gentle, grave, neat, healthy, pleasant, unexceptional" (12). This description of "ordinary, unexceptional" Eli is the central statement of Shaw's vision of the common man, lacking in external signs of greatness, but capable of heroism when pushed too far. He is the predecessor of such later Shaw characters as Robert de Mauny in *The Assassin* and Lieutenant Green in *The Young Lions*, characters who become exceptional almost despite themselves because of their inherent decency in an indecent world.

Minor figures central to Shaw's allegory are Magruder, an honest Irish cop; Angelina Esposito, Philip's boss who is determined to marry him and who is a devoted follower of Mussolini; and Lammaniwitz, "The Fat Man," a bankrupt who has lost his small business and who is used in a memorable steambath scene as a variant of the classical Greek chorus. Virtually every reviewer agreed that the steambath scene, in which Jonah and Philip plan to kill Goff rather than submit to his extortion, is a theatrical tour de force and that Lee J. Cobb, who played Lammaniwitz in the original Broadway production, was superb. To comprehend the brilliance of the Group Theatre as an ensemble company, it is perhaps only necessary to glance at the names of *The Gentle People*'s original cast: Sam Jaffe, Roman Bohnen, Franchot Tone, Karl Malden, Sylvia Sidney, Elia Kazan, and Cobb, among others.

The determination of Jonah and Philip to resist Goff comes slowly—they are, after all, "the meek." Shaw beautifully develops their gradual movement toward strength and determinism, and his utilization of a lyrical folk poetry is crucial to this development. Early in the play, they are seen luxuriating in their dream:

> [Philip:] I will get the backs of my hands browned. . . .
> [Jonah:] The fish'll bite, Philip, the fish'll bite! We will catch the fish with the spears on their noses and forget my wife and my job and what we read in the newspaper and after that I can die, God forbid, and I will raise no objections. (10–11)

This exchange is crucial to the play since it foreshadows the fact that, meek and gentle as they may be, they will not easily surrender the dream.

Some critics condemned the ending of the play, in which Jonah and Philip do kill Goff, steal his wallet, plan to make a contribution to an orphans' asylum, and keep their dream of the *Leif Ericson* alive. The critical objections were twofold: first, such a happy ending was said to be implausible; second, it apparently condoned murder. Again, critics who objected on these grounds did not understand what they were seeing; Shaw made clear that the play was a "fable" which should be viewed allegorically rather than realistically. Ironically, he may have misled such critics by the sheer force of his talent—for instance, he carefully humanizes Goff instead of leaving him a one-dimensional villain. Perhaps the intention behind the play can best be compared to that of Hawthorne's short story, "Young Goodman Brown," in which the characters exist on some plane between pure allegory and realistic characterization. Shaw, of course, is much closer to realism than Hawthorne; but it is a mistake to ignore his underlying allegory as several critics apparently did. The killing of Goff by Philip and Jonah is the murder of a gangster by two formerly nonviolent men, but it is also the allegorical destruction of fascism by the decent common men of the United States and of the world. A comparable allegory underlies Shaw's World War II novel, *The Young Lions*.

As mentioned, Shaw primarily uses his lyrical folk poetry to illustrate Philip and Jonah's initial reluctance to fight back and their gradually increasing strength and determination. Philip comments early: "If there is something good in the air, it doesn't happen to me" (4). Jonah, however, gives indication from the first of being stronger than Philip:

> Look. Soon I will die, God forbid, and on my grave they'll put, "Here lies Jonah Goodman, a good son, a good husband, a good citizen, he worked like a horse all his life and he never did what he wanted to do." (7)

Thus, one is not surprised that Jonah ultimately decides to do what he wants to do, whatever the price. The two men prefer to dream while sitting in a tiny little boat at the end of Steeplechase Pier on Coney Island. Their boat is a far cry from the *Leif Ericson*, but it serves to keep the dream alive. By the end of Act I, Jonah's determination has grown significantly:

I've been pushed too, Philip. I was pushed out of Russia, out of school, out of business, out of a house that cost me eight thousand dollars. We're getting old, Philip, we must take a stand some place. Let's take a stand in a little boat, before we're pushed right off the earth. (40–41)

Still, the two do not act until they seek recourse in the court and are denied by a corrupt judge (an act which outrages Magruder, the honest cop), and Jonah is beaten by Goff with a rubber hose. Of crucial importance, too, is Jonah's growing realization that he and Philip must destroy Goff to save the young couple, Stella and Eli Lieber. In Act II, Stella tells her father that she is "going with" Goff; and the subsequent debate between father and daughter is central to Shaw's vision:

[Stella:] He knows judges. He gives cigars to State Assemblymen. He speaks to people who get their names in the newspapers.
[Jonah:] Today that is not a recommendation for a man's character. (71)

Still, Stella persists: "When I go out with him.... I shake the curse of Brooklyn off my feet for a night."

Jonah, with a nagging, chronically ill wife and more bills than he can pay, understands "the curse of Brooklyn" far better than Stella does. But he comprehends the common, unextraordinary goodness and beauty of Brooklyn as well:

[Jonah to Stella:] You're just like the people in the subway, but that's all right. The people in the subway are good people, most of them, and you can trust them, and love them if you get to know them. (129)

This speech foreshadows the wonderful subway scene between Noah Ackerman and Hope Plowman in *The Young Lions*. Later Jonah tells Stella that

... there is one thing ordinary people can do as good as anybody. They can love each other like movie stars ... and poets. That is one reason it is not such a terrible thing to be an ordinary person, Stella. (132)

A central tenet of Shaw's aesthetic philosophy, confirmed by his own experience, has always been that, in America, poets most often do emerge from the "ordinary" people.

While Eli Lieber actually does very little in the play, his characterization still serves to underscore the thematic points Shaw is making through Jonah and Philip. As Stella's attraction to Goff grows, he does plan to confront the gangster:

> For two years I played tackle for the Boys High football team. In two years nobody gained a yard through me.... I am no cello player. (165)

Unable to talk Eli out of such a physical confrontation, Jonah and Philip feel their own responsibility to destroy the gangster even more strongly. They want the young man, with his life in front of him, to avoid danger. Most importantly, Eli personifies Shaw's point that "the gentle people" are present in all generations.

Eli works for a well-to-do uncle and has an amusing promotional speech which he delivers early in the play. In keeping with the overall "fairy tale," he and Stella are reunited at the end, while he simultaneously announces a promotion from his uncle:

> [Eli:] It is necessary to announce at this time that my uncle has decided to spread Fascination [the key word in his early promotional speech] over the United States of America. He has bought me a nice 1934 Buick and in the spring I am going West.... it will be possible to see the Pacific Ocean and Hollywood and the Arizona Desert and Kansas City, and you can take the top down and get sunburned as you ride....
>
> [Stella:] In the Brooklyn Paramount tonight, Eli, they got Gary Cooper. (209–10)

This exchange is a crucial one. Eli, like Jonah and Philip, has his dream of faraway romance and adventure—one is meant to notice the parallel between Philip's early mention of getting his hands "browned" in the Gulf Stream and Eli's vision of getting "sunburned" in the Buick. But Stella has learned from her father's advice and now understands that one can experience Gary Cooper in Brooklyn. Pushed to the wall, the "gentle people" are capable of discovering their own courage, romance, and capacity to love.

One of the most impressive aspects of *The Gentle People* is Shaw's unobtrusive extension of the Goff characterization to personify international, and especially European, fascism. The allegorical extension is achieved much more subtly and convincingly than the comparable movement from condemnation of the army to criticism of civilian society in *Bury the Dead*. One senses that *The Gentle People* might well be a difficult play to produce; but, as read, it is a superbly moving human fable. Nothing Shaw has written better exemplifies his own definition of his work as "romantic realism." The common man is capable of greatness, but all too often, he denies his own latent strength until he is finally pushed too far.

The Assassin (1946)

That *The Assassin* deserved a better fate than it received was recognized almost immediately by *Theatre Arts* magazine and, to a lesser degree, by Stark Young in the *New Republic*. *Theatre Arts* admitted that the play had "faults," but proclaimed that "in spite of its shortcomings it provided an evening of intelligent interest as well as theatric pleasures. . . . " The review editorialized that "this, in a period given over almost exclusively to mediocrity, was much to be thankful for."[18] Ironically, this editorial comment was very much in the spirit of Shaw's forthcoming denunciation of the contemporary theater. Stark Young's review was quite mixed:

> If the play does not seem to come off or get anywhere very much, despite its perilous and urgent material, it is at least literate; some of the speeches are far above the usual run of plays and the dramatist has created an intelligent hero who can express himself and whose motives are both complex and intense.[19]

The "perilous and urgent material" of the play is based upon the actual case of the pro-German Admiral Darlan. Its setting is Algiers at the time of the Allied invasion of North Africa. Shaw's "complex and intense" main character is Robert de Mauny, who achieves heroism almost despite himself by agreeing to assassinate Admiral Marcel Vespery, the fictional counterpart of Darlan. The play was written while Shaw was still in the armed services and initially subjected to some censorship; nevertheless, it was successfully produced in London before its New York failure.

Stark Young was perceptive in his insight that the complexity of de Mauny's motivations was the strongest element in *The Assassin;* it is precisely because Shaw's assassin is such an unlikely hero that he and the play are believable and fascinating. A group of supporting characters, some well rounded and some intentionally one-dimensional, effectively evoke the fear and confusion prevalent on both sides during this crucial period of World War II. Central among the Resistance figures are Helene Mariotte, a courageous woman who has lost her husband in the war and who falls in love with de Mauny despite herself; Lucien Gerard, a militant and dogmatic Communist; and Andre Vauquin, a personification of the courage and determination of the entire Resistance movement. The major pro-Nazi figures are Vespery; General Roucheau, a chilling symbol of the subordinate, bureaucratic Fascist; and Victor Malassis, a sadistic policeman. Other than de Mauny, the most memorable character is probably General Mousset, a superficially charming, but inwardly cynical and self-serving man loyal only to himself. There are other memorable minor characters: M. and Mme David Stein, a once-wealthy Jewish couple who have lost everything but their courage in the war, and M. Popinot, the common man reconciled to aligning himself with whoever is in power. Taken together, the Steins and Popinot personify Shaw's vision of the reluctant courage of the common man.

When first introduced, Robert de Mauny is a flippant, superficial young man with Royalist political views. Almost instantly upon encountering the other Resistance figures, he makes a sexual advance to Helene Mariotte and is rebuked. Before the end of the first scene, however, he has acted spontaneously to save the others from Malassis. When asked why, he replies: "There was nobody else who could." Gerard, the devout Communist, still distrusts him; but Vauquin, who virtually speaks for Shaw throughout the play, is more perceptive: "'My being saved by a believer in kings. Still, in this age, anything is possible.'" Robert analyzes the source of his heroism more fully: he likes all of the Resistance people, including Gerard, and understands that, no matter what their other political views are, they are all devoted to France.[20]

Already Robert shares a crucial insight with Vauquin—it is a confusing and corrupt age in which good and evil have transcended their old boundaries. Still, he does not yet fully understand himself and attempts to avoid further heroism. The other Resistance figures, including Helene, are arrested, however; and the cynical Mousset comes to him with a plan. Mousset explains that if Robert will agree to kill Vespery, he will be arrested, tried, and sentenced to death; but, ten minutes before the execution, he will be rescued and another man substituted for him. Robert rejects Mousset's plan until he is told that the other Resistance figures will be executed unless he cooperates. After then agreeing, he is confused as to his primary motivation: is it love for France or for Helene or simple human decency? It is, in fact, all three: Robert is another of Shaw's "gentle people" who have been pushed too far.

Vauquin understands what is behind Robert's heroism better than the young man himself. Such comprehension allows him to enunciate the play's central thematic concerns:

> The essential thing is quality. The quality of... a man's soul. Politics change. We must trust the quality of a man, rather than the color of his politics. Today that's our only hope.... That's why... I believe in the Americans. The Americans are good people.... Somehow, we all believe in the human race—that it deserves to live on the earth, that there is hope it will learn how to live on the earth. (105–6)

A key conversation with Robert further clarifies these ideas:

> [Vauquin:] ... it would look better in the history books if you were full of simple, correct reasons and eloquent democratic slogans, and terribly anxious to die in the cause of freedom.
>
> [Robert:] I'm afraid I can't oblige.

[Vauquin:] We live in a confused age and we're saved by confused heroes. (120–21)

Robert does assassinate Vespery; the others are released; but, not surprisingly, since Mousset never intended to save him, the reluctant hero is executed. Helene comes to his cell to tell him of Mousset's treachery; and, in a moving scene, the two declare their love for one another by talking about the world before the war. Shaw's lyricism is much in evidence in their farewell scene.

Before the firing squad, Robert reflects upon "the accident" which has befallen him:

We [the Resistance] can be forgotten, but only the way the acorn is forgotten in the oak, the grape in the wine.... Where is the Count of Paris this morning? I object to kings, because they do not face firing squads. My mother will not understand this, either. The honor of France is a poor exchange for a son. Where is the answer to this riddle? The son must always die and the mother always feel the bargain a bad one.... (157–58)

Clearly, Robert has grown considerably from the flippant young Royalist of Act I. Most importantly, Shaw succeeds in making this growth aesthetically convincing.

In addition, he does not always utilize the overt speech of the thesis play with which to convey his ideas about the nature of heroism. One of the best, and most understated, moments in the play involves the Steins. To secure escape to Egypt, Mme Stein is forced to sell a mink coat which symbolizes, for her, the tranquil world before the war began:

When I wear this coat I really remember what it was like to live in a country at peace. Nobody hunting you, flowers in every room, hot baths, calling for you for lunch at your office. When I wear this coat, I feel that one day it will come back.

Her husband gently responds: "The winters're mild in Egypt" and later points out that "heroism can take many symbols—a banner, a jail, a ship, a piece of fur..." (98–99).

The Assassin has some of the flaws one might expect to find in a thesis play—occasionally its propaganda is overt, and a few of the characters lack depth. These weaknesses are made more obvious by Shaw's departure from the innovative experimentation of his earlier plays. Yet, as always in Shaw, the writing is polished and sometimes eloquent; and Robert de Mauny is a complex and memorable character.

Given its quick dismissal by New York critics and audiences, it is not surprising that Shaw utilized the preface of the printed play to attack the Broadway theater. He makes the degree of his anger immediately clear:

> The critics ... had done me more harm than the German Army. It is true that the Germans had tried to kill me, but they, at least, had missed. The critics had not missed. (vii)

After thus establishing the tone of the preface, Shaw makes several specific criticisms of the current state of the theater. All too often, he says, the play as produced bears little resemblance to the play as written.

Partially, this phenomenon is a result of the power of the several unions involved in producing a play. Given his politics, Shaw made this criticism with some regret: "I am a strong union man and am almost as proud of my own union, the Dramatists' Guild, as I am of the American Army...." Still, writing, like virtually all art, is an individual achievement, and group involvement at a secondary level can mean disaster.

Much more damaging than the unions are the critics. Shaw attacks their mediocrity—"the inordinate attention paid to critics in the theatre does not come ... from the inordinate size of their talents"—and their power—"that the most promising and lively theatre on the face of the earth should suffer under this arbitrary tyranny is an evil and oppressive thing" (xiv–xviii). He accuses the "big three" critics of the New York press as poor imitators of the satiric wit of George Bernard Shaw: "When Robert Garland comes forth with *Saint Joan* I shall welcome his bad puns about my plays" (xix).

The critics, he argues, are especially damaging to writers of overtly political plays:

> I happen to be a writer who, to my sorrow, cannot help writing on political subjects. This is a savage jungle for the playwright and I regret ever having got into it. For my politics must agree with that of the critics, or I am in my grave by eleven. (xxiii)

Shaw expands this assertion to argue that the critics will accept only very safe and very uncomplicated political plays. As an example of what is acceptable to them, he mentions Lillian Hellman's *Watch on the Rhine*. While insisting that he admires Hellman, he argues that her play succeeded because it leaves the hero's politics vague, while depicting him as "flawless." Things were never that simple, Shaw insists: "The Americans in the play are charming and redeemable, and at worst childishly thoughtless. Very little is said of the guilt and murderous complicity with Fascism abroad among us then as now" (xxvi).

Essentially, Shaw's condemnation of the New York theater is that it has become cowardly, demanding simple answers to complex questions: "dramatists are in the position of Czechoslovakia, with appeasement considered the only hopeful course, and Chamberlains everywhere" (xxix). Not surprisingly, Shaw's attack resulted in some extended controversy. More important to Shaw's subsequent career than this controversy are two specific comments in his attack. As an example of the theater's cowardice, he asserts that "*The Fifth Column* by Ernest Hemingway will certainly be remembered longer than most of the successes of that year, and yet Mr. Hemingway was warned off in no uncertain terms by the critical gentry, and has heeded the warning to the extent of remaining the best novelist and short-story writer in America and leaving the theatre severely alone, as instructed" (xxvii–xxviii). Shaw hints that he intends to follow Hemingway's example: "the morbid fever of ill-health in which the theatre operates makes the writer look longingly at the comparative serenity of the novel and the charming peace of the short story" (xvi). In fact, Shaw meant what he said and turned increasingly after 1946 to the novel rather than to drama as the preferred vehicle for his longer works.

Conclusion

Even though Shaw has never enjoyed commercial success on Broadway, one regrets his abandonment of the theater. Because of *Bury the Dead* and *The Gentle People*, he will always be recognized as a major force in the revolutionary American drama of the 1930s. Shaw's most important impact upon this theater lay in his experimentation with technique. *Bury the Dead* and *The Gentle People* are innovative plays, mingling social concerns with fantasy. Consequently, while they may present special difficulties in staging, they read extremely well. Although a lesser play, *The Assassin* exhibits originality and power, largely because of Shaw's vision of heroism as an ambiguous, unpredictable human quality.

Chapter Three

The Short Stories: The Craft of Moral Fiction

For more than a decade before his first novel, *The Young Lions*, appeared in 1948, Irwin Shaw had been a major figure in the Theatre Group. In addition, he had steadily been building his reputation as a master of the modern short story. In the second half of the 1930s, his short fiction began appearing in such journals as the *New Republic, Collier's, Esquire, Harper's, Accent,* and especially the *New Yorker*. By 1948, he had contributed so regularly to the latter that he was regarded as one of the most prominent of a group known as *New Yorker* writers. His first collection, *Sailor off the Bremen*, appeared in 1939 and contained such memorable stories as "The Girls in Their Summer Dresses," "Second Mortgage," "Weep in Years to Come," and the title story. The year 1942 saw the publication of *Welcome to the City*, containing "The Eighty-Yard Run," "Main Currents of American Thought," "The City Was in Total Darkness," and "Night, Birth, and Opinion," among others. Three thematic concerns were dominant in these first two volumes: the effects of the depression on the middle and lower classes; the threat to American values inherent in the rise of fascism at home and abroad; and the moral shallowness at the core of the American success story.

In 1946 Shaw published his third collection, *Act of Faith and Other Stories*, dominated by such memorable tales of war as "Walking Wounded," "Part in a Play," "Medal from Jerusalem," and "Act of Faith." Subsequently, he has produced four other collections: *Mixed Company* (1950), *Tip on a Dead Jockey* (1957), *Love on a Dark Street* (1965), and *God Was Here But He Left Early* (1973). *Mixed Company* reprinted the best work from the three earlier volumes along with stories which had not been previously collected (e.g., "Mixed Doubles," "The Climate of Insomnia"). Reflecting his voluntary exile in Paris, *Tip on a Dead Jockey, Love on a Dark Street*, and *God Was Here But He Left Early* focus primarily on American expatriates in Europe.

Despite the importance to the American theater of *Bury the Dead* and *The Gentle People* and the position of *The Young Lions* as one of the major World War II novels and the popular and aesthetic success of such subsequent novels as *Voices of a Summer Day, Two Weeks in Another Town*, and *Evening in Byzantium*, Shaw will be best remembered as the author of an impressive body of technically superb short fiction. The frequency with which his best stories are reprinted, as well as the generally accepted evaluation of "The Girls in Their Summer Dresses," "The Eighty-Yard Run," "Walking Wounded," "Act of Faith," "Tip on a Dead Jockey," "God Was Here But He Left Early," and others as masterpieces of the form, support such an evaluation. Random House and Delacorte, Shaw's publishers for most of his career, have recognized the central importance of his short stories in any evaluation of his career. In 1961, *Selected Short Stories of Irwin Shaw*, containing twenty-three titles, was added to the Modern Library. Five years later, Random House published an omnibus collection of sixty-eight stories, *Short Stories of Irwin Shaw*. Delacorte originally planned to publish all of Shaw's stories in 1978; however, this proved to be impractical and *Short Stories: Five Decades* contains sixty-three stories, including four of the five tales from *God Was Here But He Left Early*. Shaw writes in an introduction to *Short Stories: Five Decades* that the "count" of his stories came to eighty-four and including all of them "would have meant a formidably bulky and outrageously expensive book."[1]

In this introduction Shaw also seems to recognize that his future literary reputation will rest most securely on his short fiction: "Since I am not particularly devout, my chances for salvation lie in a place sometime in the future on a library shelf. These stories were selected . . . with the hope that a spot on that distant shelf is waiting for them."[2] In addition, he introduces the sixty-three stories in the volume in a manner which will serve as a valid approach to all his short fiction. He is a "product of [his] times," he writes, and these stories can be seen as "a record of the events of almost sixty years, all coming together in the imagination of one American." The specific events which he lists are the Great Depression, the Spanish Civil War, World War II, the rise of McCarthyism, the presidency of John F. Kennedy, and the tragedy of Vietnam. The short story form has a special appeal for him: in it, one can present "disguised moralizing that will set everyday transactions into larger perspectives" and compress "great matters into digestible portions."[3]

In fact, Shaw's fiction does constitute an imaginative response to the major social and political events of the twentieth century; it is saved from polemical limitations by an underlying code of universal morality and by technical mastery. In reading Shaw's short stories, one is impressed most by the fact that virtually all of the eighty-four are clearly the work of a master craftsman. Even those stories which are not remembered in the same way as the recognized masterpieces are distinguished by an obvious professionalism.

There are thematic reasons for the superiority of Shaw's short fiction to his novels. His central vision of the world as lacking cohesive ethical values and, thus, dominated by moral and physical accidents is peculiarly suitable to the short story form. In his novels, he too often utilizes the moral and physical accidents which reflect his central vision as devices of structural unity; as a result, his longer works often lack the cohesion of his short stories. Moreover, while, with a very few exceptions, his stories consistently rest upon an underlying ethical concern which distinguishes them as serious fiction, two of his most recent novels seem to have been written primarily as entertainment. This is not to argue that in any of his writing Shaw is devoted to the didactic. Like Hemingway, he is a master of knowing what to leave out. In his short fiction, Shaw has perfected the technique of implying ethical judgment rather than overtly stating it. In his best novels, he attempts the same thing, but is not so consistently successful.

As Shaw suggests, it makes very good sense to approach the stories as an imaginative record of a turbulent half-century: most of them reflect, more or less directly, a concern with the major events of American history from the depression of the 1930s to the collapse of values underscored by the United States involvement in Vietnam. The social upheaval produced by the Great Depression inspired two kinds of Shaw stories. Predictably, given his essentially proletarian sympathies, he wrote a body of stories which depict the sufferings of the middle and lower classes. In addition, he wrote about more affluent Americans, focusing upon the spiritual and emotional shallowness of their lives. Such a focus continues in Shaw stories written after the depression; and, in fact, sophisticated examination of the spiritual hollowness at the core of affluent America is perhaps now the single motif most associated with Shaw. The stories illustrate three interrelated Shaw responses to the rise of fascism in Europe and to World War II: a group of stories morally admonishes America for ignoring the fascist threat at home and abroad; another reflects Shaw's experiences in the war; and a third contains a militantly Jewish response to the Holocaust in Europe and to anti-Semitism in the United States. Three stories represent protest against the McCarthy-inspired witch hunts of the 1950s; and "God Was Here But He Left Early" uses American involvement in Vietnam as a central metaphor for moral collapse in the twentieth century. The problems of the American expatriate in Europe become the dominant motif in stories written after Shaw's move to Europe; these stories often focus upon innocent young Americans confronting a very old and confusing postwar European culture.

Certain of Shaw's personal attachments inspire other stories. Even after he had lived for twenty-five years in Paris, he still referred to New York City as his city; and several stories are unified by the treatment of New York as a main character. Shaw's lifelong interest in sports, ranging from football to skiing, inspires the fictional use of athletics as metaphor for the corruption of American institutions. Finally, there are several memorable character studies of proud, stubborn individuals challenging either specific social institutions or society in the abstract. This chapter cannot attempt a discussion of all the best Shaw short stories, but analysis of some of the most memorable illustrations of these thematic concerns should give a sense of Shaw's mastery in this genre.

Failure of the American Good Life

As mentioned, the Great Depression caused Shaw to question the basic tenets of American idealism. Subsequent historical events only confirmed his suspicions about affluent Americans. As a result, probably the best-known body of Shaw stories depicts a spiritually and emotionally hollow affluent America. It is in this group of stories that Shaw most reminds one of the great generation of American writers that had preceded him by approximately one decade—and especially of F. Scott Fitzgerald. As in the work of Fitzgerald and the rest of the Lost Generation, Shaw's affluent Americans reside in a spiritual and ethical wasteland, unable to escape "the valley of ashes."

Perhaps no Shaw story illustrates this point more effectively, nor is more widely known, than "The Girls in Their Summer Dresses."[4] Less than ten pages long, it is a perfect example of the craft of the short story. More than any other Shaw story, it is accepted by academic critics: Cleanth Brooks and Robert Penn Warren include it in their *Understanding Fiction*. The plot can be summarized quickly: a New York City married couple, Michael and Frances Loomis, have decided to spend their Sunday together instead of with their usual circle of friends. As they walk to a restaurant, Frances notices Michael looking at the pretty girls they pass and they begin to quarrel; inside the restaurant, the quarrel becomes so uncomfortable that they decide to go to a party neither really wants to attend and, as Frances walks to the telephone to call and say they are coming, Michael examines her in the same way he has the girls on the street: "Michael watched her walk, thinking, what a pretty girl, what nice legs."

In their analysis, Brooks and Warren emphasize Shaw's skill in understating Michael's initial look at a girl passing him on the street, while still signaling to the reader that this moment will be crucial to the story. They conclude with this evaluation of theme: the story's ironic ending conveys "a serious idea—the failure of love through the failure to recognize the beloved as a person, as more than a convenience."[5] Both of these points are important, but what is most impressive about the story is how much more the dialogue implies. What one senses most strongly about Michael and Frances's quarrel is that it is a ritual. Having no real communication, they fall into the quarrel as a way of talk. This impression is conveyed through the fact that neither really listens to the other; it is almost as if they are speaking often-rehearsed lines in a play. In other stories, Shaw uses the device of the ritual quarrel to emphasize the emotional shallowness of a particular marriage.

Only once does Michael attempt to convey what the anonymous passing girls really mean to him. When he first came to the city as a young man, he says, the beautiful women were what first struck him about New York. Now that he is almost middle-aged, the women are still his symbol of the city in which he was young and full of confidence. Frances demands only that he admit his sexual desire for them. Fully giving in to the ritual, Michael answers that he does desire them. Frances pushes for more: "'You'd like to be free to....'" Michael agains seems to provide the expected response: "'Sometimes I feel I would like to be free'"; he then allows this to be interpreted as a warning that he will eventually leave Frances.

The reader recognizes the separate connotations of the word *free* as each character uses it. Michael, in effect, means that he would like to be young again and still confident of finding some excitement and lasting meaning in his life. Frances hears only that he would like to escape the restrictions of their marriage. She desperately wants reassurance that she is as desirable as the women Michael compulsively watches; and the most painful irony of the story's ending is that, to himself alone, Michael does confirm her desirability, but only after depersonalizing her as just another passing pretty girl. Because they are unable to communicate their real needs to each other, their attempt at a perfect Sunday alone will end in another party like all the parties they attend: "'We're always up to our neck in people, drinking their Scotch, or drinking our Scotch, we only see each other in bed....'" For Shaw's affluent couples, alcohol and depersonalized sex become the two great escapes from spiritual emptiness.

Shaw uses variations of the ritual quarrel device to depict emotionally empty marriages in other stories. The dialogue in "Dinner in a Good Restaurant"[6] communicates a special kind of emotional brutality. Mr. Hood, forty-three years old, has spent his life eating good dinners in good restaurants without ever working. He has been supported by financially independent women, never promising them fidelity. In the story, his forty-five-year-old wife is angry at his most recent adultery and, as they enjoy "dinner in a good restaurant," attacks him in the most vicious ways she knows. Even after she calls him a "pimp," he smiles and passively agrees, knowing that by doing so, he is hurting her and thoroughly enjoying it. As they leave the restaurant, she admits that she wants him only for sex and threatens to leave him nothing in her will when she'll have no further need for him. Right now, however, she insists that they "walk fast." Mrs. Hood, like Michael and Frances Loomis, is desperately afraid of growing older because her life's only center is sensual pleasure. There is no longer even the possibility of communication for the Hoods since he derives a brutal satisfaction from tormenting her with his passivity.

An amusing example of the ritual quarrel technique is "Mixed Doubles" (*SSFD*, 418–25). Here, instead of an actual quarrel, Shaw uses the unspoken thoughts of one partner to reveal the fragile nature of a marriage. Stewart and Jane Collins are playing mixed-doubles tennis with Mr. Croker and a pretty girl named Eleanor Burns. The Collinses are much the superior team and win the first set easily; but between sets Jane notices Stewart responding to Eleanor Burns's flirtation. The second set becomes for Jane a metaphor of their marriage: Stewart gives it away, first by needlessly forfeiting a crucial point which they clearly won, reminding Jane of how often he has threatened their security by his devotion to dramatic "gestures." As they begin losing, he blames the condition of the court. Jane remembers that he has always had an "alibi" for personal or professional failures. Finally, he double-faults set point and walks off blaming the light. Jane thinks of the many times he has failed at crucial moments in his life.

Jane attempts to remind herself that marriage is "a fragile and devious thing... not to be examined too closely"; still she cannot escape the fact that Stewart's "tennis was so much like his life. Gifted, graceful, powerful, showy, flawed, erratic.... " Shaw makes subtle ironic use of the names of the Collinses' "opponents." Eleanor Burns does make Stewart and Jane "burn" inwardly in different ways; and the unmarried Mr. Croker becomes a personification of the impending end of the Collinses' marriage. Of course, the language of tennis (*love, fault*) contributes to the verbal irony of the story.

If any single Shaw story is more widely known than "The Girls in Their Summer Dresses," it is "The Eighty-Yard Run," (*SSFD*, 1–12). Shaw does not use the device of the ritual quarrel in it, but once again the focus is on a character, Christian Darling, attempting to hold onto a symbol of confident youth after his life has crumbled into spiritual emptiness. Unlike such characters as Michael Loomis, Darling carries the added burden of professional failure. Much of the pain of the story comes from the fact that although Christian Darling never had a heroic period in his life, he believes that he had and everyone around him encourages such a belief. The high point of his life came when he played college football, and his most intense memory of that time is an eighty-yard run he once made. The run comes to represent freedom in the sense of triumph over human opposition and, most importantly, time itself; it is for Christian what young girls in summer dresses are for Michael Loomis. The reader quickly learns, however, that the run came not in a game, but only in practice, when Christian was only "a second stringer."

In fact, Christian never becomes the hero he once felt certain he would be; he was on the starting team for two years, but primarily as a blocking back for an All-American named Diederich, and in that time his longest run was for thirty-five yards at an insignificant point in the game. Still, "everybody liked him and he did his job"; indeed on campus he was "an important figure." His wealthy fiancée, Louise Tucker, then seemed to view him as possessing heroic dimensions and enjoyed showing him off. After graduation, they had married and moved from the Midwest to New York City, where her father had taken Christian into his business. From the start, he had felt alien in the city; and his resulting insecurity was manifested in occasional infidelities. Then the world changed abruptly for Darling; his father-in-law went bankrupt in the crash of 1929 and committed suicide. Out of work, with no sense of how to start over, Christian began to drink heavily because he had no other way to spend his time.

As his life collapsed, Louise began to develop in directions which were threatening to her husband's ego. She got an important job on a fashion magazine and supported them; and, through her work, she moved into a world of modern art and leftist politics which baffled Christian. When she hung prints by Dufy, Braque, and Picasso in their apartment, he was angered: "'I like pictures with horses in them. Why should you like pictures like that?'" He had pleaded with her to stop calling him by the pet name *Baby*. The climactic blowup in their marriage came when he refused to go with her and an Irish lawyer from the longshoremen's union named Flaherty to see *Waiting for Lefty*. Merely by looking at her face, he knew that she was sexually involved with the left-wing lawyer; thus, he was attempting to boycott more than Clifford Odets.

Now, faced with the fact that he may soon have to support himself, Christian interviews for a job as a tailor's representative to various college campuses: "'We want a man . . . who as soon as you look at him, you say, 'There's a university man.'" During the interview, Mr. Rosenberg, his prospective employer, asks if it isn't true that Christian was in the same college backfield as Alfred Diederich. When he answers in the affirmative, Rosenberg asks if Christian knows that Diederich suffered a broken neck playing professional football. Christian's response to this information is internal: "That, at least, had turned out well." When he asks Louise whether he should take the job, he hopes that she will say no, since it will require him to be away from home most of the time. Instead, she encourages him to take it, calling him Baby throughout the scene. Now Christian knows that their marriage is truly over.

Visiting his old campus and walking across the old practice field, he mentally reviews the emptiness of his life: "The high point, an eighty-yard run in the practice, and a girl's kiss and everything after that a decline. . . . He hadn't practiced for 1929 and New York City and a girl who would turn into a woman." He is certain that Louise is with Flaherty, "a better man" who speaks "a language nobody had ever taught him." Suddenly, he cannot resist attempting to relive his one moment of glory and begins running across the field, until he sees a boy and girl sitting in the grass watching curiously. He attempts to explain: "'I—once I played here'"—and then retreats in sweat and embarrassment to his hotel.

"The Eighty-Yard Run" is an example of Shaw's craft at its flawless peak. The ironic impact of the story is conveyed almost exclusively through understated dialogue and symbols. As a youth, Christian is everyone's "darling"; and virtually everyone wants to "baby" him. Thus, he chooses to remain a boy even when he is thirty-five years old. Completely selfish, he can only resent and be terrified by Louise's increasing maturity. His resentment of her new tastes in art and politics is really a sublimation of his terror that she has become a woman and thus cannot possibly need him much longer. He knows that she no longer sees him as "an important figure" but is instead vividly aware that he is a "second-stringer." Thus, he has only his pleasure at the downfall of the All-American, Diederich, to console him. His concluding attempt to explain himself to the anonymous boy and girl is a symbolic confession to his and Louise's vanished youth that he has never done anything but "play."

The story achieves its richness through a contrast, which works effectively on several levels, between innocence and maturity. In addition to the disparity between Louise's attainment of maturity and Christian's arrested adolescence, there is an implied contrast between the Midwest as an Edenic land of innocent games and New York City as a center of sophisticated sexual, artistic, and political experience. Finally, in a manner highly reminiscent of the fiction of F. Scott Fitzgerald, the pre-1929 America of stability and optimism is contrasted with the depression-plagued nation of the 1930s. When the dominant interest of the people around Christian switches from college football to the theater of Clifford Odets, he is simply unable to learn this new "language."

Other well-known Shaw stories depict the mental turmoil of the central character suddenly unable to cope with the pressures of external reality. For instance, "The Sunny Banks of the River Lethe" (*SSFD,* 451–61) is an ironically amusing story about a loss of memory suffered by Hugh Forester, who works as a research man for a publishing company specializing in encyclopedias and calendars. Forester, who has always had a truly photographic memory, suddenly begins to forget things. At first terrified, he soon finds that forgetfulness has its pleasures as economic demands from his wife and two chronologically adult, but emotionally and financially dependent, children accelerate. Finally, he is able to forget the reality of his existence entirely and retreat to a river where he counts boats, except ferries, in company with a little boy. The mood of the story is comic, in places similar to contemporary absurdist fiction. Nevertheless, its underlying theme is serious—Forester wants an escape from the pressures of surviving in a capitalistic economy, and his mind conveniently supplies him with such an escape. The symbolic use of encyclopedias and calendars is effective. Again like the absurdists, Shaw is implying that our civilization has too much knowledge, compromised by too little wisdom and insufficient time to absorb and make meaningful all that we do know.

Sexuality is used as the principal metaphor for affluent society's fear of the irrational in "Circle of Light" (*SSFD,* 735–56). Martin, on his way from California to Paris, stops to visit his older sister, Linda, and her husband, John Willard, in Connecticut. During his first night at their home, he sees a man outside climbing a window trying to reach the upstairs bedrooms. When Linda argues against calling the police, Martin begins to suspect that she is having an affair. The next night, the three begin a round of cocktail parties; and Martin finds himself uncontrollably exaggerating his description of the prowler: "... the remembered face was being simplified, intensified, becoming heraldic, symbolic, a racial, dangerous apparition staring out of the dark and dripping forests at the frail safety of the sheltered circle of light." His description makes the other people at the parties "... remember that there were obscure and unpredictable forces always ready to descend upon them in their warm homes..." (*SSFD,* 743–44).

Ironically, Martin recognizes the face at the window when he meets Harry Bowman, one of the most respectable members of the small, upper-class Connecticut community. Staying over an extra day, he traps Bowman into a confession; the married businessman with a family says that, although his life appears happy, it is actually "a big blank." He adds that he only watches "the happy ones," hoping that some are not "fooling" and that he will be able to discover their "secret." Such secrets are revealed only in the most intimate moments, he assures Martin. He felt it essential to observe Linda and John having intercourse because they were his "last hope." Abruptly looking at his sister and brother-in-law dancing, Martin is certain that they are happy together.

The story's basic irony, of course, is that the "racial," "unpredictable forces" threatening to descend upon these people are internal. Ultimately, what they fear is their own emotional desperation; "the circle of light" is an illusion—a facade by which they fool others and attempt to fool themselves. Linda and John personify the few exceptions to the spiritual emptiness at the core of most upper-class lives. The reader feels that perhaps Linda sees through "the circle of light"—it is, after all, pointless to call the police to protect a people from its own emotional and spiritual deadness. Harry Bowman evokes Conrad's Kurtz—miraculously set down in contemporary Connecticut, but still obsessed with the horror inside himself and in the people around him.

"Where All Things Wise and Fair Descend" (*SSFD,* 708–21) is one of Shaw's best recent stories (it was first collected in *God Was Here But He Left Early*), and it adds some new twists to his treatment of American upper-class society. He utilizes southern California as a metaphor for the values represented by the Midwest in "The Eighty-Yard Run"; like the Midwest of that earlier story, southern California projects an external image of athletic youth and physical health. Beneath the surface, however, there is something very different—physical and emotional frailty and death itself. In the story, three college-age boys symbolize different aspects of the surface illusion and the underlying reality of southern California.

Steve Dennicott is the golden boy, as yet affected by only the most transitory of sorrows:

> Nobody he had ever cared for had as yet died and everybody in his family had come home safe from all the wars.

The world saluted him.
He maintained his cool.
No wonder he woke up feeling good.

Steve personifies the sunny California with which Americans have fallen increasingly in love throughout the twentieth century. "Where All Things Wise and Fair Descend" is a variation on the initiation-story motif, however; and Steve is unable to preserve such total innocence for very long. The catalyst for his confrontation with reality is a pale thin boy named Crane, whose football-playing brother has just died in a car accident.

Entering his English class the day after the accident, Steve discovers Crane writing Shelley's eulogy to Keats on the blackboard in tribute to his dead brother. One of the reader's first clues to an innate decency in Steve is his compulsion to comfort the grieving boy even though he has never been close to either of the brothers. On the basis of this advance, Crane asks Steve to join him on a drive along a desolate California highway to the spot of the brother's fatal accident. During the drive, the frail young boy talks about his brother, painting a picture of an unbelievable young man devoted to a code of total honesty. It becomes clear to Steve that Crane admired his athletic brother for all the wrong reasons and that he feels guilty for being alive while the conventionally gifted member of the family is dead. Crane also ridicules Steve's girlfriend, Adele, and when his companion objects, insists that "friendship is limitless communication."

Still, after the ride, Dennicott realizes that he envies the frail young boy: "Crane had the capacity for sorrow and now . . . he understood that the capacity for sorrow was also the capacity for living." Seeing Adele approaching, he finds himself instinctively turning away and avoiding her, but then remembers Crane's admiring account of his brother's brutal treatment of a girl in the name of honesty and "standards." He understands that Crane had taught him much, "but perhaps not the things Crane had thought he was teaching." Nevertheless, he vows to cease waking up "automatically feeling good."

As in most of his stories about the affluent, the predominant mood of the story is ironic; however, the irony is softened here by an underlying nostalgia and sadness personified by Crane. Described as "a discredit to the golden Coastal Legend," the frail, guilt-ridden young boy exemplifies the bitter outcast who cannot fit into the southern-California ideal of physical health and intellectual superficiality. Such an ideal is an illusion, anyway. There are calendars even on the Coast; and as Steve ultimately realizes, mere physical perfection is empty unless it matures into something intellectually and spiritually wiser. The dead brother is an especially intriguing figure: while he was idolized by everyone, the reader is made aware of his inner cruelty and fondness for giving others pain. "The golden Coastal Legend" grows out of a selfish search for perpetual youth, a search which leaves no time for humane treatment of others. Symbolically, Crane's brother could never attain the sad, but essential, wisdom that Steve Dennicott is developing at the end of the story; thus, he had to die or remain a perpetual adolescent like Christian Darling in "The Eighty-Yard Run."

"Where All Things Wise and Fair Descend" is rich in subtle ironies. The title itself conveys both the idea that the quest for perpetual youth is futile and that wisdom is sacrificed in its name. Crane's dead brother is hardly a John Keats; Crane himself is much more like the brilliant, physically fragile poet. The values of "the golden Coastal Legend," however, have caused Crane to undervalue his creativity and intellect; and he is destroying these qualities in a doomed attempt to immortalize his conventionally successful brother. The story contains one hint that Crane is aware of, and bitter about, what he is doing—his brother died when his car crashed into a tree, and Crane tells Steve that he plans to enter the forestry service: "'I'm not so enthusiastic about my fellow man, anyway, I prefer trees.'" This statement seems an unconscious expression of thanks by an outcast for the destruction of an unbearably popular brother.

In "Where All Things Wise and Fair Descend," Shaw has brought his portrayal of a spiritually hollow affluent America to the opposite end of the continent from where Michael Loomis watched the girls in their summer dresses. His moral judgment of this society remains constant, however. Locked into a selfish search for perpetual youth and sensual pleasure, it is terrified by the failure to discover any transcendent meaning to existence. Thus, it creates the illusions of "circles of light" and infallible reason to protect itself from too much reality.

These stories effectively illustrate why Shaw at his best is a moral, but not a didactic, writer. They unmistakably constitute an ethical condemnation of the society depicted; however, at no point does Shaw overtly recommend any moral code. Still, the reader can deduce that values opposite from those exhibited by the characters in these stories constitute an implicit standard of morality. Thus, it seems valid to argue that Shaw's criteria for a healthy society are that individual human worth and dignity not be denied by selfishness, that men and women have the courage to face their own fears and limitations, that superficial values not obliterate spiritual and intellectual growth, and that people not try to deny those irrational aspects of human existence which no amount of materialism and technology can ever eliminate. This code, rather than constituting a profoundly original set of values, is finally a variation of the great tradition of Western humanism, a fact that does not detract from Shaw's artistic achievement. He is an artist observing the human spectacle surrounding him, and the professional craft manifested in that observation guarantees the lasting merit of these stories.

The Great Depression and the Poor

Given his background in the Group Theatre, it was almost inevitable that Shaw would produce a group of stories focusing on the sufferings of the poor after 1929. Thematically, these stories, which were especially dominant in his first two collections, *Sailor off the Bremen* (1939) and *Welcome to the City* (1942), illustrate the proletarian concerns of most overtly leftist fiction. They illustrate the ways in which economic suffering debilitated poor people's sense of self-worth and made impossible any united action by setting them against each other in the struggle for survival. As in most proletarian literature, the villain in these stories is an abstract capitalist system. Still, Shaw's craft as a storyteller and his ability to create believable characters about which one cares define them as art, rather than straight propaganda.

"Second Mortgage" (*SSFD,* 29–32), which was initially published in the *New Republic* in 1937, is a memorable example of this type of Shaw story. The narrator recounts an episode of double victimization. His father and mother no longer answer the doorbell because they know that only bill collectors would be coming to see them; as his father says, "Strangers are never friends at the doors of the poor." Nevertheless, the young boy-narrator does open the door to admit an old woman named Mrs. Shapiro, who holds a second mortgage on their house. She tells of how she gave her life savings of eight thousand dollars, accumulated from a lifetime of running a vegetable store, to a financial advisor named Mayer to invest for her after her husband's death. Mayer invested all her money in absolutely worthless second mortgages on homes like that of the narrator's family, places where the people cannot even pay their first mortgages.

The narrator's father attempts to be gentle and makes a meaningless promise to the woman that she will be paid; but his mother is bluntly honest and tells her that she will, in fact, never be paid. At the mother's words, Mrs. Shapiro faints. When she is revived, she apologizes, saying that she has been going from house to house on foot for two months and that this is the fifth time she has fainted. The mother then makes the only realistic gesture of kindness the family can afford: "My mother gave her the address of a doctor who would wait for his money. . . ."

Mrs. Shapiro comes back three more times, but the narrator's family never lets her in again. The image of the victimized old woman locked out by the equally victimized family is a powerful statement of an unfeeling capitalism's ability to divide and thus conquer the poor. The boy's father is a man destroyed by the Great Depression, making consciously false promises in an effort to retain his pride, while the mother has of necessity repressed her sympathy for others. Thus, the family locks itself inside in an attempt to escape the many threats of economic reality; obviously, it represents no revolutionary threat to the system. The story is a powerful illustration of Shaw's craft; in only four pages, he memorably characterizes the narrator's father and mother and Mrs. Shapiro.

"Borough of Cemeteries" (*SSFD,* 13–19) also emphasizes the inability of the poor to fight back against an abstract system they cannot understand. Two cabdrivers, Elias Pinsker and Angelo Palangio, are hopelessly in debt to the company for which they drive. They drunkenly discuss the hopelessness of their situation, blaming it on marriage and "circumstances." Geary, an Irish labor organizer, attempts to convince them of the importance of unionization; however, instead of listening to him, Pinsker and Palangio have "a chicken fight" with their cabs, destroy them, and go off to the movies together. Geary's reaction is predictable: "'I can't watch this.... Two workin' men.'" Like "Second Mortgage," the story derives its main strength from Shaw's ability to create, in a very few pages, memorable characterizations. For instance, it is hard to forget Pinsker's speech about his life before and after 1929: "'I had th' biggest pigeon flight in Brownsville.... One hundred and twelve pairs of pedigreed pigeons.... I got fifteen pigeons left. Every time I bring home less than seventy-five cents, my wife cooks one for supper."

"Welcome to the City" (*SSFD,* 52–61), the title story of Shaw's second collection, is unique in its comic approach to the suffering of the depression. Mixing allusions to T. S. Eliot and MGM's 1932 film *Grand Hotel,* Shaw achieves an effective absurdist tone. The story is set in New York City's rundown Circus Hotel, which emanates "the odor of age and sin, all at reasonable rates." The main character, Enders, is an unemployed actor who has just arrived in New York City from Davenport, Iowa. The story's other characters are Bishop, the hotel owner who is constantly trying to sell Enders a dead chicken for sixty cents; Josephine, a prostitute who is trying to sell him herself; and a mysterious guest named Bertha Zelinka, who looks strikingly like Greta Garbo (who played the mysterious ballerina in *Grand Hotel*).

When Enders refuses Josephine, she begins to emulate Eliot's fortune-teller, predicting the actor's death by drowning (one remembers Eliot's "Fear death by water") or suffocation in a gas oven. She assures him at any rate that the city will destroy him (one is meant to recall Eliot's description of London in *The Waste Land* as an "unreal" city and especially the line "I had not thought death had undone so many"). As Enders reflects at one point: "It was hard to read T. S. Eliot in the Circus Hotel without a deep feeling of irony."

The action of the story centers around Enders's attempt to seduce the mysterious Bertha Zelinka. An early clue that her life has not been as glamorous as she projects comes when Enders sees her "poor, poverty-stricken, ruined teeth." Still, she keeps up a pretense of success until she breaks down and reveals that she is "a specialty dancer" and that in 1936, in Miami, Florida, a drunken man at a convention suddenly reached over and put an olive in her navel and then sprinkled salt on it. Grief-stricken at the memory of this humiliation, she confesses to Enders that she has been sitting in the lobby because she has nowhere else to go. He holds her, grateful to New York City for providing him with a woman who, at least with her mouth closed, "looked like Greta Garbo, the century's dream of passion and tragedy and beauty." The story works primarily because of its absurdist tone and Shaw's ability to depict New York City as a place of magic despite its surface of poverty and despair.

If there is a Shaw story which this writer admires even more than "The Eighty-Yard Run" and "The Girls in Their Summer Dresses," it is "Main Currents of American Thought" (*SSFD,* 20–28). Obviously containing autobiographical elements, the story depicts the struggles of Andrew, a young writer, to support his mother, his unmarried sister, and himself by writing radio adventure serials (as Shaw had done for his own family). The device which makes it effective is a constant juxtaposition of the mundane pressures of the young writer's life and the fantastic situations which he is imagining for his radio characters. The title comes from his guilt over having purchased Vernon Parrington's *Main Currents of American Thought;* the irony is that, at least on one level, the radio serials are a more realistic reflection of American mentality than Parrington's influential book.

In the story, his mother is pressuring Andrew for money for a new dress for his sister, who will only buy from Saks; and his girl friend, Martha, is demanding that they get married. He stares at the increasingly neglected notes he has gathered for a long-planned play. Elements of related social protest enter the story when he considers the price he will have to pay if he marries Martha, who is Jewish ("That meant you'd have to lie your way into some hotels, if you went at all, and you never could escape from one particular meanness of the world around you."), and his own guilt for not being in Spain fighting fascism. Anti-Semitism and appeasement to fascism were also, in Shaw's view, main currents of American thought.

The story's ending is a flawless example of Shaw's craft. Andrew himself, who writes escape fantasies, wants to escape. He attempts to join a group of boys playing baseball and is suddenly made aware of his mortality. Shaw commented in a 1978 interview that the story works because of its last sentence: "[Andrew's] arm hurt at the shoulder when he threw, and the boy playing second base called him Mister, which he wouldn't have done even last year, when Andrew was twenty-four."[7] It is a beautifully ironic ending. Andrew is still a very young man; but he is trapped into writing adolescent stories, can't get to his serious play, and can't afford to get married. Still, the "Mister" is a signal that the truly young no longer accept him as one of their own. Seemingly, there is not only no escape, but also no place, for Andrew.

These depression stories work because Shaw presents characters who are too defeated or too confused by the sheer struggle for survival to protest effectively. Yet the stories themselves clearly call for drastic change in the system. The inevitable result is a cutting irony which is much more effective than overt propaganda could ever be.

Warnings against Fascism

In this period, Shaw was angry about more than economic injustice. Andrew's guilt over not being in Spain reflects Shaw's feeling that Americans were dangerously neglecting the threat of fascism at home and abroad. In this feeling, he was one with most of the socially conscious writers of the time. Shaw did not limit his condemnation for this neglect to any social class; and, as in his stories about the depression, his mastery of craft allowed him to write stories which transcended propaganda.

"The City Was in Total Darkness" (*SSFD,* 150-61) presents a character named Dutcher, who is much like Michael Whitacre in *The Young Lions* in his cynicism, self-contempt, and devotion to hedonistic pleasure. Dutcher is a writer who has sold himself to Hollywood and is currently at work on an absolutely frivolous film called *Murder at Midnight*. The story opens when another Hollywood writer, Machamer, and Machamer's girl, Dolly, invite Dutcher to accompany them on a drunken weekend in Tijuana; they promise to bring along an "actress" named Maxine for him. Dutcher accepts, and the story works by juxtaposing details of their drunken carelessness with radio accounts of the outbreak of war in Europe. One sentence effectively illustrates Shaw's contrast of the tragedy unfolding in Europe and the irresponsible frivolity at home: "Machamer turned on the radio, and a man in London said that Hitler had not as yet answered Chamberlain's ultimatum and an orchestra played 'I May Be Wrong, But I Think You're Wonderful.'"

Dutcher, however, cannot escape death and pain even in Tijuana. At the hotel, Machamer suddenly confesses to Dutcher that the trip was planned totally for Dolly's sake; she is dying of Bright's disease and is attempting to experience all the hedonistic pleasure she can. Dutcher sees Dolly as a symbol of a dying world, and his attempt to deny reality is defeated:

> ... Hollywood, Dutcher thought, if I could bear *Murder at Midnight* and all the Murders at Midnight to come. I don't want to write any more books. An honest book is a criticism. Why should I torture myself into criticizing this poor, corrupt, frantic, tortured, agony-stricken world? Later, let the criticism come later.... (*SSFD,* 160)

Dutcher's musings reveal a key ingredient in Shaw's aesthetic theory at this point in his career: "An honest book is a criticism."

The story's title comes from a radio announcer's voice proclaiming that "Berlin is in total darkness." Hollywood and its moral and intellectual superficiality, Dutcher's guilt and weakness, and the dying Dolly are Shaw's symbols of another kind of darkness, the irresponsible refusal to face the reality of a world turned grotesque and threatening, that is blanketing the United States. Dutcher will not write his criticism later; he is no longer capable of the courage and effort required to be honest.

"Free Conscience, Void of Offense" (*SSFD,* 136–43) also depicts the irresponsibility of the American upper classes in the face of Hitler's rise to power. The story goes even farther than "The City Was in Total Darkness" and suggests an American complicity with the events in Europe. Margaret Clay, a college girl, is attempting to explain to her wealthy playboy father her desire to quit school. It is the autumn of 1938, and she demands that he realize the world is about to explode. They are meeting in a restaurant, and their conversation is periodically interrupted by drunken voices from the bar celebrating Neville Chamberlain's triumph at Munich. The story's climax comes when a party from Columbia enters celebrating their team's 27–14 football victory over Yale. The Columbia party begins to sing anti-Semitic songs; and, when her father joins in the laughter afterward, Margaret realizes the hopelessness of trying to talk to him. A brilliantly understated last sentence conveys Shaw's anger: "This was in the autumn of 1938, the year Columbia beat Yale 27–14 in the first game of the season." The story clearly establishes a link between America's indifference to the threat of Hitler and its own anti-Semitism.

In contrast, "Night, Birth, and Opinion" (*SSFD,* 162–68) focuses on the American proletariat's responsibility for the triumph of world fascism. Set in a bar, the story derives its power from an imposing cynic named Lubbock, who is systematically taunting the other men in the bar: Sweeney, an Irishman; DiCalco, an Italian-American; and William Cody, the bartender, whom Lubbock persists in calling "Buffalo Bill." Cumulatively, these characters symbolize the American and world working class; and Lubbock harangues them about their responsibility for allowing dictatorships to arise and warns them that, as always, they will be victimized no matter who wins the imminent world war.

The story's ending illustrates Shaw's ability to walk a tightrope between aesthetically valid and invalid sentimentality. Just as Lubbock has thoroughly enraged the others, a girl comes into the bar searching for someone who will give blood to her sister, who is having a difficult and dangerous time delivering a baby at a nearby hospital. Led by Lubbock, they all volunteer. Lubbock is chosen; and after the transfusion, they all go off to have a drink together. The symbolism of this ending comes close to being pat and obvious—Lubbock's blood symbolizes the honesty that potentially will give birth to a unified and, therefore, stronger proletariat. It is saved by Shaw's memorable characterization of the world cynic.

In "Sailor off the Bremen" (*SSFD,* 33–41), the proletariat ceases to be passive. A young American Communist named Ernest has been beaten and physically mutilated by a group of Nazis aboard a ship. As the story opens, his family and fellow party members are meeting to plan revenge on the Nazi, Lueger, who supervised the beating. The plan calls for Ernest's wife, Sally, to meet Lueger and bring him home, where her brother-in-law, Charley, and a party member, Dr. Stryker, will ambush him. Charley is nonpolitical and is acting strictly from the motive of family revenge. The plan works perfectly, and Lueger is beaten beyond recognition.

"Sailor off the Bremen" comes as close to being strict proletarian propaganda as anything Shaw ever wrote. Besides being a member of the Nazi party, Lueger is characterized as being devoted to sadomasochistic sexual activity. The story is saved by small, delicate touches which provide elements of humanity in a thoroughly brutal situation. Dr. Stryker is a little man, terrified of physical violence, but determined to go through with his assignment out of loyalty to Ernest and to the party. Perhaps what most saves the story is the characterization of Sally, who almost backs out at the last moment, when she is no longer able to deny to herself Lueger's humanity. Precisely at this point, however, the Nazi attempts a sadomasochistic sexual approach to her; and she proceeds with the plan. The tone of the story is thoroughly ironic; for instance, Lueger is a great fan of Deanna Durbin films. It says much about Shaw's mood at this point that he made "Sailor off the Bremen" the title story of his first collection; he seems to be implying that the violent threat of Nazism could effectively be answered by more violence.

The aesthetically best of this group of stories is "Weep in Years to Come" (*SSFD,* 144–49). Barely six pages long, it portrays two young lovers, Paul Triplett and Dora, confronting the reality of a world that will inevitably shatter their dreams and plans. The story is an excellent illustration of Shaw's techniques—it combines characterization and thematic statement in a minimum of words. The opening lines establish the dominant tone: "They came out of the movie house and started slowly eastward in the direction of Fifth Avenue. 'Hitler!' a newsboy called. 'Hitler!' "

Initially, Paul and Dora are simply enjoying walking along the street, looking into the windows of expensive stores. This mood is shattered, however, when Dora says that she would like to visit Germany someday and Paul replies that he almost certainly soon will " 'at the expense of the government. In a well-tailored khaki uniform.' " Dora attempts to talk him out of such an idea, pointing out that the young men who fought in the last war were "gypped." Paul not only agrees, but assures her that the common people who join the fight against Hitler will almost certainly be "gypped" again.

Still, he explains that, while he is not interested in killing Hitler, the individual, he wants to destroy the "idea" represented by the dictator:

> "In years to come I'll cry over the young boys I've killed and maybe if they kill me, they'll cry over me. . . . Some day maybe it'll be better. Maybe some day the world'll be run for people who like Mozart. Not today." (*SSFD,* 148)

The story ends with the two lovers looking at a reproduction of Renoir's *Luncheon of the Boating Party* and Paul saying, "'It's a picture of a summertime that vanished a long time ago.'"

The mixture of idealism and cynicism expressed by Paul gives the story a tone reminiscent of the disillusioned idealism expressed in Lost Generation fiction. The distinction made between Hitler and "the idea" he represents reaffirms Shaw's concern that the threat of fascism was not limited to Germany, but was a disease threatening every nation in the world, most definitely including the United States. Moreover, Shaw's fiction presents it as only one embodiment of a larger and more pervasive threat; in none of his stories or novels does one find a world run by people who care more about Mozart or Renoir than simply possessing power.

War Stories

Shaw's war stories rarely deal with combat itself. Their focus, instead, is on the psychological suffering of soldiers, the French resistance movement, and the treachery which will inevitably result in postwar bitterness. "Walking Wounded" (*SSFD*, 203–17), which won the 1940 O. Henry Award, is probably Shaw's most famous war story. It recounts the growing desperation of Peter, a British soldier stationed in Egypt who realizes that he no longer remembers what his wife looks like. The young soldier has been chaste for three years, since his last reunion with her. Prior to that, he had experienced some of the worst of combat and then was frequently and thoughtlessly unfaithful in Paris. Reunited with her, however, he instantly regretted his infidelity: "'After France... I felt as though my wife had healed me of a dreadful disease. She healed me of mud and death and friends dying on all sides. She's most beautiful, but I don't remember what she looks like.'"

Peter has made his wife into a symbol of all that is decent and clean in life; but after three years away from her, he has difficulty in remembering such idyllic values. Then a miracle seems about to happen: some American fliers offer Peter a ride home, and he goes in search of his commanding officer to ask permission. The story's ending is the key to its effectiveness. When Peter finds the officer's address, a strange colonel, wearing a tattered bathrobe and holding *The Poems of Robert Browning*, opens the door. The colonel is perfectly friendly, but informs Peter that the young man's commanding officer has moved and left no forwarding address. Peter, who survived Dunkirk, the first hour of Tripoli, and other brutal combat zones, has finally been vanquished by military bureaucracy.

Other details contribute to the story's power; for instance, at one point, a ten-year-old boy offers Peter a " 'fine French lady.' " The story's title emphasizes that Peter's belief in such old-fashioned values as fidelity, order, and cleanliness isolates and, thereby, psychologically wounds him in the war-torn twentieth century. He is one of Shaw's people who long for a world of Mozart and Renoir.

The fragile nature of wartime friendships is the central theme of "Gunners' Passage" (*SSFD,* 221–34), which focuses on the bond between Stais, a Greek-American once shot down and presumed dead in a bombing raid over Greece, and Whitejack, a North Carolinian who attended Thomas Wolfe's funeral. Stais feels guilty because he is about to be sent home, while Whitejack faces more combat. The story's underlying point, conveyed through Stais's irrational guilt, is reminiscent of much World War II fiction. In its way, "Gunners' Passage," like James Jones's *The Thin Red Line* and Norman Mailer's *The Naked and the Dead*, stresses the idea that friendships are essential during war for the survival of some traces of civility, but they leave one vulnerable to much pain.

Shaw's incidental ironic details make "Gunners' Passage" an effective story. Given their separate backgrounds, Stais and Whitejack would never have met in civilian life. Stais, the Greek-American, knew no Greek until he had to learn five words of that language in order to survive after being shot down while bombing the home of his ancestors. Shaw makes much ironic use of a third character, Novak, an Oklahoman who constantly reminisces about a completely innocent three-week friendship with a girl from "Flushing, Long Island." Novak has never been in combat, and he keeps asking Stais, the nineteen-year-old veteran, what it is like. Whitejack's account of Thomas Wolfe's funeral plays the same thematic role here as the references to Mozart and Renoir in "Weep in Years to Come": Wolfe is the symbol of a vanished, and now almost forgotten, world of peace and art.

While "Faith at Sea" (*SSFD,* 617–28) is a much-praised Shaw story, it lacks the ironic depth of his best fiction; and its plot is somewhat reminiscent of Hollywood war films: essentially, it is the story of the enforced maturation of thirty-five-year-old Lieutenant Peter Gifford Lawrence, who, having seen only seven or eight operations in his life, is forced to perform an emergency appendectomy on a young sailor aboard a tossing ship under constant threat of submarine attack in the mid-Atlantic. What ultimately saves the story from Hollywood triteness is its ending. After the successful operation, the patient's best friend, a young sailor named Constantine, is so overcome by gratitude to Lawrence that he is unable to recite the simplest things in gunnery class and is reduced to helpless embarrassment. The effect of Constantine's mortification is to force Lawrence to turn away from the class in order to hide his own emotions.

Two stories, "The Priest" (*SSIS,* 155–60) and "Part in a Play," focus on the French Underground resistance. In the former, a Jewish man, Solomon, has survived in the underground for three years by disguising himself as a Catholic priest. As the story opens, he is meeting Maurice, a devout Catholic and resistance fighter, at a sidewalk café to plan a mission. Just after Maurice leaves, the Gestapo arrive and arrest everyone at the café; Solomon believes that he is doomed, but is glad that Maurice escaped. In prison, however, the Gestapo tell Solomon that he must hear the confession of a man about to be shot; the man turns out to be Maurice, brutally tortured, almost beyond recognition. The two get through the confession without giving away "the priest's" secret; and, as Maurice is led away, he is able to convey to Solomon that he gave away no information under torture.

The story is important as an expression of Shaw's faith. In his 1964 travel book, *In the Company of Dolphins*, Shaw describes himself as an "agnostic."[8] The belief that his writing has always reflected is best outlined in *The Gentle People*—the need for common, ordinary people to resist evil as it is manifested in the state and other large institutions and their power to do so. Solomon and Maurice are not unlike that play's Jonah Goodman and Philip Anagnos; all four characters are little men courageously defying a powerful and inhumane oppressor. Early in "The Priest," Solomon remarks, " 'If we could really get the holy men of France into the movement, we would have a system of intelligence better than any telephone network.' " In Shaw's eyes, the traditional "holy men" (the representatives of organized religions) have been replaced in our times by "the gentle people." Such a view is not dissimilar to Hemingway's faith in "men of our Lord," by which he seems to have meant individuals not associated with any organized religion who act courageously in the name of humanity.

"Part in a Play" (*SSIS,* 639-51) emphasizes the difficulties of being such a secular "holy man." Its central character is Alexis Constantin, a good French actor who is never allowed to play anything other than ridiculous supporting roles such as aging cuckolds. He lives with his friend, Philippe Tournebroche, a famous leading man. Alexis constantly dreams of getting the big part which will make him a star. One of the most interesting aspects of "Part in a Play" is its combining of the war and the theater themes. When the Germans invade, Philippe, having convinced Alexis that, morally, they must boycott the theater, then joins the underground.

Alexis joins the boycott for a while, but he is finally tempted by Lamarque, an amusing intentional stereotype of the producer who can survive anything, into accepting a big part as a French miser. After Alexis tells himself, as he told Philippe, that he is after all an actor and not a politician, he accepts the role and "becomes a tradition in the French theatre." Still, Philippe renounces him.

In July 1944, as the Americans begin to liberate Paris, Alexis searches out Philippe and begs to join the resistance; Philippe still refuses to acknowledge their past friendship but accepts him into the movement largely because of the money Alexis has made playing the miser. Even after Alexis is killed saving the lives of Philippe and others, he knows that he is "unforgiven" because of the moment of weakness when he agreed to play the miser and "had been no more than an actor." Shaw uses a motif in this story that he repeats in others—one ironic implication of the title is that Alexis is doomed always to be a supporting player, both on and off the stage. As he sacrifices himself for his friends, he knows that Philippe is now a moral "leading man." It is difficult to be one of the century's secular "holy men"—Alexis is anything but a villain, and it is difficult not to sympathize with his decision to take the big part after years of longing. Shaw is emphasizing, however, that an evil as pervasive as Nazism can only be resisted totally, a truth that necessitates the suppression of many individual ambitions.

Two other stories, "The Veterans Reflect" and "Widows' Meeting," are not, strictly speaking, war stories, but they do emphasize legacies of the war which still seriously threaten the peace obtained only after years of bloody conflict. In both, the main point is that the fascist mentality is alive and well in America, an idea that is central to much post–World War II American literature—for example, James Jones's *From Here to Eternity,* Norman Mailer's *Barbary Shore,* and Arthur Miller's play *All My Sons.*

Militant Jewish Stories

Irwin Shaw has been occasionally criticized for responding to the Holocaust in too angry a fashion; he has been condemned for allowing something like an Old Testament cry for revenge to negate the possibility for philosophical investigation of the causes and implications of the Nazi atrocities such as one finds in the fiction of Saul Bellow and Bernard Malamud. This criticism is invalid on several grounds. Shaw is not trying to be Bellow or Malamud; he was, of course, originally a social-protest writer, both in his fiction and in his plays. Moreover, anger certainly seems a valid response to the murder of 6 million people. What most invalidates such criticism, however, is that a careful analysis of his fiction does not confirm it. In a few stories, Shaw does consider violent retaliation as the only valid response to anti-Semitism, but he does not do so unthinkingly.

Probably his most angry fictional response to anti-Semitism is contained in the story "Residents of Other Cities" (*SSIS,* 124–41). First collected in *Sailor off the Bremen* and set in Kiev, Russia, in 1918, it demonstrates that Shaw's anger at anti-Semitism was present well before the Nazi atrocities. Kiev, in the story, is in the center of the struggle between the White Russians and the Bolsheviks; and a hideous pattern takes shape: each time the Czar's troops retake the city, they commit systematic atrocities against its Jewish residents. Shaw focuses on one family's attempts to survive.

Sixteen-year-old Daniel is forced into maturity during the horror, when his father advocates peace and acceptance even as the family is repeatedly beaten and robbed. Finally, a neighbor named Kirov offers the family sanctuary, only to come later with a new mob, who rape Daniel's aunt and seventeen-year-old sister and murder his uncle.

Still, the father advocates forgiveness; but when the Bolsheviks recapture the city, Daniel goes to them and demands a gun. They grant his request, and one sleepy soldier watches as Daniel shoots down, one by one, the members of the Kirov family. Clearly, the philosophical conflict in the story is between the father's passivity and Daniel's vengeance. It is equally clear that Shaw rejects the father's stance; Daniel comments early in the story: "I didn't believe in my father's prayers. My father was always at the side of God and he neglected life. I hated this insane holiness, this neglect of flesh, the denial of the present for the eternal." This judgment can be taken as accurately reflecting Shaw's faith—concern should be for man's suffering in this world, and actions should be taken to alleviate it. The concept of God as an abstraction that condones human suffering has become one of man's deadliest enemies. It is significant that the father never speaks to Daniel again and is murdered when the Czarists retake the city. His other-worldliness is suicidal.

While it is obviously preferable to his father's course of action, Daniel's revenge is not, however, clearly asserted as wholly right. It forces a break with his family and, more significantly, does not really satisfy him as he had imagined it would: "This had not been the deep pleasure I had imagined in Kirov's room. The balances were not even. They had died too easily. They had not suffered enough pain. They had come off best in the bargain, finally." Daniel has learned what Shaw knew when he wrote the story. During atrocities like the Russian pogroms or the Nazi Holocaust, the sheer weight of horror makes clear, correct answers impossible to find.

Inevitably, it was World War II and the Nazi massacre of 6 million Jews that produced Shaw's most sustained reaction in fiction against anti-Semitism. "Residents of Other Cities" is the work of a young writer, and in no other story does Shaw advocate an answer even as clear or acceptable as Daniel's revenge. Of the militant Jewish stories, probably the best known is "Act of Faith"; and it is indeed an excellent story. Often anthologized, it was included in the *O. Henry Prize Stories of 1946* and the *Best American Short Stories of 1947*. Its importance to Shaw's thought is indicated by its position as the title story of his third collection.

The central figure in "Act of Faith" (*SSFD*, 243–56) is Norman Seeger, a young Jewish-American soldier who has survived the invasion of Normandy and the liberation of Paris. Seeger is being pressured by his Gentile friends, Olson and Welch, to sell a German Luger, which had belonged to a German SS major whom he had killed. They want him to sell the gun so that the three of them will have money to spend in Paris. While Seeger is attempting to decide, he receives a letter from his father, which represents one of the angriest and most significant statements against American anti-Semitism in all of Shaw's fiction.

The letter describes Norman's brother Jacob, now hopelessly paranoid as a result of anti-Semitism in the United States Army and at home. The father, a university economics professor, then details a new virulent wave of discrimination against Jews in the States:

> "Wherever you go these days—restaurants, hotels, clubs, trains—you seem to hear talk about the Jews, mean, hateful, murderous talk. . . . The day that Roosevelt died I heard a drunken man yelling outside a bar, 'Finally, they got the Jew out of the White House.' And some of the people who heard him merely laughed and nobody stopped him. . . . "

This prejudice is having terrible psychological effects on the father. He looks hopefully among the lists of casualties for Jewish names and feels a " 'twitch of satisfaction' " that Norman and Jacob were wounded and a third brother killed in the war. Most painfully of all, he is himself developing a kind of anti-Semitism: " 'I feel [the Jews] are boring the rest of the world with their problems, they are making demands upon the rest of the world by being killed, they are disturbing everyone by being hungry and asking for the return of their property.'" The father's letter seems to refute the critical charge that Shaw's anger prevents him from a real investigation of the psychological effects of anti-Semitism.

For Norman, the Luger had previously represented a "memento" of justice won in the Allied defeat of the Nazis. Now it comes to represent more, as he contemplates a response comparable to Daniel's vengeance in "Residents of Other Cities": "If the mobs were coming down the street toward his house, he was not going to die singing and praying." As he remembers his own encounter with anti-Semitism in the army, this feeling grows stronger.

Still, he has never known anything but friendship from Olson and Welch; and, in an effectively understated last scene, they again demonstrate their lack of prejudice. Seeger then decides to place his hopes in what they have meant to him and sell the gun. It is truly "an act of faith"; except for Olson and Welch, he has no reason to believe in a more decent world after the war and, in fact, has an infinite number of reasons to expect the opposite. The selling of the Luger is reminiscent of Noah Ackerman's affirmation in *The Young Lions* that after the war, "the human beings will run the world." The preponderance of evidence in that novel and in "Act of Faith" contradicts such optimism, but in both cases Shaw is saying that one must reject Daniel's solution and that it is necessary to hope.

In the *Act of Faith* collection, however, Shaw was not ready to forgive the Germans. "Retreat" (*SSFD,* 235–42) describes the confrontation during the German retreat from Paris between a Parisian Jew who has survived the war and a German major. The major argues that he is an automobile salesman and family man and a soldier only by accident; he further asserts that the German Army had nothing to do with any atrocities, which he says were all committed by the Gestapo and the SS. He then asks: "'What can I do . . . to wash my hands?'" Segal, the Parisian Jew, answers: "'You can cut your throat . . . and see if the blood will take the stain out.'"

The faith in a humane world advocated by Norman Seeger and Noah Ackerman was to be almost instantly crushed by the horrors which attended the establishment of a Jewish state in the Mideast.

In a few stories, Shaw focuses his anger upon the Allies, especially the British, who he believes permitted and even encouraged much of the barbarous treatment of refugees from the Holocaust in Europe. Probably the best of these stories is "Medal from Jerusalem" (*SSFD,* 187–202), which focuses on the love affair between Mitchell Gunnison, a decent but superficial American from Vermont, and Ruth, a Jewish girl who escaped Berlin for Palestine.

Mitchell possesses the decency, but not the requisite strength, of Shaw's "gentle people"; Ruth, on the other hand, is tremendously strong, but the horror of her experience has left her resigned to unhappiness, if not death. Palestine itself becomes a symbol of Ruth: "They walked past the corner where the Italian bombers had killed a hundred and thirty people on a Friday morning the year before, and turned into Ruth's street.... One of [Mitchell's] strongest memories of Tel Aviv would be the strains of Tchaikovsky and Brahms and Beethoven coming through the opened windows on every street of the town..." (*SSFD,* 195). Once again, Shaw uses music to symbolize the human potential for moral strength and decency; and Ruth does indeed possess great external and internal beauty. Still, the fact that she is doomed is symbolized by the 130 people killed by the Italian bombers.

Her stories of flight from Europe are dominated by almost unbelievable horror. She tells of her own escape from Europe "in the hold of a fifty-year-old Greek ship with 700 people for over a month." When her mother had tried to join her, the British refused to let the ship land; and it blew up in the harbor, killing her mother. She assumes that the bomb was set by the refugees themselves: " 'Some people would die, but some would be saved. If the boat went back to Europe, everybody would be killed....' " Ruth has survived much; but she now assumes that it is inevitable that she will marry a sadistic Arab who will probably someday kill her. Only Mitchell could save her from this fate, but she knows he is too weak and superficial. Still, in a touching scene, she gives him a St. Christopher medal for his travels: " 'It is not in my religion, but I don't think it would do any harm to give it to you.... Something like this, something holy, might have a tendency to be more effective if it comes from Jerusalem, don't you think?' " Mitchell is touched, but knows he will forget her as soon as he is back in Vermont.

In this story there is great anger at the Allies for continuing the oppression of a people they are fighting a war to save. Still, Shaw's craft, especially in the characterization of Ruth, defines it as art rather than propaganda.

In an excellent story with an entirely different setting, "The Inhabitants of Venus" (*SSFD,* 527–46), Shaw again emphasizes that anti-Semitism did not disappear with the end of World War II. First published in 1963, it moves toward the forgiveness of the German people, as opposed to the Nazis, which Shaw could not yet offer in "Retreat." This story was adapted brilliantly for television by PBS in 1979. Robert Rosenthal, a Jew born in France but an American citizen, returns each year to Switzerland to ski. Painfully, Robert has worked at perfecting an attitude of ignoring Germans. After VE Day, he felt "an intense relief that he no longer had to *think* about them"; still they are not quite people to him, but are more like inhabitants of a distant planet like Venus. Now going up in the lift, he overhears a voice cursing and ridiculing Americans in German.

Looking toward the voice, Robert recognizes an Austrian who in 1938, when Robert was fourteen years old, left him to die in the mountains when he lay helpless with a broken leg. The Austrian had started to help, but hearing Robert's last name, had instead deserted him. Now, Robert realizes that he must kill the Austrian; however, just as he is planning his vengeance, he sees that the man has only one leg and loses all desire "to punish the already punished."

The story is vital to an understanding of Shaw's thought. Robert does strongly consider the response of Daniel in "Residents of Other Cities": "For the first time in his life he understood the profound, sensual pleasure of destruction." Recognizing, however, that there has been enough suffering already, he rejects it; watching the man ski courageously with one leg, he accepts the fact that, for him, there can be only "a cold, hopeless everlasting forgiveness."

Thus, the charge that Shaw responds with such intense anger to anti-Semitism that he is incapable of true philosophical inquiry is simply not true. There is a considerable growth in intellectual complexity from "Residents of Other Cities" to "The Inhabitants of Venus." Daniel's response is considered and rejected in the latter story, as well as in "Act of Faith." Total forgiveness of the German people for the Nazi atrocities was a great deal to ask of any Jewish writer in 1945, the date of publication of "Retreat." Still, Shaw's later stories do show a movement toward such forgiveness. It is also important to note the facts that Shaw recognizes that the Germans did not invent prejudice against his people and that he equally condemns anti-Semitism in the Russians, the British, and the Americans.

Protest against McCarthyism

The end of World War II did not bring to either Paul Triplett or his creator their ideal of a world run by people who love Mozart and Renoir. Instead, in America, the witch-hunts inspired by Senator Joseph McCarthy of Wisconsin dominated the 1950s. In *Paris! Paris!* Shaw writes:

> Bruised, but only glancingly, by the ignominious antics of the witch-hunters, you can afford to be amused when you hear that the librarian at the USIA library in Naples had hurriedly whisked your own books to the safety of the cellar just before the arrival of the famous McCarthy team of watchdogs, Cohn and Schein.[9]

It is likely that Shaw was only "glancingly bruised" during the hysteria of those years because he was in Paris. Certainly, the essentially proletarian emphasis of his drama and fiction made him a prime target of right-wing investigation and he was, in fact, blacklisted.

Shaw published three stories which deal with the phenomenon of McCarthyism; and, while one is comic in tone, he did not view what was happening in his native country with anything like amusement. In fact, it is possible that he gave "The Green Nude" (*SSFD,* 365–82) its comic tone as a device to control his anger and frustration. The story concerns Sergei Baranov, who fought for the Bolsheviks in the Russian revolution and, afterward, establishes a reputation as a popular painter of equally delectable garden products and female nudes. His demise begins when he marries Anna Kronsky, a bitter and emasculating woman who holds a high position in the Communist party; the Anna Kronsky characterization is in part a satire of Clare Boothe Luce. She totally dominates and ridicules Baranov; and out of subconscious frustration, he paints a grotesque, surrealistic green nude which everyone but Anna and himself recognizes as looking like his wife.

An art critic, Suvarnin, sees the painting, pronounces it "'Great,'" and then immediately denounces it as "'... a nauseating sample of decadent, bourgeois art.'" Baranov is shocked, but Suvarnin appears at his studio and explains that he was forced by party officials to write the negative review. Anna is immediately removed from her powerful position; and after several official threats, the couple flee the country to Germany, accompanied by Suvarnin.

In Germany, the pattern of events is repeated. During Baranov's period as a popular painter, Anna is made the head of a women's training program by Hitler. When the German green nude appears, she again loses her power and Baranov is tortured by the Gestapo and threatened with sterilization. This time, again accompanied by Suvarnin, they flee to the United States. Baranov again has a vogue as a popular painter of fruits and nudes, and Anna is "attached to a nationally circulated news magazine as an authority on Communism and Fascism.... By the end of the war...[she is] in charge of the departments of Political Interpretation, Medicine for Women, Fashion, Books, and, of course, Child Care."

Inevitably, Baranov's American green nude appears just as McCarthyism sweeps the country. He is hounded by the Treasury Department over his tax returns, investigated by the FBI, and repeatedly denounced as a subversive. The story's ending cements its comic tone. Baranov notices for the first time that his grotesque nude looks like Anna. But Suvarnin assures him that it does not; and the three plan to flee the country, as Baranov wonders aloud, "'What kind of fruit...do you think a man could find to paint in Costa Rica?'"

Shaw is having some light-hearted fun satirizing Freudian interpretations of art as well as the power of *Time* magazine. Still, two quite serious points come through clearly—McCarthyism was an outbreak of the same views that produced Stalinism and Hitler; and totalitarianism, which is devoted to intellectual death, always threatens the artist, who personifies creativity.

The tone of Shaw's two other stories which deal with McCarthyism is anything but comic. "The Climate of Insomnia" (*SSFD,* 383–98) is not predominantly a protest story, but is rather an analysis of modern, "doubtful" man haunted by the new equivalents of Greek "Fate": nerves and fear of cancer. Cahill, a university philosophy professor, comes home late to find a message that his friend Reeves has called. Afraid to awaken his wife, he stays up all night attempting to guess what the call could have been about. During this long night, he confronts several unpleasant facts and possibilities about himself and the world: he is now forty years old and no longer "witty"; he may be threatened with dismissal ("Purge by frost. Execution, university style. The polite death among the library shelves. . . . "); and another war threatens (people of "influence" seemed to want another one). Finally, he decides that Reeves could only be calling to warn him that he is the target of a McCarthyite witch-hunt currently in progress on the campus.

Cahill is not, in fact, a Communist, but he did once go to a party meeting with Reeves; and he wonders what he can do if he is called before a committee: "Just what was honorable in a situation like this? Was there honor in perjury? Or did honor lie in destroying your friends? Or destroying yourself?" The story ends with Cahill unable to find out what Reeves called about for another weekend; and "wildly, he contemplated the thought of living until Monday" (*SSFD,* 395–98).

"The Climate of Insomnia" does so many things well that it is one of Shaw's best short stories. Once again, he memorably portrays the genteel struggles of the academic. He probes the psychological terrors of the intellectual at mid-century; and even though he treats McCarthyism only briefly, he effectively analyzes the rampant paranoia which it induced. The vicious results of this form of paranoia are the sole focus of "Goldilocks at Graveside" (*SSFD,* 399–417). Shaw's craft in utilizing the devices of a story within a story and delayed information makes it art rather than propaganda. The story opens with the funeral of the former Foreign Service officer who was disgraced and forced to resign because of the McCarthy hysteria. At the funeral the officer's widow, Victoria Bryant, is shocked to see a man named Borden, a consul who had pretended to be her husband's friend but had refused to help him. Although Borden had been nicknamed "Goldilocks" because of his blond hair and seemingly irreversible good fortune, he, too, was later disgraced and forced to resign.

Seeing Borden stirs Victoria's old memories; and returning home, she begins to read a fictionalized account of her husband's sufferings which she wrote, but was never able to get published. Her story, entitled "From the Desert," details the conflicts among herself, her husband, and Borden. Initially, she hoped that it would be published and that it would revive her husband's interest in living: "Writers of the first class, I have read somewhere, are invariably men or women with one obsession.... I share that one thing with them.... That obsession is my husband and it is of him that I shall write." After three rejections, however, she gave up submitting it: "Wishing does not make a writer, nor education, nor injustice, nor suffering."

Through Victoria's short story, the reader learns that Borden was the man responsible for Bryant's destruction; he had acted out of terror when Victoria had stumbled onto knowledge of the consul's homosexuality. John never knew Borden's treachery; and Victoria was not certain until the day of the funeral. Still, when the consul was disgraced, they were pleased. Remembering their pleasure, Victoria is disturbed anew: "In a time of sharks, must all be sharks?" It is a tribute to Shaw's craft that the reader is not certain of the depths of Borden's deceit until the last line of the story. "Goldilocks at Graveside's" theme is that, in a time of carefully cultivated paranoia, people who are not habitually vicious will become so; the central horror of the McCarthy years was that this phenomenon occurred repeatedly.

"The Green Nude," "The Climate of Insomnia," and "Goldilocks at Graveside" all emphasize Shaw's revulsion over the McCarthy years. It is significant that the three stories are of considerably more aesthetic value than his 1951 novel, *The Troubled Air*, which deals with the same concern. *The Troubled Air* is clearly "a thesis novel" and suffers from the limitations of that genre. Once again, Shaw's vision makes him consistently more effective with the short story than with the novel.

Stories of American Expatriates in Europe

As described in *Paris! Paris!* Shaw's voluntary exile in France began more or less by accident; still, one suspects that such outrages as the McCarthy witch-hunts encouraged him to extend it for twenty-five years. In that time, he began to write a new kind of short story. The collections *Tip on a Dead Jockey* and *Love on a Dark Street* are dominated by fictional accounts of the adventures of American expatriates in Europe. These expatriate stories largely abandon the social protest underlying his earlier fiction. One feels that Shaw had been pleading for a world run by lovers of Mozart and Renoir since the depression, and the McCarthy phenomenon represented his last disillusionment in such a hope. Thus, the expatriate stories work from a different kind of moral basis; they are very much in the tradition of Henry James in their depiction of innocent Americans bringing harm to themselves or others in sophisticated Europe.

"A Year to Learn the Language" (*SSFD,* 328–54) is an amusing example of this kind of Shaw story. Nineteen-year-old Roberta James (one wonders if the character's last name could be a veiled tribute to Henry James) has come to Paris for a year to study painting. She wants excitement in Paris; but she also wants to avoid accidents. ("'I want to be *precise*. I don't want anything to be an accident. . . .'") Typically for a Shaw character, such a mixed ambition leads her into a series of accidents.

Early in the story, a gallery owner named Patrini establishes a contact for her with a wealthy baron whose name she never learns. Patrini gives her a hidden warning about the Baron, the import of which she misses: "'The Baron has a famous collection, as you know, of course.'" After buying two of her paintings, the Baron invites her to dinner; and she decides to break a date with her French boyfriend, Guy, in order to go. ("' . . . Artists must be ruthless, or they are not artists. Remember Gauguin. Remember Baudelaire.'") At the dinner party, the Baron shows her that he has hung her two paintings with a Matisse drawing between them.

Initially pleased, she suddenly realizes that she has been invited by the Baron solely as an object of amusement for sophisticated French society, and she rushes to find Guy. Having refused his sexual advances several times, she now tells Guy that she is ready to sleep with him. Guy takes her to a cheap, freezing hotel and then breaks down and confesses that he is a sixteen-year-old virgin, after which he falls asleep.

The story makes use of the innocence-experience theme on several levels. Roberta, the American, is innocent enough to fall into the trap of being ridiculed by sophisticated French society; but ironically, she is much more experienced than Guy, whom she has thought of as representing European sexual experience. As is appropriate for the heroine of an initiation story, Roberta loses much of her own intellectual, if not her sexual, innocence because of the accidents which she experiences.

"Then We Were Three" (*SSFD,* 559–82) is an excellent story also dominated by the loss-of-innocence theme. It concerns the attempt of three expatriate young Americans—two boys, Munnie and Bert, and a girl, Martha—to establish an Edenic existence together. Set in Europe, it does not utilize that continent as the symbol of destructive experience. Munnie, Bert, and Martha have agreed to live together on a strictly platonic basis; but their own sexual tensions destroy such an arrangement. Munnie, the decent one, has fallen in love with Martha, but struggles to be faithful to their agreement. It is time for him to go home, but his "gift of instantaneous nostalgia" tells him that life will never be as good again, and he delays his departure for a day.

For their last day, the three decide on a picnic near the sea, during which Munnie realizes how thoroughly he has been tricked and used by the other two. Shaw had already given the reader hints of a strain of cynicism and brutality in Bert, and he confirms those suspicions during the outing. First, he analyzes the "gifts" of the three. Martha has "beauty," he says, which she should "use" on a man; Munnie's only "gift" is "virtue," which is obviously worthless; Bert himself has two "gifts," "charm" and the ability not to care, both of which are of great worth. After this analysis, even the innocent Munnie begins to suspect that he has been duped and walks away from the other two and looks out at the sea.

Seeing an overturned boat and a man and a woman in the water about to drown, he calls to Bert and Martha, who make it abundantly clear that they do not care if both people drown. Munnie, in contrast, plunges naked into the sea to save the endangered couple. Afterward, his two friends laugh at him. Even though Munnie is now certain that Bert and Martha have been breaking the rules from the first, he blames himself for "letting the summer go on one day too long."

The story is beautifully told, supported by an underlying Garden of Eden imagery, which is both thematically crucial and consistently understated. For example, Munnie's nudity, linked with his knowledge of Bert and Martha's betrayal, clearly associates him with Adam. He has, in all innocence, tasted of the Tree of Knowledge. One would have to search through a great deal of fiction to find a familiar pattern of symbolism more effectively understated.

The title story of Shaw's 1957 collection, "Tip on a Dead Jockey" (*SSFD,* 500–26), is probably the most critically admired of all his tales of expatriates. Set in Paris, it is a wonderfully comic account of the confrontation between Lloyd Barber, a thirty-year-old American ex-flier and present-day drifter in Europe, and a masterful con man, Bert Smith. Barber is approached at the race track by Smith, who gives accurate tips on all the races. Smith knows all about Barber; and when the American asks how, the con man only replies: "'. . . Paris is a small city.'" Finally, Smith reveals what he wants from Barber—he needs someone who can fly a plane to smuggle "close to a million and a half dollars" from Egypt to France.

The ex-flier is considering the offer when Smith invites him to a steeplechase race and, as usual, gives his tip. He claims that this information comes directly from the jockey. In the race, the horse falls and the jockey is apparently killed; Barber takes this accident as an omen and backs out of the smuggling scheme. Barber's friend Jimmy Richardson arrives, however, and Smith starts to work on him. Barber is confident that Richardson is too stupid to be used for such an elaborate scheme, until the friend suddenly disappears for several days. Then, in a perfect ending, Richardson returns, suddenly quite wealthy; and Barber realizes that his friend's very stupidity was the special insurance Smith always carries.

It is time to go home, he decides: "This continent is not for me." The story is an especially ironic treatment of the theme of the innocent American in sophisticated Europe because, before meeting Smith, Barber has considered himself to be not only experienced but jaded. Smith is an example of the charming con man who appears in such novels as *Nightwork*.

"The Man Who Married a French Wife" (*SSFD,* 462–78) illustrates another variant of the same theme. Not at all comic, it focuses on the thirteen-year marriage of the American, Beauchurch, and the Frenchwoman, Ginette. Beauchurch has spent years perfecting a facade of calmness and rationality in order to gain his material and political goals; he has succeeded at the expense of suppressing a strong temper and capacity for irrational rage. Vacationing in France, he discovers Ginette in conversation with a French journalist named Mestre. He suspects Ginette of infidelity and begins to hate Mestre. To him, Mestre is " 'the perfect model of the French intellectual' " in that " 'he's self-important and impressed with his own intelligence, and he has a condescending attitude toward Americans.' "

From Ginette, he learns that Mestre fears for his life because of an anticipated revolution in France and wants Beauchurch to smuggle some money out of the country for him. Beauchurch hesitates until Ginette confesses that Mestre was her first and only lover before himself and that she had once promised to marry him. Beauchurch's long-controlled temper almost explodes; but then he realizes that his marriage has been made stronger by Ginette's revelation and that Mestre, and not himself, is the real victim of infidelity.

"Love on a Dark Street" (*SSFD,* 601–17), the title story of Shaw's 1965 collection, is not only comic but absurdist in tone. Nicholas Tibbell, a thirty-year-old American, has been stationed for six months in Paris; hopelessly shy, he has missed out on the excitement of Parisian life and, in nostalgia, he places a call to his American fiancée to ask her to marry him. Waiting for the call to go through, he witnesses an argument on the street among an old man, M. Barnary-Cointal; his daughter, Moumou; and her lover, Raoul. Raoul and Moumou have been living together and she is pregnant, but Raoul plans to marry someone else because she is never at home.

Their conflict intrudes on two lovers in a darkened doorway across the street. Ultimately, Moumou attacks Raoul with her handbag, driving him away, and then assaults his motorcycle. At this point, a Spanish woman and "a man in a dark suit" appear, also arguing. The man claims that the woman has tricked him into buying her some flowers for sixty cents and demands to be repaid. M. Barnary-Cointal intercedes between them and almost has to fight "the man in the dark suit"; at this point, someone suggests calling the police, and Tibbell is told by the overseas operator that Betty in America is not home. He feels relieved because he no longer wants to marry anyone. The story reads almost like a brief absurdist parody of such complex James works as *The Ambassadors* with their male American spectators watching, but afraid to join in, the spectacle of life around them.

Whether comic or serious in tone, these expatriate stories are an important part of Shaw's achievement. The protest of the earlier stories is missing, but the craft is still present. In one late masterpiece, "God Was Here But He Left Early," Shaw combines the best ingredients of the protest stories and the expatriate tales. Before it is discussed, however, three types of earlier stories should be briefly treated. Before his twenty-five-year residence in France, Shaw was a New Yorker, and he often pays tribute to that city in his fiction. He also loves sports, especially football, and admires proud, stubborn individuals in conflict with powerful institutions.

New York City Stories

In Irwin Shaw's fiction, New York City is a magical blend of the delightful and the grotesque—a city where one may encounter virtually anything. In "The Indian in Depth of Night" (*SSFD*, 304–8) good-natured O'Malley goes walking alone in Central Park and is initially accosted by a homosexual and then by an Indian ex-prizefighter named Billy Elk, who threatens to rob him and then to turn him in to the police as a homosexual. When a police officer is found, Billy Elk only asks directions to the nearest reservation and disappears. The last sentence makes the story: "O'Malley walked home slowly, breathing deeply the clear morning air, pleased to be in a city in which Indians roamed the streets and went to great lengths to prove their friendliness and goodness of heart" (*SSFD,* 308).

A similar absurdist tone is found in "Material Witness" (*SSFD,* 309–13), in which a mediocre little man named Barnum walks home from work one day, turns at the wrong corner, and witnesses a gangland execution. Excited, he begins to tell a crowd about it and is put in jail for a year as a "material witness." During the year, he loses his family and his job. Shaw's mastery of endings is again the key to the story's success: on the first day out of jail, Barnum witnesses a car accident but walks quickly away, refusing to say anything. The story illustrates Shaw's accident theme in an absurdist fashion. Comedy is also found in "Lemkau, Pagron and Baufox," in which three short, unattractive businessmen extend their partnership to include dinner with a beautiful showgirl.

The atmosphere of New York City is crucial to many of Shaw's other stories. Before Paris, it was, because of its infinite variety of dramatic human activity, the only true writer's city for him. The title of his second collection is, after all, *Welcome to the City;* and until 1951, "the City" for Irwin Shaw could only be New York.

Corruption in Sports

Shaw played quarterback for Brooklyn College and later played as a semipro. Since he has always loved the game of football, it is not surprising that in a few stories he uses its commercialization as a symbol of the corruption of American institutions. "'March, March on Down the Field'" (*SSFD,* 132–35) is an amusing satire of a semipro football owner, Scheepers, who makes his team dress in a freezing locker room; cuts their pay 50 percent because of a small crowd; forces them to play without helmets; and then, as a final insult, orders them to charge out onto the field to a recording of a college fight song.

"Whispers in Bedlam" (*SSFD,* 669–707) and "Full Many a Flower" (*SSFD,* 722–34) satirize the hypocrisy in contemporary professional football. "Whispers in Bedlam" is actually a novella written in a mood of fantasy. Because of a freak ear operation, its main character, a thoroughly mediocre player, develops the ability to hear other people's thoughts and becomes an overnight star. The characterization of the coach, who mixes right-wing politics, fundamentalist religion, and military discipline to achieve success, is, however, the most amusing aspect of the story.

One suspects that the satirized coach in "Whispers in Bedlam" is based on Tom Landry of the Dallas Cowboys; and this suspicion is confirmed by "Full Many a Flower." In the latter story, Carlos Romanovici is an "unutterably rich" gypsy who owns the state of Vermont. Still, he has "a psychic wound": he was once dropped from a National Football League team. Romanovici's "psychic wound," of course, parodoxically evokes Ernest Hemingway and the psychology of the entire "lost generation." To gain revenge for his wound, the owner of Vermont builds an entire rival league from NFL castoffs. The climax comes when his league champion, Montpelier, challenges and defeats Dallas, the NFL champions, by playing strictly improvised football which the professional, computerlike Dallas team cannot comprehend. The winning touchdown pass is caught by a Montpelier player wandering aimlessly around the field suffering from a concussion. Tom Landry and the Dallas Cowboys have long been main targets of liberal sportswriters because of their systematic, computerized approach to football. Shaw seems to be joining this attack because of his understandable belief that football should, above all, be fun. Other sports also come in for comparable satire from Shaw; for instance, "Stop Pushing, Rocky" is an amusing satire of corruption in boxing.

Portraits of Stubborn Individuals

Irwin Shaw is, in essence, a believer in the traditionally American ideal of the worth of the individual; and it is not surprising to find among his work a group of stories which celebrate absolutely stubborn characters often in defiance of some external system. For instance, "The Monument" (*SSFD,* 76–81) depicts a bartender who defies his employer and absolutely refuses to serve inferior liquor:

"'. . . in my bar, good drinks are served.'" "Triumph of Justice" (*SSFD,* 98–106) and "The Dry Rock" both present characters who baffle everyone else by simply demanding justice.

The central character in "Triumph of Justice" is Mike Pilato, an immigrant farmer who identifies with and trusts nature: ". . . the duplicity of Nature was expected and natural. Also no documents were signed in the compact with Nature. . . ." When he is cheated out of some money by his neighbor, Victor Fraschi, he astonishes everyone by acting as his own attorney. He wins the case when he forces a confession from Fraschi by threatening to hit him with a chair. Pilato's fundamental concept of justice wins him the applause of the courtroom spectators; but in a typically ironic Shaw ending, his wife upbraids him for embarrassing her in a law court.

"The Dry Rock" (*SSFD*, 286–93) is a largely comic story with a serious underlying theme. Leopold Tarloff, Russian-born but a resident of the United States for twenty-five years, has his cab run into by a car driven by Mr. Rusk, a gangster. In the ensuing argument, Rusk punches Tarloff in the nose, but then tries to buy him off for ten dollars. When Tarloff demands to go to the police "for principle," Rusk brings in a lawyer, a Russian, and two fellow gangsters in an attempt to intimidate the cabdriver. Tarloff will not be moved; but his case depends totally on his passengers, Mr. and Mrs. Fitzsimmons, who are late for a dinner party. Claude Fitzsimmons finally backs off from the complexities of a trial; and Tarloff says he understands, but still asserts: "'There is a principle. The dignity of the human body. Justice. For a bad act a man suffers. It's an important thing.'" Irwin Shaw, of course, would agree with Leopold Tarloff.

"The Kiss at Croton Falls" (*SSIS,* 483–87) and "The Lament of Madame Rechevsky" (*SSFD,* 111–16) are primarily character studies of wonderfully eccentric individuals. "The Kiss at Croton Falls" centers around Frederich Mull, "a huge rollicking man," who is hounded by his wife throughout their marriage because, one day in 1921, she saw him on a porch in Croton Falls kissing a red-haired woman. For the remainder of their marriage, she accuses him of infidelity and attempts to trap him in the act. After his death, the wife reports to their married daughter Clarice that Mull is visiting her from the grave. These "visits" take an ugly turn when Mull begins to appear with the woman from Croton Falls and a baby boy who looks just like him. Finally, the wife tells Clarice that she had to order him to leave. Clarice Smalley is struck by a passion that could survive years of marriage and even death and knows that her timid, respectable husband will never arouse such passion in her. The story ends with Clarice going alone to a saloon near the corner where, as a child, she watched her father drive a trolley car (*SSIS,* 483–87).

"The Lament of Madame Rechevsky" (*SSFD,* 111–16) is a moving study of the widow of a great star of the old Yiddish Theater. Madame Rechevsky regularly visits the grave of her dead husband in order to berate him:

> "I taught you how to act, Abraham. The Great Actor, they said, the Hamlet of the Yiddish Theater.... I played opposite you better than any leading lady you ever had, I gave you a child every two years and fed all the others other women gave the rest of the time. With my own hands I polished the apples they sold during intermission!" (*SSFD,* 115)

The story gains its strength from Shaw's genius in conveying the passion of the widow for her dead husband (which is comparable to that of Mrs. Mull for Mr. Mull) and the idea that even she no longer knows whether her memories are true or not. An added irony is the presence at the graveside of their actress daughter, who is totally uninterested in the memory of her father or of the old Yiddish Theater.

"God Was Here But He Left Early"

"God Was Here But He Left Early" (*SSFD,* 583–650), the title story of Shaw's most recent collection, can serve as a summary of all his short fiction. Because of the American involvement in Vietnam, he returns to protest, although the story focuses on American expatriates in Europe. It is a masterful tale which touches on all the major themes of Shaw's earlier work; the title itself symbolizes his belief that, since traditional religion has been invalidated, secular holy men are needed. It is reminiscent of F. Scott Fitzgerald's *Tender Is the Night* in its use of sexual perversity to symbolize general moral decadence. The story repeats the theme of moral accidents on "a bawdy planet" which runs through most of Shaw's novels.

Rosemary, a thirty-six-year-old American divorcée and buyer for a department store, has become pregnant through a meaningless affair with a married Frenchman, Jean-Jacques. ("Absurdity, too, has its limits.... two meaningless nights during a snowstorm.... The vulgarity was inescapable.... It was so banal.") The story opens with her failed attempt to get an abortion in Switzerland. Back in Paris, she contacts Jean-Jacques, who promises to get her the abortion, although she will have to wait a week. While waiting, she is invited to dinner by an Englishman, Harrison, a friend of her homosexual friend Bert, who likes "rough trade."

At dinner, Harrison is accompanied by a Polish girl named Anna, who tells a story of being arrested in Poland and put in a cell with two prostitutes who invent a substitute penis. The three are then joined by Carroll, an American photographer-journalist, and Rodney, a gentle-looking Englishman. Carroll has just returned from Vietnam with a photograph of an old beggarwoman, a starving child, a haughty prostitute, and the graffito GOD WAS HERE BUT HE LEFT EARLY scrawled on a wall behind them. The picture inspires Harrison to tell horror stories of having been a prisoner of the Japanese during World War II.

Feeling ill, Rosemary starts to leave; but Rodney stops her and apologizes for Harrison, claiming that the prisoner-of-war stories are Harrison's way of pleading with her as an American to stop the horror of Vietnam. Rosemary simply replies, "'I'm not doing anything in Vietnam.'" She returns to the table just in time to hear Harrison's story of an especially sadistic Japanese guard, Brother Three-Iron, who used to torture him with a golf club. When he had a chance, Harrison refused to take revenge on the sadist. The reader understands, though she does not, that this detail is a further appeal to Rosemary as a representative American to end the horror in Vietnam. She leaves with Rodney, consciously using him as protection against the terrifying world outside.

Walking along the street, they pass a movie theater: "On a giant poster above the entrance, a gigantic girl in a nightgown pointed a pistol the size of a cannon at a thirty-foot-tall man in a dinner jacket." The poster further disturbs Rosemary: "The various uses and manifestations of the flesh. To caress, to mangle, to behead.... To protect and destroy.... Violence, costumed, pursues us. Rosemary shivered." She needs Rodney to make love to her gently; instead, he asks permission to spank her, and she submits: "Who was she to be spared?" The next morning, she laughs "coarse, unstoppable laughter."

The story captures Shaw's vision of a century devoted to unceasing violations of the flesh and the spirit. The "horror" will not cease, even after Vietnam. The world is dominated by an insanely selfish absurdity; the "gentle people" have been defeated; and Harrison, the secular holy man, is unheeded. Finally, no one will be spared.

It may seem inappropriate to devote such a long discussion in a short book to Shaw's short fiction. His eighty-four short stories, however, represent his greatest achievement as a writer. More than *The Young Lions* and the other novels, and more than his plays, they will constitute the heart of his future literary reputation. Not all are masterpieces (although a great many are), and a very few are lacking in the highest literary seriousness, but all are clearly the work of a distinguished professional. Cumulatively, they represent a vision of some of the most dramatic decades of American history told with great mastery of the craft of fiction.

Chapter Four
War and Moral Allegory: *The Young Lions*

Shaw's first novel, *The Young Lions*, appeared in 1948, after he had established a significant reputation as a short-story writer and as a member of the Group Theatre. *The Young Lions* is a panoramic World War II novel detailing the experiences of three major characters: Noah Ackerman, a Jewish-American; Michael Whitacre, a dissolute, guilt-ridden Broadway type; and Christian Diestl, a German soldier. All three are introduced on the eve of the New Year, 1938. In addition to the stories of these men, Shaw presents such major events of the war as the Nazi occupation of Paris, the Battle of North Africa, the Allied invasion of France, and the liberation of Paris. *The Young Lions* appeared in the same year as Norman Mailer's *The Naked and the Dead*, three years before James Jones's *From Here to Eternity*. While all three novels are big books in length and artistic ambition, Shaw's devotion to historical panorama creates a major difference between *The Young Lions* and the Mailer and Jones novels. Much of *The Naked and the Dead*'s ironic power derives from the absolute military unimportance of Mailer's fictional Pacific island, Anopopei; the novel's only relief from a carefully cultivated claustrophobia is in its "Time Machine" flashback sections. Much of *From Here to Eternity* is devoted to Jones's simultaneously brutal and nostalgic depiction of the old peacetime army that vanished after the Japanese bombing of Pearl Harbor. Shaw's ambition was to create a fictional overview of the war in Europe from three distinct perspectives.

Initially, Shaw's concept for the novel was even more ambitious. In an interview with the *Paris Review*, he comments that he "started off with a very grandiose idea indeed, one that eventually proved not to be feasible." This "grandiose idea" was a plan to link the Ackerman, Whitacre, and Diestl characterizations with "a fourth character—a bullet—the bullet fired by Whitacre in the Black Forest which kills Diestl":

> I wanted to show it as lead in the ground, the miners that got it out, the engineers, the smelters, the sorters, the packagers, then the long chain of supply in the army that put the bullet finally in Whitacre's cartridge belt. My idea was to show how we are all linked in this world—soldiers, civilians, the most sophisticated, the most primitive—the link being, in our time, death. There are other links, of course, but the strongest and most fundamental one in our century is killing.[1]

Shaw has shown this writer the original prologue to the novel, which he discarded and which does focus upon the "fourth character" of "the bullet."

Despite Shaw's abandoning of his "grandiose idea," the scope of the published novel still leads to structural complexities; in fact, the structural soundness of *The Young Lions* is a hotly debated critical issue. Shaw attempts to create unity through the utilization of minor characters who serve as links connecting Diestl, Whitacre, and Ackerman and through reliance on parallels in the experiences of the three characters. The novel initially received largely favorable reviews. In his 1951 critical study *After the Lost Generation,* however, John W. Aldridge attacked it, partly on structural grounds. Aldridge argues that the characters' parallel experiences do not grow organically out of the novel's meaning, but are "a system of carefully contained parallels, near-parallels, and pseudo parallels" which give only "an appearance of unity."[2] In a more recent study, Peter G. Jones finds a subtle mythological substructure in the novel which he believes creates "a tightly integrated book."[3]

These almost polar critical positions reflect the risks Shaw took in aiming at an extremely fragile unity. Margaret Freemantle is the published novel's most important linking character, a function Shaw foreshadows when he makes her the first character introduced in the novel. A beautiful young American girl, Margaret is in an Austrian ski resort in 1938. After a night of drinking and singing, she is almost raped by an Austrian named Frederick. On her escape, she is comforted by the ski instructor, Christian Diestl. She and Diestl argue about the evils of Nazism, and Margaret leaves with her lover, a Jewish doctor named Joseph. She reappears later in the novel at a horrible party given by Michael Whitacre in Pennsylvania at a time when the Whitacre marriage is disintegrating and the radio is carrying reports of the imminent Nazi occupation of Paris. Subsequently, she and Michael have a long and meaningful affair.

Appearing so infrequently in the novel, Margaret Freemantle still carries much of the novel's structural load. Shaw uses her argument with the extremely polite Christian Diestl to expose the inner corruption of the handsome ski instructor. Ironically, critics as sound as Aldridge and Jones have missed the point of this scene. Later in the novel, Freemantle functions as the personification of Michael Whitacre's conscience. The most subtle touch is her relationship with Joseph, the threatened European Jew; it foreshadows the introduction of Noah Ackerman, an American Jew who is killed in Europe. Such unobtrusive, but still heavily symbolic, unity occasions comments by both Aldridge and Jones about the novel's allegorical quality.

Shaw does still more with Margaret Freemantle. In the opening scene, she enjoys, with clear American condescension, the quaint innocence of the Austrian villagers until they break into the Horst Wessel song, whereupon she runs away in tears. Moreover, the supposedly quaint Austrians are shown as devoted to American popular culture, especially films and music. At the Whitacre party, Margaret is outraged at any suggestion of America's entering the war even as the radio brings the news of the inevitable occupation of Paris. Michael says to her: " 'You're living in the wrong year, lady . . . you and me, both.' "[4] Broadcasts about the tragedy in France are constantly interrupted by commercials for soap and deodorant. Clearly, Margaret is meant as a largely sympathetic character; however, she also represents an American innocence which Shaw finds dangerous because it is made possible by underlying arrogance and superficiality of intellect. The negative aspects of her character, which symbolize those of her country, are underscored by emphasis upon the mass media in both of her major scenes in the novel. Thus, while she first brings out and attempts to refute the inner monstrosity of Christian Diestl and while she serves as Michael Whitacre's moral guide, her limitations of intellect and perception are severe. The word *allegorical*, then, is probably more applicable to her than to any other character in the book. She is the decent American—well-intentioned, but dangerous because of her refusal or inability to comprehend reality. Having served her linking and allegorical functions, Margaret Freemantle soon disappears from the novel.

In addition to Shaw's dependence on subtle, partly allegorical unification, there is another major reason for the critical controversy over the structural soundness of *The Young Lions*. The novelist has mixed success with his three central characterizations: Christian Diestl is drawn with chilling convincingness, and Noah Ackerman is largely believable. But the character of Michael Whitacre verges on triteness. Correspondingly, the novel seems most unified in the Diestl segments, least in the Whitacre sections.

Even so, persistent critical misinterpretation clings to the Diestl characterization. Aldridge sees him as a "bravely dedicated but ultimately defeated German soldier" who is gradually brutalized by war.[5] Peter G. Jones summarizes the characterization in two rather puzzling sentences: "[Christian] is a good man who dies in the service of a cause unworthy of him. His weakness is that the abstract concepts of order and [German] nationalism mean more to him than human lives."[6] Shaw, in fact, has been praised for presenting a sympathetic Nazi in a novel which appeared so soon after the war. But in a 1978 interview he expressed indignation at Marlon Brando's interpretation of Diestl in the 1958 film version of *The Young Lions*: "Brando wanted to play an innocent, and the character is a monster."[7] When one understands the Diestl character as progressing from latent to active monstrosity, Shaw's point is easy to see.

The central theme of *The Young Lions* can be summarized as the necessity of ethical choice. Noah Ackerman and Michael Whitacre move from an avoidance of moral commitment to devotion to principle. In contrast, Diestl begins with an abstract, but still monstrous, set of ethical values and increasingly acts upon them. In his first scene, he is contrasted to Frederick, the would-be rapist of Margaret Freemantle. The contrast is not made to stress his decency, as Aldridge and Jones seem to believe, but to suggest his still latent capacity for brutality. Diestl condemns Frederick, but there are hints in the opening scenes that his condemnation is merely the first step in his own plans for a sexual encounter with her. Margaret, the oblivious American innocent, inevitably misses these hints.

More than his sexual hypocrisy, the moral values which Christian proclaims to the American woman reveal his capacity for monstrosity. First, citing Austria's poverty, he asserts that " 'people cannot live forever in humiliation. They will do whatever they have to do to regain their self-respect.' " Once a Communist, he states his newfound knowledge that " '. . . nothing will ever be accomplished by reason' " and then argues that, while any form of socialism is absurd, " 'if the only way you can get a decent and ordered Europe is by wiping out the Jews, then we must do it. A little injustice for a large justice. . . . The end justifies the means' " (18–19). Describing the extermination of the Jewish people as "a little injustice" is surely the sign of a potential for unlimited depravity. It is not impossible that Shaw intended such remarks by Diestl as satire of the Nazi perversion of the philosophy of Friedrich Nietzsche. In the remainder of the novel, Diestl's surface, and superficial, decency is destroyed by his inner monstrosity. Shaw utilizes allegory in order to demonstrate this process: the artist Brandt personifies the apparent decency; and Christian's immediate superior, Lieutenant Hardenburg and his wife, Gretchen, personify the inner monstrosity. For the purposes of Shaw's allegory, it is appropriate that Brandt, despite his devotion to impressionistic painting and his sense from the beginning of inevitable German defeat, is more than a little corrupt himself. His corruption, however, pales beside that of the totally degenerate Hardenburgs.

A crucial first step in Diestl's movement from latent to overt monstrosity comes when his jeep is ambushed by some members of the French underground just outside Paris. The scene is an especially well-written one, incorporating Shaw's recurrent theme of dangerous innocence. A young German soldier named Kraus is killed in the ambush immediately after bragging that he will kill a Frenchman to avenge his father, who lost a leg in World War I. Kraus is eating cherries as he is killed; and, in death, he "looked very young and healthy, and there were red stains around his lips from the cherries, like a small boy who comes guiltily out of the pantry after pillaging the jam jars" (72). The several layers of Shaw's allegory are indicated in the fact that another member of the ambushed party is Sergeant Himmler, a laughing mediocrity rumored to be related to Heinrich Himmler. The naive, boyish Kraus, intent on killing, embodies mid-century Germany's potential to be led into unprecedented areas of subhuman action by mediocrities like Heinrich Himmler, the bureaucratic mass murderer.

During the ambush scene, Christian kills his first Frenchman and does not "feel anything special" (72). Brandt later tells him that he is " 'a good model for a German soldier, except for the hair' " (78). Diestl, Brandt, Sergeant Himmler, and Hardenburg go together to a Paris brothel, where Hardenburg requests to be whipped. Sadomasochism is only one of the sexual aberrations practiced by the lieutenant and his wife. Christian initially dislikes Hardenburg, but it is essentially the dislike of the enlisted man for the officer. After an adulterous and perverse affair with Gretchen Hardenburg while on leave in Berlin, Diestl increasingly emulates his military superior. During a North African ambush of some British soldiers, Hardenburg is humming as he waits to give the signal to open fire. Diestl, tense because of the abnormally long wait, is outraged by the lieutenant's humming. Later, in a parallel scene, Christian hums to himself before giving the order to fire on some exposed American troops. Phrases comparable to "he didn't feel anything special" occur regularly during Christian's metamorphosis into overt monster. After rounding up some French underground members for the SS and listening to their screams as they are tortured, he sits at Hardenburg's desk and thinks "it hadn't been so bad" (147). A person who possesses the ability to minimize genocide as "a little injustice" has the capacity to feel that virtually anything is not "so bad."

The Hardenburgs' function as allegorical characters becomes increasingly clear as Diestl becomes virtually a reincarnation of the lieutenant after Hardenburg's death. Shaw builds this crucial symbolic metamorphosis through a sequence of dramatic events. Christian's Berlin leave with Gretchen Hardenburg introduces him to deviate sexual modes he had never before imagined. She works for the Nazi Propaganda Ministry and is a favorite sexual partner of high-level party members. Her husband is, therefore, kept carefully away from Berlin. In one crucial passage, Shaw describes the material possessions which she has collected from her influential lovers: "A student of economics could have pieced together the story of German conquest in Europe and Africa merely from the stores tucked away carelessly in Gretchen's apartment . . ." (163). Christian decides that she is "above ordinary morality, beyond it" (165). Gretchen Hardenburg is the symbolic whore of Nazism; the description of her closet, full of material possessions, recalls the passage in *Tender Is the Night* in which F. Scott Fitzgerald denounces the excesses of American capitalism by describing the world's economy as functioning only for the pleasure of Nicole Diver. Compared to Gretchen Hardenburg, however, Nicole is angelic, just as Nazism, of course, represents an evil considerably in excess of laissez-faire American capitalism.

Diestl decides that, while he would never wish to marry Gretchen, he would enjoy being "a kind of private Prince Consort" on her large estate after the war (166). With supreme irony, such dreams are smashed when Nazi officials order Gretchen never to be seen with Christian again because of his Communist past, a mistake which also prevents his receiving an officer's commission.

In North Africa after his leave in Paris, Christian privately gloats at having seduced his lieutenant's wife. But during the ambush of the British soldiers, his attitude toward Hardenburg shifts to unmitigated admiration and his gloating turns to guilt. He can never confess his disloyalty although he comes close. The North African campaign turns; Christian's company is trapped and Hardenburg decides they will desert the others. A clue to the Aldridge-Jones view of Diestl as a sympathetic character is perhaps contained in the sergeant's reaction to the order to desert. For a moment, Christian considers staying behind, but only for a moment: "really nothing would be gained by that" (263). Christian has repeated momentary decent impulses, but he is able to subdue them with very little struggle. Working from his basic ethical premises—"a little injustice for a large justice"—and "the end justifies the means"—one could easily rationalize any act.

It is during the desperate retreat on a motorcycle driven by Hardenburg that Christian is tempted to confess his affair with Gretchen. But he lies instead and says that in Berlin, he slept with a "'girl who worked in an airplane factory'" (273). Later the motorcycle is hit and Hardenburg is mutilated; his face is literally blown off. In the hospital, the lieutenant attempts to maintain an illusion of confidence with Diestl, saying the doctors have promised him a new face and that his wound will help his postwar career in politics. Announcing that he desires "'disciples,'" he lectures Christian on the future of Nazism: Europe must be kept in a constant state of war; Germany is not yet harsh enough ("'We kill Moses, but pretend to tolerate Christ. . . .'"); "'Killing is an objective act and death is a state beyond right and wrong.'" (Again, a parody of the Nazi perversion of Nietzscheanism could be intended in Hardenburg's philosophy.) Hardenburg then abruptly blurts out that Germany is led by madmen and his future would be brighter if he had ever suffered from epilepsy or amnesia or paranoia (290–93). Hardenburg is, of course, himself a madman; and his last outburst is an ironic and incongruous moment of sane insight. Diestl does not recognize this and commits himself to the discipleship his lieutenant has asked.

He leaves the faceless man in the hospital and returns to combat, increasingly absorbing Hardenburg's obsessive love of killing. After the ambush of the American troops (the parallel scene to the North Africa ambush of the British), Diestl muses that Hardenburg "will be pleased . . ." (370). The allegory reaches its climax when Diestl returns to Berlin, now in the chaos of imminent defeat, and visits Gretchen again. There he learns that the lieutenant has sent his wife a picture of his mutilated face with a letter outlining his future plans. Gretchen answered that he should not return, but instead accept hospitalization for the rest of his life. After receiving her letter, Hardenburg commited suicide " 'with a pocket knife.' " Diestl asks for his lieutenant's picture: " 'I owe a great deal to him. He taught me more than anyone else I ever knew. He was a giant, a true giant' " (425–26).

Hardenburg has his face blown away, metaphorically exposing inner monstrosity. Neither he nor Gretchen can live with such a hideous revelation, but Christian can and thus requests the photograph. Diestl has become more than his lieutenant's disciple. Symbolically, he is the monster resurrected and magnified.

Again, Shaw's allegory contains several levels. "The new face," which is constructed for Hardenburg and which sickens Gretchen, is the true face of Nazism. While she has been able to profit from Germany's evil, she cannot, unlike Joseph Conrad's Kurtz, find courage enough to face the horror.

For the remainder of Diestl's story, the German army steadily crumbles, while Christian schemes and struggles to stay alive. In a puzzling scene, he is accosted by a German soldier named Behr, who tells him that the war is virtually over and that the Germans have justifiably been defeated: " 'The animal is slowly being driven into his last corner, the human being is preparing his final punishment' " (432). Behr suggests an army rebellion against Hitler and then a negotiated peace with the Allies: " '. . . the Germans themselves must get the tigers out' " (433). Diestl seems to listen seriously to Behr and even has a puzzling momentary vision of Margaret Freemantle. Before he can commit himself either way, however, an Allied plane strafes the beach on which the two men are resting and Behr is seriously wounded.

Diestl's apparent consideration of Behr's plan is another moment in which he may seem to verge on becoming a sympathetic character. Shaw is, of course, continuing the novel's panoramic effect—Behr's plan is based on the actual attempt by certain high-ranking members of the German army to assassinate Hitler late in the war. The cumulative effect of the Diestl character prior to this scene and his actions immediately afterward suggest strongly that Christian is momentarily tempted by the idea of overthrowing Hitler out of thoroughly pragmatic reasons.

Christian goes for help, leaving the wounded Behr on the beach. When two bicycling Frenchmen appear, Diestl tries to enlist their aid but fails. He returns to Behr to discover that the Frenchmen have killed the wounded man. Subsequently, he falsely identifies two Frenchmen, selected by the SS at random, as the murderers and watches their execution after they have been hideously tortured. He remarks on observing the execution: "'I didn't mind it'" (448). Thus Christian's pattern of cold, emotionless response to brutal events continues. His motivations in the Behr incident are complicated, however, by the momentary vision of Margaret Freemantle, since, despite her naivete, she personifies a capacity for decency. If there is a decent element in Christian's brief temptation by Behr, it is significant both that he is puzzled by it (he finds the image of Margaret "confusing and tiring" [434]) and that, shortly afterward and in response to Behr's death, he behaves barbarously. The always subverted element of decency in Diestl's personality heightens, rather than lessens, his monstrosity. He is not a freak, born without the capacity to comprehend right and wrong like Steinbeck's Cathy Ames in *East of Eden;* rather, he is a man who constantly and willfully chooses evil. This pattern of behavior is emphasized again when during a general retreat, "without thinking," he murders a French boy to get his bicycle (553). He is then given a ride away from the combat zone by the painter Brandt and for a moment considers leaving the bicycle behind in case someone might need it. Quickly he rejects the generous impulse: "'What could I have been thinking of?'" (562).

The climax of the allegorical aspect of Diestl's characterization comes when he identifies Brandt, who has rescued him from the front, to the SS as a traitor. Significantly, he does it in the name of Hardenburg: "Better friends than Brandt had died beside him for four years; should Brandt be left alive to suck on Hardenburg's bones?" (578–79). Brandt, though not without his own degree of corruption, still personifies art and muted opposition to Nazism. Christian sacrifices him in Hardenburg's memory; metaphorically, he chooses barbarism over decency. Such a choice was inevitable for

Diestl. It is the completion of his progression from latent to overt monstrosity. Since he operates initially from a corrupt ethical basis, he can only degenerate. With the character of Christian Diestl, Shaw seems in part to be answering the question: "How did it happen?" Diestl is the personification of an ethically shallow Germany waiting to be transformed into overt monstrosity by Hardenburgs. His given name carries considerable irony.

Diestl's personal barbarism is tied directly to Germany's national guilt in a concentration camp scene near the end of the novel. The German army is in complete disarray; he is involved in his own retreat, personal survival his only goal. He is now contemptuous of Hitler and the Nazis because they lost the war by refusing to be harsh and brutal enough. The Nazi government is now reduced to fighting against battalions of well-armed, well-fed invaders with "Rhetoric and myth": "Hardenburg had understood, long ago, but Hardenburg had killed himself. Yes, there would be a use, after the war, for men who had been cleansed of rhetoric and who had been once and for all inoculated against myth" (662–63). Diestl stumbles into a Nazi concentration camp in his retreat. Instead of any moral pain at the sight of gas ovens and skeletal figures in prison uniforms, he is outraged by the smell of the camp and by the incompetence of its commanders.

The camp, in fact, is in a state of rebellion; and, to save himself, Christian knocks one prisoner unconscious, perhaps killing him, and then, to convince the rioting prisoners that he is one of them, methodically slits the camp commandant's throat. By now he is an animal, devoid of any traces of humanity. It is allegorically sound for this final stage of his metamorphosis to take place in a setting symbolic of the twentieth century's most infamous capitulation to brutality. The theme of Shaw's novel is the necessity for humankind to choose and then attempt to live by a viable ethical code. Diestl begins with an inhuman set of values ("a little injustice" is acceptable) and increasingly acts on that code until his monstrosity becomes total.

Noah Ackerman, in contrast, begins by trying to deny the need for an ethical code; but he is forced by circumstances and his own innate decency to formulate one. That acceptance of, and pride in, his Jewishness are the heart of Noah's code causes John W. Aldridge to read the novel as "a dramatic affirmation of faith in the struggle of the Jew for equality in the modern world."[8] As a comment about Noah Ackerman, this is somewhat valid. As a summation of the entire novel, it is a simplification.

Noah is introduced at the deathbed of his father, Jacob, in Santa Monica, "on the western edge of America" (42). Like so much in the novel, the scene is extremely allegorical. Jacob Ackerman, since coming to America, has drifted across the country, failing at one semilegitimate job after another. Now dying in the West, he is dictating a letter to his brother, Israel, in Hamburg, Germany: " 'They are burning my brother Israel in the furnace of the heathen' " (45). Noah, forced to write down his father's words, is repulsed by the lies the old man is sending his brother, just as he has always been disgusted by his father. Jacob begins by dictating to his German brother an account of a life of material success and social prominence; he also claims to have seven children when in actuality Noah is his only child.

Shaw's skill in narrative technique is especially clear in this scene. In the midst of the old man's lies are hidden truths which, though not as Jacob envisions them, become the code of ethics for which Noah ultimately lives and dies: " 'Don't smile, my son, my brother is burning for you' "; " 'The times are getting more difficult and a Jew must behave as though the life of every other Jew in the world depended on every action of his' " (46, 49). Seconds before he dies, Jacob abruptly reverses himself and states the truth about his life in America: " 'I have led a miserable life and I have cheated everyone and I drove my wife to her death and I have only one son and I have no hope for him . . . ' " (49).

There is little reason to have hope for Noah at this point. Most of all, he wishes not to be defined by any Jewish legacy; and his initial response to his father's death is relief at being freed from the weight of his heritage. Leaving the dead Jacob, he goes to a bar and tries to arrange cremation, immediately encountering anti-Semitism from a funeral director. The irony is intensified by the wife of the undertaker he telephones: " 'He don't burn Kikes. Happy New Year' " (53). The line of course recalls Jacob's words about the burning of Israel in Europe. But Noah, in a condition of denial and suppressed panic, hangs up the phone and occupies himself by picking up a drunken woman at the bar. He tells her he is an Indian. Significantly for his later development, he leaves her before there is much more contact between them.

Other characters and historic events will force Noah into an acknowledgment of the importance of his Jewishness. His lack of meaningful identity has resulted in a complete absence of confidence. He has no identity to rest confidence on. As his New York friend, Roger Cannon, says about him, when he does gain a sense of self, he will become " 'a wonderful man' " (115). Four characters—Cannon, Michael Whitacre, a young soldier named Johnny Burnecker, and most of all, Hope Plowman—will support him in his struggle to attain pride and identity. Negatively, the corruption of the United States Army, which he decides to fight back against, will cement his maturation.

Roger introduces Noah to the worlds of art and intellect. He also introduces Noah to Hope Plowman. The courtship of Noah and Hope has been denounced as sentimental and even mawkish by John W. Aldridge and other critics. But in fact, Shaw successfully walks in these scenes a very fine line between legitimate romanticism and sentimentality.

Hope's first name is, of course, part of Shaw's allegory; for she embodies the hope of self-transcendence of Noah, just as Margaret Freemantle does for Michael Whitacre. The still insecure young man meets her at a party given by Roger Cannon and immediately attempts to impress her by quoting some of Cannon's worldly philosophy as his own—New York City is " 'unalterably provincial,' " he says, and " 'Continental women' " are preferable to their United States counterparts because they understand how to " 'submit' " to men (118–19). There follows a wonderfully comic scene in which Noah, knowing New York City not at all well, has to take Hope home to Brooklyn on the subway. After innumerable changes of trains, he believes that they have surely reached their destination when she says, " 'Now . . . we take the street car' " (122). Finally arriving at her aunt's home, he stumbles over an attempted confession of his inexperience and then suddenly kisses her. She stops him, denounces him as " 'an arrogant, opinionated, self-satisfied young man,' " and sends him away (124).

In disgrace, Noah attempts a retreat, but immediately realizes that he is completely lost and has no idea of how to get back to the apartment he shares with Roger. Thus, he has to return to Hope, plead with her to open a window and talk to him, at least long enough to explain how to get back home. Laughing, Hope comments: " 'You're a terrible fool... aren't you?' " Noah agrees: " 'I am shy... and I don't have a single opinion in the whole world, and I don't know why I kissed you. I... I just couldn't help it.' " This time when they kiss, he discloses his love for her (125). It is easy to imagine the scene as one of Shaw's short stories celebrating the gentle people—two strangers meeting, baffled and intimidated by the strange city (Hope is from Vermont), and, out of a comic mixture of shyness and a need to appear sophisticated, failing initially to communicate. The delicacy with which it is written saves it from excess sentiment. (The scene was one of the few moments in *The Young Lions* which the 1958 film presented in its original form; and, as played by Hope Lange and especially by Montgomery Clift, it is the film's best moment.)

Noah at this point in fact has no opinions; but the positive inspiration of Hope and the negative impact of the United States Army will force him to acquire some. Hope and Noah marry, after a scene in which he goes to Vermont to meet her father. Again, Shaw's delicate writing makes what might have been a mawkish scene a subtly moving one. Noah is prepared, by the nature of small-town Vermont, for some expression of anti-Semitism. He and Mr. Plowman go for a walk during which the father talks about how far back his family's New England Yankee heritage goes and admits that he would have preferred Hope to marry someone with similar, defined roots. Noah, whose own father was a personification of the homeless "wandering Jew," listens in despair as Mr. Plowman expresses his ignorance, and suspicion, of Jewish people. Abruptly, the older man says that it is obvious that Noah and Hope intend to marry, there is nothing her father can do about it, and that Noah should come home for Sunday dinner. What saves the scene is Shaw's artistic instinct in having Noah say virtually nothing throughout the entire discussion. The incident is balanced so delicately on the edge of sentimentality that any outburst from him would inevitably have marred it.

After Pearl Harbor, Noah enlists in the army despite Hope's objections, which are based on his eligibility for a medical deferment. Still, this enlistment has nothing to do with any sense of Jewish pride; Noah simply feels that it is the proper thing for a young American to do. Later, he speculates on the inevitability of anti-Semitism: "Must stop thinking about the Jews. If you let yourself fall into a reverie, on no matter what subject, it finally came around to that" (227).

Immediately after induction, Noah learns that "it finally came around to that" whether one thinks about it or not. Sent South for basic training, Noah immediately becomes the target of harassment by two anti-Semites, Captain Colclough and Sergeant Rickett. Symbolically, Colclough appropriates three books from Noah—Joyce's *Ulysses* ("'It's a filthy, dirty book.'"), *The Collected Poems of T. S. Eliot*, and a collection of George Bernard Shaw's dramatic essays (299–300). Colclough, representative of totalitarian ignorance, attempts to destroy the intellectual ambitions awakened in Noah by Roger Cannon. Colclough and Rickett, then, inflame the rest of the company into a systematic mental and physical harassment of Noah.

In this section of the novel, Shaw treats a theme that is also dominant in Jones's *From Here to Eternity* and Mailer's *The Naked and the Dead*—the fascist element in the United States Army. Like much American fiction of the late 1940s and early 1950s without a military setting (William Styron's *Lie Down in Darkness*, for instance), all three of these war novels express a common fear that the United States is moving toward a totalitarian mentality that throws a hypocritical light on its crusade against Hitler. To the disapproval of a critic like John Aldridge, however, Shaw does not finally express this idea as forcibly as either Jones or Mailer.

Nonetheless, he creates a harsh setting. Noah has only one ally in his battle against the company, which quickly becomes his battle against the entire United States Army. Michael Whitacre has been drafted into the same company and is sickened at the harassment of Noah. Especially during a visit from Hope, during which the two are refused a room in a cheap roominghouse, the military lock arms, with ten of the biggest soldiers mockingly confessing to a ten-dollar theft from Noah's locker: "We took it, Jew-Boy" (322). Noah insists on fighting, one at a time, all ten. He asks Whitacre to be his second; and with self-punitiveness much like that of *From Here to Eternity*'s Robert E. Lee Prewitt, insists that there be no rounds, referees, or gloves. Noah, at 135 pounds, is predictably beaten brutally during each of the first eight fights. A ritual evolves—Noah will be beaten senseless, the rest of the company will jovially congratulate the victor, and Whitacre will carry his unconscious friend to the hospital. Colclough, despite Whitacre's appeal, refuses to intercede and stop it.

After the eighth fight, Noah is visited by the only other Jewish soldier in the company. Private Fein is physically large enough to be safe from the brutality Noah is receiving; and he urges on the injured man the same kind of passive acceptance of anti-Semitism which Noah has so persistently endorsed. Now, unconsciously echoing his dying father, Noah refuses Fein's advice: " 'I want every Jew . . . to be treated as though he weighed two hundred pounds' " (330). Events have forced Noah into a strong embrace of his Jewish identity; as a result, he begins to have very strong opinions.

The ninth and last fight is with a man named Brailsford, whom Noah soundly beats. Afterward, the other men do not congratulate the victor. They walk away in silence, and on the following day Noah deserts. His crusade has been to win, however painfully, the respect of the other men; and he takes their refusal to acknowledge his triumph as a sign that such respect cannot be won.

Back in New York, Noah gives himself up to the army and is imprisoned at Governor's Island. He says that he is wrong to have deserted and requests only a transfer. In a beautifully written satiric scene, an army bureaucrat named Lewis explains to Hope, now pregnant, that because of the " 'extenuating circumstances' "of Noah's desertion, the army will not press charges, but that he must return to his old company (345–46). Lewis is one of Shaw's decent men forced by his situation to advocate an indecent position, and Hope stabs at his obvious embarrassment. Noah has not known of Hope's pregnancy; when she visits him, he realizes that he has new responsibilities and agrees to return to Colclough's company. It is not the same Noah who returns, however. This time, he carries a switchblade which he threatens to use at any sign of intimidation. The other men are seemingly different too. They greet him with the news that after his desertion three other men followed suit, resulting in Colclough's upbraiding by his superior. In addition, they give him a package—the three books appropriated by Colclough. Noah feels that some sort of resolution has been attained: "he realized that his personal armistice with the Army had been made. It had been made on lunatic terms, on the threat of the knife and the absurd prestige of his opposition to authority, but it was real..." (353-54). The concept of Noah's personal armistice recalls Frederick Henry's separate peace with World War I in *A Farewell to Arms.*

However, in the remainder of the novel, the resolution of Noah's war with military harassment is not as clear-cut as this climactic incident might lead one to expect. This is in part a result of Shaw's softening his satire of military corruption in some quite significant ways. Colclough's humiliation by his superiors after Noah's desertion foreshadows his final fall from military grace. At the Normandy invasion, the lieutenant rides ashore wearing "a pearl-handled forty-five" in a "fancy leather holster"; but he has to be virtually forced off the landing craft, almost immediately gets his men trapped behind the German lines, and collapses in hysterical fear. Lieutenant Green, a brave and humane officer, replaces him. The degree to which Colclough's replacement by Green represents a significant lessening of Shaw's attack on the army can be seen by comparing this novel to *From Here to Eternity* and *The Naked and the Dead.* Jones's Dynamite Holmes, a corrupt officer advocating control through fear, moves up in the military echelons to become an associate of the thoroughly totalitarian General Slater; and Mailer's General Cummings, a spokesman for postwar fascism, receives credit for the final capture of Anopopei, even though he had nothing to do with it.

Shaw also gives Michael Whitacre a crucial speech which further weakens the novel's attack on the army:

"I believe in the war. That doesn't mean I believe in the Army.... You don't expect justice out of an army, if you're a sensible, grown-up human being, you only expect victory. And if it comes to that, our Army is probably the most just one that ever existed. . . . It is much less corrupt, for example, than the German Army." (387)

While Shaw's initial depiction of the army does not sustain this judgment, he does have Colclough replaced by Green; and Noah immediately begins to be treated in a decent and humane way.

In the *Paris Review* interview, Shaw sheds some significant light upon the reasons behind his relatively muted attack upon the army:

War has now been taken out of all human contact. We can hardly conceive or bear to think of the faculties now achieved for mass destruction. This isn't even the kind of killing with regret, with compassion, that I tried to write about in *The Young Lions*.[9]

The discarded prologue to the novel does emphasize our present age of mass technological killing, introduced at Hiroshima. One reason for Shaw's abandoning the prologue could well be that such a theme does not smoothly harmonize with the comparably nostalgic depiction of World War II as an example "of killing with regret, with compassion." Of course, the published novel does contain, especially in the climactic concentration camp scenes, moments which foreshadow the present age of technological destruction.

The change in Noah's relationship with the army is, however, not a total one. He learns painfully that while Green's leadership will assure him fair treatment, it cannot gain him respect from such a man as Sergeant Rickett. Colclough's breakdown after the invasion endangers all his men. Noah is able to escape from behind the enemy lines only by a sequence of courageous acts, during which he draws, on the back of a photograph of Hope and their baby, a map of crucial enemy positions. Upon his return to the company, he is promised a medal by a Lieutenant Colonel, but Rickett only stares at him and mutters, "'Oh, Christ, we still got the Jew'" (509). Noah's reaction to Rickett's insult constitutes the last phase of his personal armistice with the army. He now realizes that his enemy lies much deeper than the corrupt authority personified by Colclough. The enemy is the cumulative anti-Semitism of the company's enlisted men. Thus, Rickett has "absolved" him from ever trying to prove anything again; he will now do no more and no less than any of the other men and will hope only for survival.

Even so, his desire for survival is not passive. While the army will offer him at best a limited acceptance, he hopes for much more from the world that will emerge after the war. Just as he depicts a Green largely negating a Colclough in the officer class, Shaw creates a human, decent enlisted man, Johnny Burnecker from Iowa, to balance the brutally insensitive Rickett. Burnecker's friendship with Noah is cemented as they struggle to escape from entrapment behind the German lines. Burnecker subsequently becomes obsessed with the idea that, as long as he and Noah stay together, they will be safe. Moreover, the two have made plans for a life after the war—Burnecker's uncle owns a newspaper in Johnny's small Iowa hometown and has promised to hire Noah as a reporter; Noah, Hope, and the baby will live quietly in small-town mid-America close to Johnny Burnecker. Implicit in the characterization of Burnecker, as in that of Hope and her father, is a romantic faith in a fundamentally decent America. Small-town Iowa, like small-town Vermont, is conceived as a refuge not only from the war, but from the anti-Semitism of prewar America. To be sure, Shaw is not blindly optimistic: the heart of America is not only Johnny Burnecker; it is also Rickett and the other enlisted men who will never respect Noah as a human being.

Besides the promise of a medal and Rickett's insult, Noah is greeted by something else upon his heroic return to the company. Hope has sent a copy of a journal which has published one of Noah's poems. He had enclosed the poem in a letter to her, and without telling him, she had submitted it for publication. The poem symbolizes Noah's largely unrealized capacity for artistic creativity. Roger Cannon says of Noah that when he attains self-awareness, he will be " 'a wonderful man.' " Noah has been struggling, against heavy opposition, for self-awareness throughout the novel; and Shaw utilizes artistic creativity as a means of showing how far he has come (the army did attempt unsuccessfully to appropriate his literary property). Implicit in Noah's struggle for maturity might be the idea that pride in his Jewish identity is related to his capacity to create art. The poem Hope succeeds in getting published is, however, a love lyric; and the remainder of the novel makes extended discussion of any concept of a connection between ethnic pride and the creative process pointless. It is certainly of thematic significance, though, that Noah shows the poem to Johnny Burnecker before he collapses in exhaustion.

The reader next sees Noah through the disbelieving eyes of Michael Whitacre. During the time Noah went AWOL after the succession of brutal fights in Florida, Whitacre had requested and received a transfer out of the infantry. Through an elaborate sequence of events, he rejoins the old company after Normandy and after Noah's heroism and rejection by Rickett. Meeting Ackerman again, he is astonished by how much the young Jewish soldier has changed: Noah now wears a Silver Star pinned on by Viscount Montgomery in the presence of General Eisenhower and General Patton; the decoration is the outer symbol of an inner change: "... [Noah] seemed to have found some inner balance, a thoughtful, quiet maturity..." (621).

This maturity is momentarily shaken by the death of Johnny Burnecker. Burnecker's spine is shattered, producing a collapse of the nervous system. Wounded himself, Noah is separated from the company when Burnecker is hit by the shell. He immediately goes to his dying friend, feeling responsible for having violated Burnecker's mystic faith that, as long as they stayed together, they would be safe. This sense of responsibility is augmented when the collapse of Burnecker's nervous system is manifested in extreme paranoid thinking—Burnecker begins to scream that Noah has been sent to murder him. Afterward, when Noah describes the event to Michael Whitacre, it becomes clear that his newfound "balance" and "quiet maturity" are not complete: "'I've had two friends in my whole life... A man named Roger Cannon.... He got killed in the Philippines. My other friend was Johnny Burnecker. A lot of people have dozens of friends.... Not me. It's my fault and I realize it. I don't have a hell of a lot to offer'" (642). In this speech Noah indirectly pleads for Michael's friendship; and it is promptly and unequivocally offered. Both literally and symbolically, Whitacre has, in fact, more to gain from such a bond than Noah. The

Jewish soldier has already experienced combat and is an expert on surviving its horrors; he proceeds to guide the onetime New York City playboy safely through the Battle of the Bulge. More importantly for the novel's symbolism, Whitacre's life has been a struggle to develop an ethical code which his selfishness and weakness will not dissipate. Noah Ackerman gives him a model for such a code; and the playboy begins progress toward the attainment of strong moral fibre.

The Noah Ackerman and Michael Whitacre characterizations climax at the same concentration camp in which Christian Diestl finally reverts to complete brutality. The camp is the realization of that vision of horror prophesied by Noah's dying father; and the Jewish soldier must exercise extreme self-control simply to walk through its horrors. This hard-won and delicate self-control is not shaken until one of the camp's rabbis requests permission to hold religious services and an Albanian diplomat, one of the non-Jewish prisoners, advises Green to deny the request because " 'The other prisoners will not stand for it' " (677). Green orders that the services be held and further states that machine guns will be aimed at the other prisoners to insure that there is no interference.

John W. Aldridge objects to the dramatic role played by Lieutenant Green at this stage of the novel, arguing that Shaw has not prepared the reader to see Green as such a force of strength and decency. In fact, Green's characterization must be seen in conjunction with that of Johnny Burnecker as evidence of Shaw's faith that decency exists in the American heart. Neither Green nor Burnecker is an outwardly impressive man, and both can be described as intellectually mediocre. Still, they are two of Shaw's gentle people who find strength in their basic human decency. Michael Whitacre, observing Green's ability to restore a sense of order to the holocaust around him, thinks: "There was nothing, not even the endless depravity and bottomless despair which the Germans had left at the swamp-heart of their dying millennium, which could not be remedied by honest, mechanic's common sense and energy of a decent workman" (675). Noah, close to emotional collapse during the Albanian's speech, gains a new assurance from Green's answer. Afterward, he goes for a walk with Whitacre and begins to shout: "'When the war is over... Green is going to run the world, not that damned Albanian.... The human beings are going to be running the world.... The human beings! There's a lot of Captain Green's! He's not extraordinary. There're millions of them!'" (680). The novel's ending considerably undercuts Noah's prophecy. Still, one point seems clear: Green's importance lies precisely in the fact that "he's not extraordinary," that human decency is not defined by, or limited to, genius or unusual talent. Like evil, it is an inborn propensity of the human heart. This prophecy completes the characterization of Noah Ackerman and seems to refute John W. Aldridge's emphasis that Shaw's main theme is "the struggle of the Jew for equality in the modern world."

Noah has arrived at a vision of a future decent world. To him, the undeniable fact that the only world he has ever seen is hideously indecent has been offset by Green's integrity; the friendships of Roger Cannon, Johnny Burnecker, and Michael Whitacre; and the love of Hope. Coming to terms with his own Jewish identity was the essential step in his struggle for self-awareness and self-acceptance. Finally, though, that self-acceptance is the means by which all the world's "human beings" can be embraced. Thus, Noah Ackerman balances Christian Diestl; without an ethical code, one is something less than "a human being."

The Michael Whitacre characterization completes Shaw's theme; still, it is the weakest aspect of the novel simply because it is difficult to care very much about Whitacre. Certainly, Shaw was writing about a type he knew when he created the New Yorker, but the character rarely rises above the level of a type. Before the war, Whitacre is a product of Broadway theater; his life is one of too many cocktails, too many drunken parties, and a degenerating marriage. He does, however, have a potentially decent side. In a 1978 interview Shaw commented accurately that the 1958 film version completely missed a crucial dimension of the character—"He's supposed to be an intellectual, to a degree at least"—whereas Dean Martin had played him strictly as a playboy.[10] Whitacre is more specifically a liberal intellectual who is perennially tormented by an inability to follow through on his decent impulses.

He is introduced at a New York party where a man named Parrish, who has just returned from fighting against Franco in the Spanish Civil War, shames him into donating money to the Loyalist cause. Later, at the party, Parrish saves a drunken playwright from suicide while Michael, helpless to act, stands by. Parrish, because he has the courage to go to Spain and fight for freedom, is a living reproach to Whitacre, who is unable even to help prevent an alcoholic friend from killing himself. Contributing money to the Loyalist cause is a desperate attempt to hide his weakness and cowardice. After the near suicide, Whitacre faces the meaninglessness of his life: "There was no honor to this life, no form . . . " (40). For the remainder of the novel, he searches for "honor" and "form" and finally discovers them with the help of Noah Ackerman.

The attainment of honor and form is a difficult process, however. Most of all, Michael has to overcome the weakness of his own character, which, like the Broadway world that produced him, is quick to resort to cynicism in the face of complex and difficult problems. For example, when he learns of Pearl Harbor, he instinctively wonders if there could be "a war that ran as long as *Tobacco Road*" (183). The first crucial moment in Michael's struggle for meaning is a chance meeting with Margaret Freemantle which results in a two-year affair. This affair is significantly different than the others he has known—he honestly loves Margaret and, as a result, begins to come to grips with his own habitual cynicism and weakness. Thus, he enlists in the infantry instead of one of the Special Services which his Broadway connections could easily have obtained for him.

After serving as Noah's second during basic training in Florida, he idealistically decides to become an officer and protect the Ackermans in the army. However, his request for Officer Candidates' School is denied when the FBI discovers his financial contributions to the Spanish Loyalists and labels him a subversive. Shaw, of course, intends considerable irony in the fact that the money Whitacre contributed in an attempt to salve his conscience results in the destruction of a later legitimate idealistic impulse. There is also a parallel to Christian Diestl's failure to become an officer because of his Communist past. This parallel is much more than the arbitrary unifying device that Aldridge calls it. It is important to remember that Diestl's desire to join the officer class was inspired by the thoroughly corrupt Gretchen Hardenburg. What the two failed applications show about the totalitarian mentalities in both governments is less significant than what they reveal about the characters making them. Whitacre has the capacity for honor and form, Diestl the potential for ethical monstrosity.

Still, the weak side of Michael's character has not disappeared; and, in outrage at the unfair treatment of Ackerman and himself, he requests a transfer out of the infantry. Subsequently, he becomes a Civil Affairs Officer under a colorful commander named Pavone. He feels guilty about his noncombatant status, however, and vows after the war to marry Margaret Freemantle and "stop wasting his life." He considers politics as a future field of endeavor, but knows that he has not earned the right to be listened to: "You could not merely spend the war being a chauffeur for a Civil Affairs Colonel" (527). As she does throughout the novel, Margaret Freemantle again personifies Michael's conscience. Still, Michael suppresses his impulse to ask for a transfer back to an infantry company even though he worries that "...a man...should have been able to emerge with a key, a key to wars and oppression, a key to unlock the meaning of Europe and America" (587).

The idealistic and the selfish sides of his nature continue to war with each other. In a scene ironically reminiscent of his inability to save the drunken playwright from suicide, he finds himself momentarily trapped in a German ambush in an occupied French village, but cannot act to protect the villagers or even himself. In fact, an accident is required to liberate the idealistic side of his nature. Following the Allied occupation of Paris, Michael is drunkenly celebrating with Pavone and two women when he and the officer are run over by a taxicab. Pavone is killed, and Michael suffers a broken leg. After his leg heals, Michael is arbitrarily assigned back to the infantry because he does not hold the rank of an officer. He is, however, awarded the Purple Heart.

Throughout Shaw's fiction, the motif of accidents either creating or resolving ethical difficulties is dominant. The irony of Michael's receiving a Purple Heart for being run over by a Parisian taxicab symbolizes the fact that Michael would never have been able to act had external events not interceded. Still Pavone, who personifies the weak side of his character, is now dead; and Michael is about to be reunited with Noah Ackerman. One recalls that he once vowed to become an officer in order to protect the Noah Ackermans of the world. As discussed, it is Noah who contributes most to Whitacre's ethical development. The young Jewish soldier overtly teaches the intellectual New Yorker how to survive combat. He also serves as a prototype of the moral strength Whitacre has been struggling to find in himself.

The novel's ending has been denounced by John W. Aldridge as Hollywood melodrama; yet it is essential for the completion of Shaw's moral allegory. Immediately after his shouted prophecy of a postwar world run by human beings, Noah is shot and killed by Christian Diestl. The 1958 film version changed this ending and allowed Noah to live; in 1978, Shaw expressed strong disapproval of this revision.[11] The novel has its idealistic core, but it is not an attempt to disguise reality. The Nazis did murder 6 million Jewish people; it is impossible even to estimate the effect of such a monstrous act upon a people's legacy. Noah has to die to symbolize the incalculable horror of the Nazis' crimes against the Jewish people and against humanity.

Noah, however, leaves his own legacy: Hope and the child, his published poem, and the moral courage which Michael Whitacre has acquired through his friendship. Thus, Whitacre, who at one time could not even act to prevent a drunken suicide, tracks Diestl down and kills him. The novel's closing hope is that Michael will be one of the "human beings" who run the world. Diestl's dying words, " 'Welcome to Germany,' " symbolize his total capitulation to cynical animalism (689). He is welcoming Michael to the hideousness of the concentration camp and to the senselessness of his shooting Noah. After killing the ethical monster Diestl, the now mature "human being" carries Noah's body " . . . personally, to Captain Green" (689).

Shaw attempts a great deal in *The Young Lions*—in some ways, more than the authors of the other major American World War II novels. The book is both a broad panorama of the major events of the European theater and an allegory of the crucial role of ethical choice in the attainment of human decency. While the Michael Whitacre characterization is stereotyped, Christian Diestl and Noah Ackerman emerge as memorable creations. Moreover, Shaw's unifying devices are not nearly as arbitrary as John W. Aldridge claims. The novel lives, not only as one of our major fictional re-creations of the most total and decisive of wars, but as an investigation of the human potential for good and evil.

Chapter Five

Moral Accidents on a "Bawdy Planet"

Since *The Young Lions,* Shaw has published ten novels, virtually all of them popular successes. In 1951, he responded to an immediate postwar sociopolitical crisis with *The Troubled Air,* a thesis novel attacking Senator McCarthy-inspired "witch-hunts" in the radio industry. In that same year, he became an expatriate in Paris; and, inevitably, his subsequent novels are less directly inspired by the external social and political realities of American life. As mentioned in Chapter 1, John W. Aldridge has asserted that Shaw's departure from America destroyed him as a major writer. While such a dismissal is not valid, Shaw's novels after *The Troubled Air* are the works of a markedly different writer than the angry leftist of the 1930s and 1940s.

In a manner that parallels his short stories, one observes a shift in the morality underlying his post-1951 novels. Increasingly, the emphasis is on Americans attempting to find ethical values in Europe and in a milieu of comfort and wealth. *Lucy Crown* (1956) depicts the ruinous consequences of a casual summer adultery. *Two Weeks in Another Town* (1960) describes the attempt of a onetime American movie star to recapture his past in Rome; *Evening in Byzantium* (1973) is a similar novel thematically, with the main character an American film producer attending the Cannes film festival. *Nightwork* (1975) is a comic novel which recounts the exploits of an innocent American expatriate and a charming European con man.

Four other Shaw novels, for different reasons, cannot be accurately placed in this group. *Voices of a Summer Day* (1965) is a nostalgic work in which a Jewish character mentally reviews the injustices he has experienced and perpetrated during a lifetime in

America. The Jordache saga, *Rich Man, Poor Man* (1970) and *Beggarman, Thief* (1977), sprawls across three generations and two continents and was apparently intended in part as entertaining popular fiction. The immense popularity of its television adaptations demonstrates that Shaw succeeded in this goal. His more recent novel, *The Top of the Hill* (1979), is thematically reminiscent of *Two Weeks in Another Town* and *Evening in Byzantium,* but it does not revolve around a personality from the entertainment world; and it is set entirely in the United States.

As mentioned in Chapter 1, Shaw criticism tends to be quite divided concerning the lasting value of his work. The novels which have appeared since *The Young Lions* provide the best framework for a thorough analysis of some of the more serious critical attacks upon his writing. There is a general consensus that he is a master of the modern short story (Diana Trilling appears to be one of the very few dissenters from this judgment).[1] His early plays, especially *Bury the Dead* and *The Gentle People,* are generally accepted as being significant moments in the history of the American theater of protest. While it has its detractors, *The Young Lions* is included in virtually all lists of the major American World War II novels. In contrast, the emphasis upon material wealth in most of these recent novels, along with the distinctly popular appeal of *Nightwork* and the Jordache saga, has had much to do with the virtual dismissal of Shaw as a serious writer by academic critics.

While Aldridge has been content to say simply that Shaw has been ruined by living away from the United States, many other academic critics have quit mentioning him at all. Three critics who have discussed his work since the move to Paris have had somewhat dissimilar responses. The most puzzling comment is by Ihab Hassan in *Radical Innocence*—in a chapter on Saul Bellow, Hassan refers in passing to the "pallid caricatures" of Jews in Shaw's work.[2] If Hassan is referring to the short stories, such an evaluation is incorrect and, if he has the novels in mind, it simply makes no sense. *Radical Innocence* appeared in 1961, at which time the only Shaw novel with a Jewish main character was *The Young Lions.* Subsequently, *Voices of a Summer Day* has been the only other novel focusing primarily on a Jewish character. Leslie Fiedler has been the most persistent, if not the most perceptive, critic of Shaw's work. It was Fiedler who, in 1957, classified him as a "middle middlebrow" Jewish writer.[3] The previous year, the same critic published a long derogatory evaluation in *Commentary*. Shaw has value as "a sociological touch-stone," Fiedler writes; however, the "slickness" of his style and the "sentimentality" of his intellect make him a "symptom" of the mediocrity of the times, rather than "a first-rate writer." In fact, Fiedler charges, the result of Shaw's "slickness" and "superficiality" is a kind of "half-art."[4]

Fiedler's attacks are interesting and even valuable in that they are extreme statements of recurrent misjudgments of Shaw's work. The "middle middlebrow" remark begins the curious assessment, which was to be repeated by Hassan and by Chester E. Eisinger in *Fiction of the Forties*, of Shaw as an emotionally militant Jewish writer. In fact, an accurate reading of Shaw as a specifically Jewish writer would be to place him in the middle of two extremes—on one side, such writers as Saul Bellow and Bernard Malamud who almost always write about Jewish characters and, on the other, Norman Mailer who, though Jewish, practically never depicts Jewish characters. In his novels since *The Young Lions*, Shaw falls much closer to the Mailer side than to that of Bellow and Malamud.

Fiedler's "half-art" comment is of more significance because it seems to have gained a wide enough degree of acceptance that a critical neglect of Shaw has resulted. Even Eisinger, who is, in many ways, a perceptive reader of the early Shaw, picks it up in a modified way: "I should say in passing, however, that Shaw's notion of maturity involves a knowledge of modern painting and the theater, of politics and labor, but does not include a profound knowledge of the human heart."[5] Since it has had such a wide acceptance, Fiedler's evaluation needs a close examination. First, one notices a curious tone of anger in the *Commentary* essay. Fiedler remembers "screaming in ecstasy" at *Bury the Dead* and feeling that it was "our play"; however, he has subsequently been annoyed at Shaw's alleged proclivity since the late 1930s for always being on the correct liberal side of every issue at exactly the right time.[6]

On balance, however, it must be said that not all the Shaw novels since *The Young Lions* seem to have been written with the highest of literary intent. William Startt has written perhaps the most objective recent essay about Shaw. Startt asserts correctly that Shaw is a natural dramatist and short story writer whose talent is sometimes strained by the demands of the novel. He evaluates *The Troubled Air* as a "sincere," but ultimately disappointing, "thesis novel." *Lucy Crown* does, in fact, read like "popular fiction," not, however, because of Shaw's intent, but because of the failures of his technique. Startt analyzes *Two Weeks in Another Town* as a quite serious and generally successful novel, which is underrated because Shaw's style seems, at times, "too clipped," too controlled.[7]

All of these evalutions seem correct. Ironically, Shaw's mastery of style, juxtaposed with his occasional problems with novelistic structure, is a factor in the recurrent evaluation of his work as superficial. He generally writes so effortlessly that one has a tendency to underrate the seriousness of what is being said; this is especially true if the overall structure of the novel seems somewhat contrived. In the words of Startt: "Still, Shaw the writer, rather than Shaw the novelist, makes excellent reading."

The question of literary seriousness is the simplest to deal with. *The Troubled Air* is a most serious thesis novel which ultimately fails aesthetically because of structural flaws and the overt nature of its political statements. *Lucy Crown* was meant as a serious study of the problems of what might be considered a "liberated" woman, but, as has been documented, Shaw had difficulty in controlling it from the beginning. *Two Weeks in Another Town* and *Evening in Byzantium* are quite serious, and highly underrated, studies of men associated with the motion picture industry attempting to discover some meaning for their lives. *Voices of a Summer Day,* Shaw's only lyrical novel, is a memorable study of the effects upon one man of the injustices and mistakes of a lifetime. *The Top of the Hill* attempts to analyze the psychological instability of a man dedicated to seeking encounters with death. While these novels are not completely successful, their underlying intent is serious; and it is a mistake to dismiss them in such terms as "half-art" and semi-serious.

Shaw's artistic aim does seem lower in *Nightwork* and in *Beggarman, Thief,* the second volume in the Jordache saga. The former is written in the tradition of picaresque comedy, and its few comments about the morality of our culture read almost like afterthoughts. *Beggarman, Thief,* too, feels melodramatic. Both can be seen as well-made popular entertainment. Again, Shaw is hardly the first serious writer to have occasionally written in such a mode; Somerset Maugham quickly comes to mind as a comparable figure.

It seems an obvious mistake to dismiss the total work of either man as unimportant because they do not always write in a mood of high seriousness. Yet that is precisely what many critics have done to Shaw.

An underlying vision does unite all of the novels, as well as most of Shaw's short stories. It can best be introduced by two quotations, one from *Lucy Crown* and the other from *Two Weeks in Another Town*. In the former, Oliver Crown has just learned that his wife, Lucy, has been unfaithful to him. A deliberate, almost emotionless man, he attempts to comprehend what has happened by logical reflection and by reading Shakespeare. In *The Winter's Tale*, he finds these lines:

> "Should all despair," ... "That have revolted wives, the tenth of mankind Would hang themselves. Physic for 't, there's none; It is a bawdy planet."

He proceeds to torture himself with thoughts of Lucy lying next to him in bed planning her deceit and feeling contempt for him, "the twisting, stubborn inhabitant of the bawdy planet."[8] In *Two Weeks in Another Town,* Jack Andrus visits the Sistine Chapel with his ex-wife, Carlotta, years after their acrimonious divorce.

As he stares at the ceiling, a sequence of bitter thoughts passes through Jack's mind.

> He could believe in Michelangelo ... but he could not believe in God.... Man is flesh, God is flesh, man makes man, man makes God, all mysteries are equal.... Salvation was the caprice of the usher who made out the seating plan on the last day.

Suddenly, Michelangelo's nudes remind him of photographs "of thousands of naked women being paraded before SS doctors in the German concentration camps." For a moment, Jack considers the possibility that "God is an SS doctor, and Michelangelo had advance information." Once outside, however, Jack rejects total cynicism and tells Carlotta: " 'There is a God.... But I don't think He has any interest in us. Or at any rate, not the interest that any religion says He has.... It does not affect Him whether we murder our fellow man or honor our father and mother or covet our neighbor's wife.' " He then proposes the view that one should " 'hope that God is a pre-1940 scientist [and thus not responsible for the bomb], Whose hand perhaps has slipped a little, but Whose intentions are still reasonable.' "[9]

It would undoubtedly be a mistake to argue that Jack Andrus's theology corresponds exactly to his creator's; nevertheless, the 1980 interview with Shaw substantiates the fact that he shares many of Andrus's beliefs.

Throughout his work, a limited kind of faith is posited in humanity and its potential for transcendent works, especially art. Shaw often seems to share the view of nineteenth- and twentieth-century existential thinkers that man created God as a shield against a cosmic void. The atrocities of the Nazis and the potential total devastation of the bomb make inevitable consideration of the possibility of a truly sadistic God. Shaw, like Jack Andrus, seems to reject such a vision. While Andrus falls back on the concept of a disinterested God, Shaw generally avoids consideration of any kind of God. Man, in his universe, is capable of great acts because of an underlying decency; however, that decency is a fragile thing, which can be totally submerged in the appetites of the flesh. Since the early optimism of his dramatic "fable," *The Gentle People,* Shaw has progressed to "the despair" of the short story, "God Was Here But He Left Early," in which "the various uses and manifestations of the flesh" have destroyed underlying decency. *Two Weeks in Another Town* and other novels fall in between these two extremes of faith and despair.

Given this vision of a world in which man, without the support of any divine force, struggles to save his potential for ethical behavior from the ever-present manifestations and abuses of the flesh, it is not surprising that moral and physical accidents are so central to Shaw's fiction. Such accidents are the central metaphor of his fiction. In a world of chance, where weakness sometimes overtakes the best of people and completely controls the worst, mistakes will happen. Increasingly, Shaw seems to believe that an individual's worth is determined by how he or she deals with such mistakes. Anyone can drift into moral accidents on "this bawdy planet"; the best people, however, accept their responsibility afterward and work at salvaging something from their lives.

While the accident metaphor is perfectly suited to the form of the short story, it is not to the novel. Shaw's novels sometimes seem structurally weak because they are held together by a series of such accidents and, thus, appear lacking in authorial control. Marital infidelity is a common ethical accident into which his characters lapse. Still, adultery is not, as Leslie Fiedler suggests, Shaw's desperate substitute for old leftist politics. It is a prime example of the abuses of the flesh and spirit. This chapter will discuss Shaw's novels to date since *The Young Lions,* except for *Rich Man, Poor Man* and *Beggarman, Thief,* which constitute an extended family saga and thus necessitate a separate analysis. The unifying focus for the analysis in this chapter will be the theme of moral accidents on a "bawdy planet."

The Troubled Air (1951)

In the 1980 interview, Shaw made structural distinctions among *The Troubled Air, Voices of a Summer Day,* and his other novels. Only these two, he said, were "cause and effect" novels and not dependent on the accident concept for underlying unity.[10] As a thesis novel warning against the threats to democracy posed by both the far right and the far left during the McCarthy era, *The Troubled Air* could have been nothing other than a "cause and effect" novel. In it, the cause is a right-wing magazine's blacklisting of five people associated with a popular radio program. The effect is the attempt of the program's director first to prove, in an allotted two weeks, that the five are innocent of Communist involvement and then to discover just what degree of guilt the five do possess.

The director, Clement Archer, has been described by Bergen Evans, among other critics, as "a resurrected Michael Whitacre."[11]

After some qualification, such an evaluation seems accurate. Rather than a Broadway playboy, Archer is a former academic, and he is never handicapped by the moral and intellectual superficiality which Whitacre battles. Still, he does represent the same kind of liberal faith in humanity. In fact, his handicap is a special kind of innocence resulting from blind faith in individual goodness. Shaw, once blacklisted himself, said in the 1980 interview that he had always known that the McCarthy hysteria would die out in America because of the fundamental decency of the United States. He added that Michael Whitacre personifies that decency which often has to be prodded into action but does finally act.[12] Clement Archer represents the same kind of decency; in fact, his problem is essentially that he carries it too far. Archer places faith not only in an abstract America, but in virtually all individuals. Such faith ruins his career in the novel, but, after being considerably modified, saves his soul.

Shaw leaves no doubt as to his contempt for such right-wing viciousness as blacklisting and other forms of character assassination by innuendo, but the novel's most memorable villain is its dedicated Communist, Vic Herres. Herres had been a favorite student of Archer's in college and had later recruited his former professor for radio work. A bright student and quarterback on the football team, Herres had been one of Shaw's apparent "golden boys," to whom seemingly nothing bad could ever happen. But, in a well-written flashback sequence describing the origin and history of the Archer-Herres friendship, Shaw warns the reader of something very dangerous about the real Vic Herres. Herres, now the star of Archer's program, has always been completely ruthless and unconcerned about other individuals. Because of his own peculiar kind of innocence, Archer is unable to see this aspect of his friend until it is too late.

The novel's comparable right-wing villain is Lloyd Hutt, the president of the advertising agency which puts Archer's program, "University Town," on the air. Hutt is never as real a character as Herres because he works strictly in a Machiavellian fashion and is too much the personification of right-wing viciousness (" 'Today

... we are living in a fearful, vindictive, unforgiving time. The rules of the game are being changed. One strike and out.' ")[13]. When Archer learns, near the end of the novel, that it was Hutt who started the movement to blacklist the five, he is relieved that it was not the government. One of Shaw's central points in the novel, however, is that men like Hutt have become, in the 1950s, a kind of invisible government, if anything more powerful than the legal one.

Archer has few problems in denouncing Hutt when he discovers the agency president's real role in the blacklisting. Hutt promises to ruin the director's career; but Archer, as a representative of the innate decency of America, will not let that intimidate him. Repudiating Herres is much more difficult, however. Old friendships and personal debt trouble Archer even when he is certain that Herres is the only real Communist among the five and is indeed intent on overthrowing the government of the United States and destroying anyone, including Archer, who gets in his way. Shaw's thesis, though, is that Herres must be renounced no less than Hutt because both are enemies of American and democratic values.

The novel is structured through an alternation of confrontation scenes and passages recounting Archer's periods of introspective searches for the truth. In the best of Archer's internal monologues, he wonders, while facing his tapped telephone, if there is "... a new philosophy, created for these confused times, which is based on the concept of unconscious crime?" (255–56). In an argument in which he is defending the validity of comedy as an art form, he asserts that " 'The idea of comedy ... comes from something that's just as real as despair—the conception that men are fundamentally good—or at least that some men are fundamentally good ... ' " (248). Even after his final confrontations with Hutt and Herres, which leave him financially and professionally ruined, Archer, like Irwin Shaw, clings to this belief.

The novel's most believable secondary character is Manfred Pokorny, a Jewish refugee and composer of the program's music. Pokorny is absolutely nonpolitical, but his Jewishness and immigrant status make him an inevitable victim of Hutt's purge.

Pokorny, whose parents died in Nazi crematoriums, did join the Austrian Communist party in 1922, but quit almost immediately when the party attempted to dictate the kind of music he wrote. His American wife is a militant and vindictive Communist. In an excellent early scene, Pokorny attempts to warn Archer of Hutt's viciousness and of the hopelessness of attempting to defend a Jew, however innocent he may be. Archer refuses even to believe that anti-Semitism is involved, but Pokorny insists: "'. . . I have had experience . . .'" (163).

The composer's prophecy that it is hopeless to attempt to help him is correct, and he commits suicide. Archer is shocked when Pokorny's wife and other party members use the dead man as a symbolic martyr to their cause: ". . . God, Archer thought, the Communists don't understand anything because they are not human" (293). After Noah Ackerman in *The Young Lions* and Benjamin Federov in *Voices of a Summer Day,* Pokorny is the most memorable Jewish character in any of Shaw's novels. His subplot is comparable to that of the short story "The Green Nude," except that the comic tone of the shorter work is absent. Like Sergei Baranov, Pokorny is the Jewish artist who wants simply to be left alone to produce, but who is hounded by vicious anti-Semitism no matter what country he is in.

Externally, Clement Archer loses virtually everything in *The Troubled Air,* but feels, at the end, that he has won something important. He has kept his integrity, the love of his wife, and his belief in the decency of at least some people. He is not the same man he was, however. Much of the innocence which once blinded him to reality and made him a potentially easy victim is dead (symbolized by the stillbirth of his son, in the last few pages of the novel).

William Startt is correct in calling *The Troubled Air* a "sincere" thesis novel. It is undeniably worth reading both as a record of the hysteria of the McCarthy years and as a statement of Shaw's faith in the potential of human decency to triumph over extreme ideologies of the right and the left. Still, it lacks the aesthetic subtlety of much of Shaw's short fiction—for example, "The Green Nude" and "Goldilocks at Graveside."

Lucy Crown (1956)

More than one critic has commented that the tone of *Lucy Crown* is marred by an aesthetically incongruous bitterness. Certainly, it is the one Shaw novel in which the writing sometimes feels forced and unnatural. Shaw, in fact, encountered more difficulty in writing it than he had with any of his other novels. In her biography of her husband, Dorothy Commins reproduces an exchange of letters between Shaw and Saxe Commins in which Shaw proposed giving up on the book. The novelist's professionalism and Commins's encouragement persuaded him to finish it, however. The editor's reaction to the finished work was interesting; he admired its art, but felt that it would probably not sell very well: "partly it lacks the violence expected of Shaw and partly it restates a theme that is now none too new." Commins saw the novel as a contemporary restatement of the central themes of Ibsen's *The Doll's House* and George Bernard Shaw's *Candida.*[14]

In fact, *Lucy Crown,* while not a fully realized work, is important as the first Shaw novel in which the theme of "moral accidents" is fully explored. It opens with Lucy, now widowed, accidentally seeing her son, Tony, in a bar in Paris. Much of the remainder of the book is a flashback describing the disastrous summer of 1937 in which the Crown family stability was destroyed. During that summer, Tony, then thirteen, was recuperating from rheumatic fever, which had almost killed him and which had left him with poor vision and a heart murmur. The family had gone to a summer cottage in Vermont, hoping to restore Tony's health. Shaw quickly sets the mood for what is to follow in a paragraph outlining a concept of "decisive" moments in human lives during which everything is irrevocably changed:

> The moment may be just that . . . or it may be a long afternoon, a week, a season, during which the issue is in doubt, in which the wheel is turned a hundred times, the small, accumulating accidents permitted to happen. For Lucy Crown it was a summer. (12)

The reader then learns that Lucy's husband, Oliver, is a prototype of such later Shaw characters as Rudolph Jordache, a decent man devoted to the work ethic and the American ideal of material success, but unable to express emotion or affection.

Shortly after Oliver's marriage, however, his father had committed suicide and the family business, always thought of as secure, had been discovered to be quite shaky. Oliver, then, had to move away from New York City to the family home in Hartford, Connecticut, and Lucy had to give up her scientific ambitions, which Oliver had never taken seriously. When they had a child, Oliver believed that the roles of wife and mother should satisfy her.

In fact, Oliver has for years been making the decisive accident inevitable by treating Lucy as a child, refusing to allow her to make even the most basic family decisions. During the crucial summer, he insists on hiring twenty-year-old Jeff Bunner as a companion for Tony. He instructs Bunner to win the boy from Lucy (Oliver fears that Tony is unnaturally devoted to her). When Oliver leaves, Bunner immediately falls in love with Lucy, then thirty-five.

Initially, Lucy attempts to laugh off Jeff's sexual advances. But a key scene between Lucy and Oliver just prior to the husband's departure warns the reader of what will inevitably happen. Oliver asserts that he is " 'an old-fashioned husband and father.' " Lucy then asks: " 'What if one day I decided to turn into a new-fashioned wife?' " Still, Lucy does not sexually give herself to Bunner until she receives a phone call from Oliver in which he cruelly scolds her for having forgotten to pay a bill; then, she takes the initiative in arranging her seduction. Afterward, she again treats it lightly, calling it a summertime affair. Nevertheless, the real disintegration of the family begins when Tony, through a series of further accidents, sees Jeff and Lucy in bed together and calls his father to come down immediately. It is only when Lucy becomes unmistakably aware of her son's implacable hatred for her that she begins to realize the seriousness of what has happened.

To this point, the novel is virtually flawless. Lucy has been characterized as an intelligent and inwardly strong woman whose potential has been frustrated by a husband unable and unwilling to treat her as a mature human being. When Oliver returns to ask for a reconciliation, however, the unnatural bitterness of which critics have complained begins seriously to flaw the novel. In a well-written scene, Lucy lays down the terms of any reconciliation. She first tells Oliver that he has " 'converted' " her, and she is now devoted to total truth. She then informs him that he has never sexually satisfied her, that Jeff made her remember what pleasure felt like and she most certainly will be unfaithful again, and that Tony must be sent away never to see her again: " 'he's my enemy . . . ' " (191). Oliver accepts these terms. Despite the smoothness of the writing, this scene simply contains too many improbabilities which are crucial to the direction the novel will take.

The novel picks up two years later when Oliver over the Christmas vacation, goes to visit Tony in the private school at which he is exiled. Not surprisingly, the fifteen-year-old boy is embittered, given to drawing cartoons in class and making certain that he has no friends. Touched, Oliver decides to take Tony home.

Tony's visit ends on a bitter note after he observes a boorish visitor, an authentic son of Babbitt, patronizing and humiliating Oliver. He goes back to school, leaving behind a note blaming Lucy for the obvious disintegration of his father.

One last meeting between Oliver and Tony is described in the novel. The war has started; and despite his age, Oliver has succeeded in enlisting. Tony, because of the damage of his childhood illness, is still a civilian. The scene is a long one and, to a degree, works because of the irony of a son sending his father off to war. Oliver is drinking heavily throughout the scene, and Tony becomes increasingly certain that this is further evidence of complete psychological disintegration. Increasingly embarrassed by his father's drunken behavior, Tony becomes intent upon escaping him.

However, Oliver insists upon telling Tony what he needs to tell him. First, he accuses the now twenty-year-old man of having developed " 'confidence' " by hating everyone; he then asks Tony to be " 'original' " and love his father. Pathetically, he asks his son to take care of Lucy while he's gone and to count the " 'guests.' " Later, in a hotel room, Oliver describes his own father's suicide and explains that, like most men, he wanted a son to give him " 'optimism' " again. He then describes his own recent sexual infidelity, the first of his marriage, and outlines a Crown family shield: " 'Suicide, Failure and Adultery.' " He has joined the army hoping to die. Suddenly transcending his self-pity, Oliver apologizes to Tony for all the ways in which he and Lucy failed the boy and gives his son the watch his father gave him two weeks before the suicide. Tony then agrees to an attempt to phone Lucy, but she does not answer (287–99). Tony then leaves, never to see his father again.

The reader learns that Oliver returned home, only to discover that Lucy has had many affairs; she assures him that there will be more in the future. Oliver explodes and beats her until she is nearly unconscious. In the war, Oliver is killed because he insists on taking unnecessary chances. Especially in the Oliver-Tony scene, the level of writing is excellent. Still, a central problem with the novel is the characterization of Oliver. Although one understands that he is committing a form of indirect suicide and understands the parallel with his father, the change in his character is too total and abrupt to be aesthetically plausible.

The story returns to the present time of its opening. Lucy, after the accidental sight of Tony in the bar, decides that she must seek him out. When she goes to Tony's apartment, she meets his wife, Dora, and learns quickly that Tony is still an embittered man. He makes a living drawing satiric cartoons under another name, refuses to return to America because he became an exile while still very young, and is thoughtless of his wife and his one child, a four-year-old boy.

When Tony arrives, he agrees to have a drink with Lucy, at which time she tells the details of Oliver's death in the war and asserts that she does not believe Tony is as unfeeling as he pretends. She then challenges him to go with her to visit Oliver's grave in France. Recounting in a long speech all the "accidents and errors" of the "decisive " summer, she argues that while accidents befall everyone, " 'It's what you do with them, how you come out of them, how you repair the damage, that's important. Well, I did the worst possible thing. I made my accident permanent.' " Since her last night with Oliver, she has been chaste. After his death, she tried to adopt children, but couldn't. Now she works for a United Nations children's committee: " 'I'm not satisfied—but I'm necessary' " (381–87).

At Oliver's unmarked grave, Tony initially remains contemptuous of both his dead father and of Lucy; but when Lucy trips and falls painfully to the ground, he suddenly sees her as an aging, vulnerable woman attempting to heal old and destructive wounds. No longer viewing his mother as "the enemy," he is now free to give love himself. Upon returning home, he is determined to become a real husband and father. Lucy's fall is, then, the healing accident which starts to undo some of the damage of the "decisive" summer.

Lucy Crown is an ambitious novel in which Shaw attempts to delineate the consciousness of a complex modern woman. It is flawed by improbabilities of characterization and by the fact that, for the only time in Shaw's career, the difficulties of writing show. Still, it is valuable for its several well-crafted scenes and as Shaw's first novel to explore the full ramifications of moral accidents.

Two Weeks in Another Town (1960)

In a sense, two novels constitute the peak of Shaw's achievement as a novelist—*Two Weeks in Another Town* and *Evening in Byzantium* (1973). While they do not offer the ambitious panorama of *The Young Lions,* they are structurally tight, convincing novels. Each is a much-underrated work of art. Their respective settings (Rome, where an American company is making a film, and the Cannes film festival) probably play a part in the failure of academic critics to appreciate them. Even though the worlds they depict may be chic and artificial, both novels are investigations of moral concerns long central to Shaw's fiction. In fact, they thematically resemble *Lucy Crown* in their depiction of central characters struggling to exorcise the guilt resulting from past mistakes and failures.

Two Weeks in Another Town focuses on Jack Andrus's struggle to overcome the inhibiting bitterness caused by the destruction of a major part of his past. In the novel's present tense, Jack is an employee of the United States government stationed in Paris. He is married to a French wife, Hélène, with whom he has had two children. He has had two former lives, however, both of which ended in bitterness. Once an ambitious young Broadway actor, he had been married to an aspiring but untalented actess, Julia. Even though he and Julia had a child, Steven, their marriage was doomed from the first by her obsessive jealousy of his greater talent. This life was ended and a second begun by a dynamic Hollywood director, Maurice Delaney.

During a try-out in Philadelphia, Delaney had suddenly entered the dressing room of a theater in which Jack was appearing in a play. He had persuaded the writer and producer of the play that it was no good and that they should forget it and come to California with him. Almost as an afterthought, Delaney had hired Jack as well. From the first, Julia had "hated what Delaney meant to Jack" (66).

Once in Hollywood, Jack allowed the studio to change his name to James Royal; starred in three successful Delaney films; soon became the director's sole confidant; and fell in love with Carlotta Lee, a beautiful actress in the first Delaney film, *The Stolen Midnight*. Having a " 'peculiar sense of honor. . . . in those days' " (177), Jack, after falling in love with Carlotta, had refused to sleep with her until he flew back to New York to tell Julia that he was about to begin an affair. Looking at their sleeping child, he had promised himself to find time someday to love Steven. Six months later, Julia agreed to a divorce, and he married Carlotta Lee. Shaw's craft is manifest in his conveying the point, primarily through brief, memorable bits of dialogue, that marriage to Carlotta represented the high point of Jack's life: " 'In California, I find . . . they have wonderful California mornings in the morning. Don't you find?' " (188). Five years after their marriage the war came; and Jack's James Royal life crumbled. In the service, he accidentally learns at a poker game that Carlotta is being regularly and openly unfaithful to him. He is accidentally abandoned in a farmhouse which is shelled and almost dies, but lives to undergo eighteen operations over a two-year period. His life is saved; but his face is marred and his acting career thus destroyed.

Still, he is determined not to lose Carlotta until she visits him in a hospital and is seemingly most upset that her dog has been poisoned: "'He's the one really near and dear thing I've lost in the war'" (196). Jack's realization that he must find a new life is later confirmed by Delaney, who comes close to admitting that he, too, slept with Carlotta during the war. During the divorce settlement, Carlotta is ruthless and virtually destroys Jack financially.

Most of this background information is conveyed in a brilliantly constructed long chapter near the middle of the novel. As the book opens, Jack is in Orly airport with Hélène and their two children. He is preparing to answer a summons from Maurice Delaney, with whom he has had no contact since the war destroyed his acting career. Suddenly Delaney, making a film in Rome, has wired Jack that he needs someone to dub the voice of his leading man. While Jack has not heard directly from Delaney for years, he has read that the director's career is going steadily downhill. Jack's farewell with Hélène is tense; he has not slept with her for two weeks, and they have never reconciled a fight a year before in which she had accused him of being uninvolved and "remote" in all his relationships.

Inwardly, Jack acknowledges the truth of this accusation and fears that his third marriage is about to fail. He cannot really explain to Hélène why he is answering Delaney's call; but the reader ultimately understands that Jack must see the director again because, next to Carlotta Lee, he was the most significant person in Jack's past. Subconsciously, Jack is reaching for a cure for his remoteness.

He finds such a cure, but not in a manner he would have expected. Almost immediately upon his arrival in Rome, Jack is physically attacked by a drunken American whom he has never seen before. This senseless incident forcibly brings home to Jack the chaotic nature of the postwar twentieth century, and he begins to have a series of agonizing nightmares which prophesy the imminent death of someone. He is unable to divine whether the foreshadowed death is his own or that of someone close to him. The nightmares produce in Jack a terror of being alone; and, when he meets a beautiful young Italian girl, he has an affair with her.

Jack is introduced to Veronica by his friend Jean-Baptiste Despière, a French journalist whose specialty is war correspondence. Despière is one of several memorable secondary characters in the novel, a cynical but attractive man who knows that the chaos of his age must inevitably destroy him. Jack's affair with Veronica is the first time he has been unfaithful to Hélène, and he initially does not understand why it is happening so casually. Soon, however, he decides to quit attempting to analyze it: "this way (O, benevolent accident) no harm would come to anyone, and maybe a great deal of good. What the hell, he thought, it's only two weeks" (77). Veronica disappears almost immediately after the affair has begun, and Jack is made painfully aware of what she has represented for him—as he lies in bed one night unable to sleep because Death is "back in the room with him. . . ." he knows that "if she were here . . . it would all be different" (206). The girl's youth and beauty have represented temporary escape from the terror produced in Jack by his nightmares.

Besides these nightmares, Jack encounters more in Rome which creates a sense of impending doom. Initially upon meeting Delaney again, Jack is certain that the director wants more from him than he has asked. After watching the film Delaney has shot, Jack is shocked by how "lifeless" it is: " 'it's all skillful embroidery. On top. Under it, it's chaotic, accidental . . . ' " (251). Jack soon realizes that Delaney wants more from him than can ever be given: reassurance that his talent is still intact and, most of all, a rebirth of the director's great years when he worked with, and confided in, James Royal. That James Royal died long ago is one implication of Jack's recurring nightmares.

Two characters serve to put Jack's fears and uncertainties to rest. As mentioned, Veronica disappears shortly after she and Jack begin their affair. She does not reappear until near the end of the novel to announce her marriage to a wealthy but emotionless Swiss. She primarily functions as a symbol of Jack's lost youth and as a device for introducing another, more important, character, Robert Bresach. Bresach is Veronica's young, insanely jealous American lover; and his entrance into the novel is dramatic. Confronting Jack with a knife, he threatens to kill Andrus for taking Veronica away from him.

Even in this initial scene, Jack is struck by how much Bresach looks like his son, Steven, whom he has never found the once-promised time to love. Steven has, in fact, renounced his father as a corrupt agent of a corrupt government. In a later meeting, Bresach repeats the same charge and adds that Jack's present life is made even more unforgivable by the fact that he was once a talented and dedicated actor. When Jack is able to attain the necessary distance, he begins to view the erratic young man as a surrogate for his son. Bresach's appearance seems to Jack a second chance to feel and express the love he promised Steven as an infant.

This, however, is perhaps the least important symbolic level on which the Bresach characterization functions. Jack soon discovers that the young man has come to Rome in order to study film and that he has already written a script. Bresach continues his verbal abuse of Andrus for a while and even leaves the threat of physical assault as a future possibility, but Jack knows that the young man is harmless. After reading Bresach's script and concluding that it is "brilliant," Jack realizes the full complexities of his relationship with the eccentric young man. Andrus sees in him the potential for saving Maurice Delaney. The intensity of the young American's devotion to film as the twentieth century's dominant art form reminds him of the young, uncorrupted Delaney. Even more significantly, Bresach comes to personify for Jack his own youthful ambition and integrity—that lost past with which he is struggling. With wry amusement, he observes that while the young American may be slightly mad, he has a faith in art and a code of personal integrity which the vanished James Royal shared. Thus, Bresach soon begins to act as Andrus's conscience—quoting from da Vinci's transcription of Pliny, he leaves Jack a note warning him to "cleanse" himself and then "salute the planet" (208). Later, he lectures the older man:

> "You are a civilized man. . . . At the end, no matter what happens, you must not be able to say to yourself, 'I didn't know. It was an accident.' " (239)

The accident motif enters to move the novel toward its climax. Delaney is injured while recklessly jumping a horse and then suffers a heart attack. In the hospital, he asks Jack to take over the film and, having previously read Bresach's script, to " 'use' " the young man. Delaney has already come to see the young American's script as his means for a comeback. Primarily because of Bresach's dedication, the film begins to fall into place; his dedication inspires everyone, even the drunken leading man for whom Jack is dubbing the dialogue. It is at this point that Andrus is forced into making the novel's central moral decision. Carefully weighing loyalties, he tells Bresach not to let Delaney touch his script and then gets the director to agree that, as a young man, he would have given the same advice. Jack has chosen loyalty to what he and Delaney once were over what they have become. Thus, he has accepted partly that vanished past which has long haunted him.

Still, the peace Andrus has come to Rome to find is not complete. Partially because of Veronica's sudden disappearance, he has realized that much of his remoteness stems from his deep hatred for Carlotta Lee. He understands that Carlotta's promiscuity, which contributed so strongly to the destruction of their marriage, came from her terror over the prospect of growing older and the reality of a slumping career. However, he cannot forgive her heartlessness when she visited him in the hospital and during the divorce settlement. After Delaney's injury, she arrives in Rome and calls Jack, asking to see him again; he assures her that he does not hate her, but initially refuses any meeting.

When he does agree to visit the Sistine Chapel with her, their conversation is dominated by a scarcely veiled hostility.

> [Carlotta:] "I didn't leave you.... You left me."
> [Jack:] "It's amazing... how many different opinions eyewitnesses can have of the same accident." (313)

She asks forgiveness for her hospital visit and attempts to explain her greed during the divorce settlement (the money saved her from becoming a high-class prostitute), but Jack refuses to listen. At a later meeting, she admits to sleeping with Delaney during the war and says that he gave her more pleasure than any other man ever did. Still, she pleads with Jack to like her; again he responds coldly.

Events external to his relationship with Carlotta soon accumulate, however, and result in Jack's finding the capacity to forgive her. Clara Delaney, the director's bitter, frustrated wife, convinces her husband that Andrus and Bresach are betraying him by remaking the film the way they want it. Delaney orders Jack to leave town. Thus, it is no longer possible even to pretend that the old Maurice Delaney can be brought back to life. Earlier, Jack has learned of the senseless death of Despière in Algeria. The prophecy in Jack's nightmares was actually of two deaths—Despière's, and the symbolic death of Maurice Delaney's integrity and decency. Feeling desperately lonely, Jack hears the voice of a drunken man crying outside his hotel room: " 'Oh God, I'm all alone.... Won't anyone help me?' " and the jeering laughter of two prostitutes (366–67).

Without really knowing why, Jack rushes to the phone, calls Carlotta and asks to come to her room. They make love in a forgiving, healing manner rather than as an act of revenge. Afterward, Jack realizes that he has cleansed himself and can now salute the planet by returning to Hélène and his children no longer haunted and crippled by the past. Waiting at the airport for a plane back to Paris, he encounters the young Bresach, terrified that he is on the verge of success. Affectionately amused, Jack tells Bresach that the secret of avoiding personal corruption is to " 'Be delighted' " (372). Thus, Bresach and Carlotta Lee have liberated him from his remoteness.

Two Weeks in Another Town is a rich, well-structured work. It contains several memorable secondary characters: among others, Despière; Jack Holt, one of Shaw's decent if naive Americans from the nation's heartland; Barzelli, a sensual and heartless Italian actress. The novel constantly alludes to the accidental nature of life in the chaotic twentieth century—a fatal helicopter accident in the Alps is mentioned twice; and, when visiting the Forum, Jack remembers some lines from Cicero: "What an age! What morals!" William Startt interprets the novel as being primarily about the problems faced by the out-of-fashion artist;[15] and Shaw does give Despière some crucial lines elaborating the difference in European and American attitudes toward art:

"The intermittent failure, the cadenced rise and fall of the level of a man's work, which is accepted and understood by the European artist, is fiercely rejected as a normal picture of the process of creation. A dip is not a dip to an American artist, it is a descent into an abyss. . . ." (292)

In the 1980 interview, Shaw emphasized that no writer is ever consistently successful—not Faulkner, not Hemingway, not even Tolstoy.[16]

Thus, while the novel's main focus is on Jack Andrus's struggle to find peace with his past, the nature of art is clearly an underlying theme. Part of its message is this: while reality is chaotic and accidental, art should not be. There are rules of fiction, and Irwin Shaw has always believed in the necessity of following them. He believes that fiction should communicate the accidental nature of reality, but not imitate it.[17] *Two Weeks in Another Town* succeeds beautifully in this objective.

Evening in Byzantium (1973)

Published thirteen years later, *Evening in Byzantium* is a thematically and structurally comparable work. Jesse Craig, a man also struggling to find peace with the past, is the analogous figure to Jack Andrus. He is a once-prominent Broadway and Hollywood producer whose career is in eclipse. In the novel's present tense, he has arrived at the Cannes film festival with a screenplay supposedly written by an unknown named Malcolm Harte. Cannes functions in this novel much as Rome does in *Two Weeks in Another Town,* a rich, exotic background where creativity and financial power struggle for a satisfactory balance. Much as with Jack Andrus, Jesse initially does not quite understand why he has made his journey; but events will soon force him to make crucial, live-saving decisions.

Almost instantly upon settling into his Cannes hotel room, he is visited by a persistent young American girl, Gail McKinnon, who introduces herself as a journalist specializing in "interesting people."[18] Jesse, who disapproves of the abrasiveness and values of Gail McKinnon's generation, attempts to dismiss her; but she insists upon leaving with him a questionnaire and some background material concerning the life of Jesse Craig. Reading it, he is stunned to discover how much the girl knows about him. Still, he tries to ignore her and her questionnaire, but encounters her wherever he goes in Cannes. Her attitude toward him wavers inexplicably between overtures of friendliness (" 'You are not really as remote a man as you try to appear.' " [p. 106]) and hostility. When he finally does start to read her questionnaire, its first question forces him to confront some unpleasant realities. " 'Why are you in Cannes?' " Gail has written. Jesse answers, " 'I am in Cannes to save my life' " (106–7).

As in Jack Andrus's story, Shaw then intersperses flashback sequences with present tense action to convey how Jesse Craig has arrived at this stage of desperation. The extreme financial pressures he is under have already been described in the novel's opening pages. Only gradually, however, does the reader learn the details of how these pressures accumulated. Inextricably interwined with his money problems are moral dilemmas, which are of more significance to both Jesse and his creator. Craig wants to achieve an internal reconciliation with the past wrongs he has suffered and the mistakes he has made.

Jesse Craig's career and his moral struggles began simultaneously when he met Edward Brenner in a poker game on a troopship returning home from World War II. Brenner had written a play, *The Foot Soldier,* which he allowed Jesse to read; and, with his inheritance from his father, Jesse produced it approximately one year after both men's army discharge. He chose a young director named Baranis, and things went smoothly during production except when Brenner violently disagreed with Craig's and Baranis's selection of Penelope Gregory for a part in the play. The play was an instant success; Jesse married Penelope Gregory and quickly produced two more successful plays.

During the summer of 1949, Jesse, Penelope, and Edward Brenner spent an apparently idyllic summer on the Cote d'Azur. It was at the end of this summer, however, that the first signs of inevitable personal problems appeared. As Jesse prepared to leave, Penelope launched a vicious verbal assault upon the suddenly penniless Brenner, demanding that Craig force him to leave the villa. Jesse talked her out of it and left, watching his wife and friend "standing side by side on the platform in the dusk waving to him" (84).

He agreed to produce Brenner's next play, even though he knew it was "stillborn, irretrievable" (85). Made confident by his first success, the playwright saw no signs of failure, even when the rehearsals were disastrous, and married Susan Lockridge, a complete newcomer to the theater. When the play failed, Brenner accused Jesse of destroying it and hinted that the producer had an ulterior reason for doing so. Many years later, Jesse understood what Brenner had been implying when, during a quarrel, Penelope confessed to having slept with Brenner during the idyllic summer: "She meant to hurt him, and she managed it" (87).

Everything Brenner wrote afterward failed. Finally, Susan Brenner sent Jesse another play by her husband, explaining that Edward did not know what she had done and pleading with Jesse to produce it despite the " 'painful memory.' " He read it, felt it too failed, and called Susan to tell her so. Her reply was brief and sharp: " 'I thought you were a better man' " (137). Someone else did produce the play and it did fail; but when Jesse went to see it, he realized that he had been wrong—that the play itself was good and, if produced correctly, would have succeeded and restored Brenner's reputation. Backstage, he explained this to Brenner and pleaded with the playwright to allow him to produce the play correctly a year later. Bitterly, Brenner told Craig to get out of his life and walked away. Jesse never saw him again. Part of what Jesse is struggling to reconcile in Cannes is Susan Brenner's implicit accusation that Jesse subconsciously refused to save Brenner out of anger at his adultery with Penelope. This question has become all the more necessary for Jesse to answer since he too has experienced professional failure.

Brenner had not been Penelope's only betrayal of Jesse. Standing in the lobby of a theater after the disastrous preview of one of his films, the producer learned that his longtime director, Baranis, had slept with Penelope the night before her wedding. In addition to infidelity, Penelope became increasingly given to outbursts of insane jealousy and extravagant shopping sprees. She drove away all of his interesting friends and populated his house with dull acquaintances. Still, he did not press for a separation until she announced one night that she would no longer have sex with him; and he did not demand a divorce until he accidentally learned of her infidelity with one of the most mediocre of their acquaintances. During the legal battling over the divorce settlement, Penelope had been unreasonable; "she had become a lawyer's creation, sticking for gain, advantage, revenge" (131). Penelope had become virtually psychotic, but Jesse knows that he must share the responsibility for their ruined marriage. He had sometimes slept with other women, always telling himself that he was still faithful to the marriage because the affairs meant nothing to him. Now, in Cannes, he realized that "he had been wrong. He and his wife had avoided candor, and they had drained their marriage" (129).

Jesse has come to Cannes both to save a deteriorating career and to reach a vantage point from which he can calmly view the wreckage of his personal life. Attaining necessary objectivity is made difficult by too many sharp reminders of the past following him. Besides the mysterious Gail McKinnon with her questionnaire and background information, he must deal with his daughter, Anne, and his mistress, Constance. Anne inevitably reminds him of his traumatic marriage and of the 1960s counterculture toward which Jesse (like Irwin Shaw) feels much hostility. Anne has, in fact, dropped out of college in San Francisco because of her own misgivings about this movement; still, she is chronologically part of the generation which created it. She abruptly decides to join her father in Cannes where she instantly becomes devoted to Gail McKinnon and, even worse, to Ian Wadleigh, a drunken, self-pitying writer and onetime friend of Jesse.

Constance is an American living in Paris who had eventually saved Jesse after the damage inflicted by Penelope: "'... once more he enjoyed the entire [female] sex. It was not the least of the gifts Constance had brought him'" (48). Thus, he is sincerely devoted to her; but she too makes some demands which initially distract Jesse from his purpose in Cannes. On balance, however, she gives more than enough to compensate. The Malcolm Harte screenplay is actually Jesse's, based on a true story he heard from Constance. Jesse has signed it with the name of a soldier killed in the war so that it will be read and judged on its own merits, rather than as the work of Jesse Craig.

The screenplay represents Jesse's attempt to recapture his former professional magic; but, since he has been a producer and not a writer, he has little certainty about its worth. One of the novel's most effective metaphors is of an aging Spanish matador who is too old and too rich to still perform, but insists on continuing to face the bulls anyway: " 'It is the only thing that deeply amuses me. It is my only playground. . . . So—I cannot permit them to drive me from it' " (109). Jesse's screenplay is his attempt not to be driven from his own playground. Upon reading it, his agent and friend of many years brutally rejects it as old-fashioned and uncommercial. After this rejection, Jesse shows it to Walter Klein, one of the new powerful men in the world of films. Klein likes it, wants to produce it, and begins to push Jesse to get a commitment from Malcolm Harte. Significantly, Jesse escapes Cannes at this point and goes to Constance.

Her name is symbolic—Jesse believes that she is the one unfailing constant in a chaotic world. While they spend an idyllic time together, however, Constance announces that she is moving from Paris to San Francisco, a change which cannot help but adversely affect their relationship. Shaw's point is that, in fact, there are no constants in the world. Earlier in the novel, the novelist has symbolically foreshadowed this truth by stressing Constance's record as a poor driver: "She had never had an accident, she boasted. She should have had twenty" (110–11).

When Jesse returns from the idyllic retreat with Constance, Klein offers him a deal: a prominent director, Bruce Thomas, is excited about filming the Harte screenplay, although he wants Ian Wadleigh brought in for revision. After confessing that he is Malcolm Harte, Jesse again realizes "the joys of power" (286). Having salvaged his career, Jesse is now assaulted by new personal problems.

He has started having sex with Gail McKinnon: "Another ordered life was to begin for him tomorrow. He had one last night to enjoy the pleasures of chaos" (312). After their first lovemaking, however, Gail makes the chaos less than pleasurable by leaving a note accusing Jesse of having slept with her mother and implying that he has just committed incest. At this point, Craig does not even know who her mother is. Ultimately he learns that the girl is the daughter of a woman who worked in his office years ago and whom he had scarcely noticed. The woman had constructed an entire fantasy life around him and had deserted her family. Gail's original animosity toward Jesse came from the mistaken assumption that he had corrupted her mother.

Earlier, Jesse has discovered that a critic bears him a long-standing grudge because of a disparaging remark which the producer does not even remember making. In this incident, as in the story of Gail and her mother, Shaw is analyzing the power of the creative man to affect the lives of people without realizing that they exist. Art is a powerful force, with its total implications beyond the control of even the artist. A related thematic concern here is the modern tendency for people to live vicariously through the triumphs and failures of celebrities. Both an artist and a celebrity, Shaw has direct knowledge of these phenomena.

While Jesse is still trying to unravel the mystery of Gail's mother's identity, Anne runs away with Ian Wadleigh. In a letter, she cites her father's behavior with Gail as a precedent which legitimatizes her action. Painfully, Jesse is learning again that actions do not occur in isolation and that their consequences are unpredictable. Thus, when his agent explains the producer's role in Penelope's hysteria, he understands:

> "... you were the center of attraction. She was always in the background. There was one way she could stop being in the background. And she took it."
>
> "And she took it." Craig nodded. (292)

Shaken by the scare from Gail and Anne's potentially disastrous behavior, Jesse leaves Cannes for New York. He has learned of Edward Brenner's death in poverty and obscurity; and in an act of symbolic guilt, he registers at the Manhattan Hotel, where he had stayed while producing Edward Brenner's first play. While his personal life is only becoming more complicated, he is still determined to save his career. Shortly after checking into the hotel, he collapses from a massive bleeding ulcer and has to be hospitalized.

Symbolically, the blood which rushes out of him represents the moral impurity of his life.

After Jesse undergoes a successful operation, the novel moves swiftly toward its conclusion through a sequence of farewell scenes—with Penelope (Jesse weeps because "he didn't feel anything when he said good-by, not even rage" [359]) and with Constance ("She was the best girl he had ever known, and she was gone" [365]). Finally, he leaves the hospital with the doctor ordering him to "'eat yeast'" and "'uncomplicate'" himself (366).

Like Jack Andrus, Jesse Craig is one of Shaw's decent men who have made a number of mistakes and are forced to struggle for a reconciliation with their own past. *Evening in Byzantium* also contains a number of memorable secondary characters: David Teichman, a once-powerful figure in Hollywood dying of a brain tumor and gallantly wearing a toupee to hide the scars of surgery; Natalie Sorel, a beautiful and sexually promiscuous actress who decides to become respectable by marrying a wealthy Texan; and Tonio Corelli, a handsome and totally self-centered Italian actor.

The novel effectively utilizes recurrent symbolism to convey the erotic and exotic ambience of Cannes—for instance, a plump woman lying on the beach with her legs spread apart and Jesse Craig seeing Picasso sitting by himself in a restaurant. The instability of the film industry is graphically conveyed through effectively concise summaries of complex power shifts. A beautifully written "overture" describes the absurd self-centeredness of the entire film festival in a world poised on the brink of destruction.

As in *Two Weeks in Another Town,* a subtheme in the novel concerns the special difficulties of the artist. At one point Jesse Craig scolds the self-pitying Ian Wadleigh: "'Come on, Ian.... Every artist has his ups and downs. Just about everybody goes in and out of fashion in his lifetime. If he lasts long enough'" (101). Later Jesse says: "'A book is one thing.... The man who writes it is another. More often than not a book is a disguise, not a description'" (251). Shaw, through Craig, is again saying that the writer must convey chaos without imitating it in the form of his work. Here, he is adding another commandment for the survival of the artist: ignore the critics when they pronounce your work to be irrelevant and passé. Irwin Shaw has, of course, gone in and out of fashion several times during his career, but works like *Two Weeks in Another Town* and *Evening in Byzantium* insure that he will never go permanently out of fashion.

Voices of a Summer Day (1965)

Published between *Two Weeks in Another Town* and *Evening in Byzantium, Voices of a Summer Day* is a very different kind of novel, although it bears superficial resemblances to the other two works. In 1980 Shaw made two revealing observations about *Voices of a Summer Day*: it represents his only return to the "cause-and-effect novel," instead of the novel of accident, since *The Troubled Air;* and it is his only novel that neither the critics nor the public liked. The book's relative unpopularity may be a result of its mood and tone not being those one normally expects from Irwin Shaw. *Voices of a Summer Day* is a distinctly lyrical, rather than dramatic, work; and its predominant mood is one of nostalgia. Perhaps more than any of his novels, it shows the strong influence of the English Romantic poets, an influence Shaw stressed in the same interview.[19]

Its similarities to *Two Weeks in Another Town* and *Evening in Byzantium* are essentially structural. The novel opens in 1964 with Benjamin Federov, now fifty years old, watching his thirteen-year-old son, Michael, in an informally arranged baseball game on Long Island. The opening description of Federov sets the novel's tone: "He was no longer young, ..." and he gave "the impression of melancholy" and of "a man who permitted himself to be cheated in small matters."[20] Events in the baseball game trigger associations in Federov's mind and send him into prolonged reminiscence about the past.

These reminiscences are predominantly personal and focus upon Federov's relationships with his father, brother, and son; his adolescent loss of ideals; and his record of marital infidelity. But Shaw uses historical events to give them emphasis. Much of the critical disapproval of the novel may have resulted from Shaw's treatment of Federov, the first Jewish main character in one of his novels since Noah Ackerman in *The Young Lions*. While the novel certainly contains protest against anti-Semitism, Federov is depicted as a man grown tired of anger and demonstration: " 'I do not have enough anger left for all causes. I must ration it wisely' " (37). Moreover, Federov's Jewish identity, while certainly not repudiated, is ultimately made secondary to his American nationality. Ironically, the book may have been resented because of this subordination of Jewish identity—Shaw has been condemned for being too militantly Jewish.

Despite its lack of popular or critical acceptance, *Voices of a Summer Day* works on the level on which it is written; while it might seem to break down under extensive rational analysis, it has a strongly evocative lyrical power. For instance, Shaw uses the 1927 execution of the Italian immigrants Sacco and Vanzetti in Boston, the 1963 assassination of President John F. Kennedy, and World War I to symbolize the dark side of American life. Baseball is his recurrent metaphor of the basic decency of the American character. On a strictly rational level, this seems an obvious imbalance, especially when, as nearly always in Shaw, the novel's final thrust is that the American character is more good than bad. In an abstract statement, baseball, when compared with the tragedies of Sacco and Vanzetti, the JFK assassination, and World War I, seems insignificant.

Finally, the novel works because Shaw is able, on a lyrical level, to make baseball an effective symbol of family tradition. Federov's memories start when the inevitable cry of " 'Kill the umpire' " reminds him of the stories he has heard of Dallas schoolchildren cheering the news of Kennedy's death. Without knowing that he is going to, he leaps to his feet and yells, " 'Stop that' " (10–11). Then the memories begin, with the most moving ones centered on his father, Israel, and the concept of family tradition.

Israel Federov had come to America from Russia at the age of six and "had grown up amongst the usual terrors and sweated labor on New York's East Side . . . " (14). Finally, he had become moderately successful in the automobile-accessory business. The father had come to love the game of baseball instantly: "Israel Federov was made into an American catching behind the plate bare-handed in the years between 1895 and 1910" (142). He came to love everything about America and, in fact, grew into a superpatriot. In 1917, he insisted upon enlisting in World War I despite the fact that he had a family and quarreled bitterly with Samuel, his younger brother who refused to go to war. Israel's participation in this "bungled, unnecessary and disastrous [war]... was the one purely selfish act" he ever committed (15).

Ten years later, he had another bitter quarrel with his brother-in-law, George. Uncle George had been beaten by the police for protesting against the executions of Sacco and Vanzetti; and Israel Federov could only see this as a family disgrace which would unleash anti-Semitism in his American Legion post. Israel's patriotism was not even shaken when, in 1931, his partner's dishonesty resulted in the bankruptcy of his business and he was ultimately reduced to making his living by door-to-door peddling. During the depression, the family barely survived, although Benjamin's mother defied "the chaos that threatened each day to engulf them all" by keeping the house immaculately clean (73–74). Still, she came close to losing her faith when Benjamin, after being unjustly denied a teaching position, took a laborer's job as a shipping clerk; the son did not have the heart to tell her that he got that kind of work only by giving his name as "Bradley Faye" since the advertisement specified "only white Gentiles need apply" (78).

In 1942, Israel saw Benjamin off to World War II and recalled his own enlistment twenty-five years earlier: " 'The band played as we sailed out of the harbor. And I came back' " (143). In 1957, Israel died in a cab on the way to Yankee Stadium with Benjamin. His dying words proclaimed that Bill Dickey and Al Lopez were the best catchers he ever saw. At the funeral, Benjamin resolved many of the complex feelings a son inevitably has for a father. He did not share Israel's devotion to Jewish cultural traditions, and he realized that his father had been wrong about many things—Sacco and Vanzetti and his uncritical patriotism in general. Still, he is confident, in 1964, that his father had been "heroic in his way... the heroism had come from the endurance of a world that had battered at him with a thousand small, ugly blows that no photographer would have had any interest in recording" (146). This concept of heroism has always been a dominant motif in Shaw's work, receiving its fullest expression in *The Gentle People*.

Benjamin is annoyed by the ceremony of the funeral ("He's dead and gone and this is merely theatre." [148]), but he does see Uncle George there for the first time in years ("Death binds families, transiently and too late." [195]). It is Uncle George who helps him put into perspective Israel's mistakes. The meeting with Uncle George also results in a brilliant long chapter which could easily stand alone as a short story. George introduces him to a man named Sternberger who has his own Sacco-Vanzetti story. In 1927, Sternberger was studying philosophy at Columbia. Abruptly, his mother ordered him to go to Montreal to attend to his Aunt Elsa, who was dying. Sternberger had been shocked because his aunt was a family disgrace—an internationally famous anarchist who had gone to Russia during the Revolution and had been an advocate of free love. In Canada, he finds the old woman near death, but outraged that she cannot be in Boston facing execution instead of Sacco and Vanzetti: "'They are victims, not martyrs. THEY DO NOT KNOW THEIR GLORY . . .'" (203).

In 1957, remembering Sternberger's story, Benjamin had confronted some young people in a bar, demanding to know if they had ever heard of Sacco and Vanzetti. Most had not: "'They don't give that course in good schools.'" Only one young girl, originally Belgian, had ever heard of them. Her father and mother had been European aristocrats and had made up a family joke about Sacco and Vanzetti involving a particular kind of stroke in croquet (205–7). Thus, Benjamin realizes that, while his father was wrong about the two victimized Italians, Israel's mistake had not been the result of cruelty or heartlessness.

Two moving scenes indirectly convey the full impact of Benjamin's relationship with his father by focusing upon interaction between Benjamin and his son, Michael. Federov recalls taking six-year-old Michael to the boy's first major-league baseball game at the old Polo Grounds and that Israel had taken him to his first game at the same stadium when he was six: "An uprooted people . . . we must make our family traditions with the material at hand." The scene is made more evocative by the fact that, in 1964, the Polo Grounds no longer exist: "Nobody played baseball in the Polo Grounds any more, and they were tearing it down to put up blocks of apartment buildings." Thus, Benjamin meditates on the difficulty of establishing family traditions in a time and place as young and unstable as the twentieth-century United States. Still, he thinks, there may well be one unfailing "tradition": he fully anticipates someday seeing Michael off to war (152–55).

When Benjamin is driving his son home after the pick-up game, Michael suddenly chastises him for making a one-handed catch in the stands and thus becoming " 'conspicuous.' " Knowing that Michael's criticism constitutes the universal moment of a son's first rebellion against a father's dominance, Benjamin remembers the first time he openly criticized Israel. At family gatherings, Israel delighted always in doing a difficult Russian dance. When Benjamin was eleven, he had walked scornfully out of the room while his father danced. His mother, Sophie, had followed and sternly lectured him; his father's dancing delighted the people, she said, because it reminded them of " 'some of the good things of their old life' " and warned him never to say anything to Israel about it and not to " 'grow up to be an Englishman' " (161–63). Thus, Benjamin can accept Michael's criticism in nostalgic amusement.

Benjamin recalls also disillusioning experiences of his youth, the most painful one occurring when, as a freshman in college and involved in the first love affair of his life, he gave up a New Year's Eve date with his girl, Patricia Forrester, in order to earn some money. A "casual friend" named Dyer, whose father managed a country club, promised Benjamin and several other boys fifteen dollars and tips if they served as waiters at a country-club dance. At the club, the waiters immediately discovered that their own food and lodging were inadequate and dirty. More painfully, they discovered the contempt of the young rich for them.

During the dance, Benjamin envisioned one especially beautiful blond girl as representing hope for some decency in these disdainful young aristocrats. The girl, however, regularly went upstairs with different men throughout the dance; and when Benjamin later found evidence that she had used his own bed for sex, he simultaneously hated and lusted for her: ". . . he knew he was never going to marry Pat and that, for a longer or shorter period of his life, he was going to be promiscuous and probably perverse and, for a long time and perhaps forever, incapable of fidelity" (62). The reader already knows that his prophecy has come true.

There were yet more disillusionments to come after the dance. The waiters were cheated on their pay; and an old female Irish servant lectured them not to complain but to accept their " 'place' " (57). In revenge, Benjamin broke into the club's private store of food and liquor; still, he knew that the experience had emotionally and psychologically scarred him: "The night had put its mark on Benjamin. . . . He was ashamed of himself. Filthy people had behaved filthily to him and he had become filthy himself" (66).

For the rest of his life, Benjamin does have difficulty in being faithful to any woman. His engagement to Patricia Forrester did end and he found himself involved with a Miss Prentiss, who could " 'only have an orgasm with a bestial Jew' " (66–68). Years later, almost immediately after his marriage to Peggy Woodham during the war, he began an affair in Paris with an American woman, Leah Ross. Benjamin truly loved Peggy, but the war made everything seem temporary. In the novel's present tense of 1964, he is still married to Peggy; but their union is a shaky one. Leah Ross is now Leah Stafford, a neighbor and family friend of the Federovs on Long Island; and, although he has by 1964 ended it, Benjamin had continued his affair with her for some time after the war. Peggy knows this and is constantly suspicious of her husband; Benjamin feels that she "smothers" him.

The theme of Benjamin's sexual infidelity is the least successful aspect of *Voices of a Summer Day*. As discussed, Shaw traces his character's failing back to the disillusioning New Year's Eve party and specifically to the beautiful rich blond who used Benjamin's bed for intercourse. Obviously, Benjamin is a man severely disillusioned by his first direct encounter with anti-Semitism. The primary symptom of that adolescent trauma is an inextricable mingling of love and hate for Gentile women. While this may be sound psychology, Shaw does not make it aesthetically plausible.

The novel's ending does successfully bring all its different elements together. Benjamin, at home alone, finds a letter in Peggy's handwriting with the heading "Dear Friend." He remembers when she was almost killed in a traffic accident in Paris and how he had promised himself never to hurt her again. In much mental anguish, Benjamin goes for a walk along the beach and sees a group of boys playing foolish and dangerous games in the water. This results in a memory of a summer camp in 1932. This camp had been run by a penny-pinching man named Kahn, whose refusal to take adequate safety precautions, coupled with the carelessness of a lifeguard named Olson, had resulted in a senseless drowning. Afterward, Kahn was able to persuade the doctor to list the cause of death as a heart attack.

As Benjamin remembers Kahn's camp and watches the boys' careless play in the Atlantic Ocean, Shaw repeats the phrase "Death by Water," an allusion to T. S. Eliot's influential poem "The Waste Land." Benjamin's sense of existing in a moral wasteland is reinforced when he asks two old ladies having tea on a veranda to call someone to help him save the boys. The two reply that the boys are not "'members'" of their club and look away. Shaw then summarizes the entire novel with the distinction between members and "nonmembers." Dyer and his father, Kahn and Olson, the beautiful blond at the New Year's Eve dance, the old Irishwoman, the aristocratic Belgian croquet player, and the high-school students in Dallas who had cheered John F. Kennedy's death were members. In contrast, Sacco and Vanzetti, his father, his own wife and son, Patricia Forrester, Sternberger's Aunt Elsa, and his Uncle George were nonmembers (219–21).

There is a subtle but effective irony in this distinction. The "members" are essentially those who deny their bond with the human race and thus hurt others, often without knowing it. The "nonmembers" are those who strive for a union with the rest of humanity, but are denied their goal. With this new knowledge, Benjamin Federov saves the boys and then hurries home to Peggy and his family: "There are harbors left" (223). Much of *Voices of a Summer Day* might not stand up under a strictly logical evaluation;

but it does, nevertheless, have an undeniable lyrical power. Despite some flaws, it is an underrated novel.

Nightwork (1975)

In contrast to *Voices of a Summer Day, Nightwork* was a quite successful novel. Nevertheless, it does not seem nearly as memorable or significant a work. In the 1980 interview, Shaw described it as a "fantasy" and commented ironically upon the inability of many critics to accept such entertainment from "serious writers."[21] Judged strictly as witty, literate entertainment, *Nightwork* does generally succeed.

Solidly in the fictional tradition of the picaresque, *Nightwork* could well be subtitled "The Education of Douglas Grimes." When the novel opens, Grimes is one of Shaw's American innocents; he stutters and is inexperienced and tentative with women. But he lives on our "bawdy planet," which is dominated by accident. Shaw's theme of accidents controlling individual fate is at least as dominant in *Nightwork* as in any of his other novels. The novel is most memorable for its treatment of the accident motif and for the characterization of one of Shaw's elegant con men.

Accidents control Grimes's life from the beginning. Formerly a pilot, he now works as a night clerk in a rundown New York City hotel called the St. Augustine. Consequently, Grimes no longer believes what he was taught in English literature courses—that one's fate is the direct consequence of his character and that "failures" and "rewards" result from "faults and virtues." Instead, he feels "the ruling law was simple—accident."[22]

Soon another accident occurs that again changes the course of Grimes's life: a man dies of a heart attack in a room of the St. Augustine and, in the course of his investigation, Grimes finds a mysterious tube filled with one hundred thousand dollars. In the 1980 interview, Shaw emphasized that, even though *Nightwork* was written as a "fantasy," it contains a serious underlying theme—that of the power of money to affect, if not permanently change, human character.[23] The money immediately begins to change Douglas Grimes. He quickly decides to hide it from the police and is amazed that he does not stutter at all when lying to them. Later, he realizes that his life will now necessarily be devoted to "travel" and anticipates the inevitable day when someone will come to claim the money.

The education of Douglas Grimes really begins when he encounters Miles Fabian. Fabian functions in the novel as a virtually surreal character; only gradually does the reader learn much about his background. Initially, one learns that he had been born to a poor family in Lowell, Massachusetts; he had met a wealthy English girl during World War II and married her shortly after his military discharge, but had been unable to control his passions for gambling and other women and was forced to agree to a divorce; and he has subsequently made his living by gambling. Still, he is discontent because he has never succeeded in getting far enough ahead (" 'It is rasping to the soul to be committed to the company of the rich without being rich yourself.' "[158]).

Throughout the novel, in a series of "approximately legal" business ventures, Fabian makes investments for himself and Grimes. The investments include buying gold and a racehorse, as well as financing a pornographic film. Grimes's adventures on the set of the film constitute the novel's most amusing scenes. Grimes is at heart puritanical; and, sensing this, the film's female director asks him to perform in her picture. She argues that his innocence would come through as " 'beautifully perverse' " and that it would add " 'a new dimension' " to pornographic films (173). Grimes has not even been able to watch the rushes without blushing, and the director's suggestion of a new career terrifies him. Further, the film's star is Priscilla Dean, an American girl supposedly studying comparative literature at the Sorbonne. Shaw is, of course, having satiric fun with the girl's wholesome-sounding name and its peculiarly American associations. Priscilla Dean propositions Grimes, as well as virtually every other male on the set. Shaw's hero is relieved that he was too modest to accept when he learns later that the girl has a venereal disease.

Miles Fabian quickly detects Grimes's lingering innocence and consciously sets out to educate him: " 'Ah, Douglas . . . you have a long way to go, a long, long way. . . . But you'll make it, I guarantee you'll make it'" (180). Specifically, he plans to teach the innocent how to "calculate" (222). There then evolves an internal struggle in the soul of Douglas Grimes. He is strongly attracted to Fabian and the life-style he personifies. ("Partially against my will he had established himself in my imagination as a looming father-figure, capriciously powerful, solver of problems and mysteries, mover of men and laws." [269]). Moreover, he finds many of Fabian's arguments quite persuasive, especially those concerning money and its attendant morality: the surrealistic con man lectures that since the world is "'... a place of infinite injustice,'" most people are "'victims'"; all any one individual can do is to avoid being such a victim since world misery cannot be alleviated; and not being a victim means having money and the "'freedom to move.'" Fabian summarizes this lecture in a consciously cynical manner: "'None of this is particularly admirable, but I'm not running as an admirable entry...'" (196–97).

One passage in particular reveals that the onetime pilot and nightclerk begins to share such cynicism. The traditional heroic virtues of "courage, generosity, guile, fidelity, and faith" are not possible "in our uneasy time," he decides. Thus, all that is left is "aplomb," and "whatever Miles Fabian may have lacked, he had aplomb" (204–5). Grimes's awe of his mentor is increased when he learns that even though Fabian does not look to be much more than forty years old, he is, in fact, almost sixty (274). The con man's apparent agelessness adds to the surrealism of his characterization. It is only when Fabian is accidentally shot and lies dying at the end of the novel that one learns the details of his background. During the war, he had been a heroic and much-decorated pilot. In 1944, his personally ambitious commanding officer had forced him to fly a needless mission, during which he and his best friend were shot down. The best friend died and Fabian was captured by the Germans, who were responsible for his horrible scar. When he was rescued, he weighed only one hundred pounds. As an old friend, Lady Abbott, concludes: "'That's when he decided... that he had done his last deed for humanity. That explains something of the way he lived....'" She adds: "'He's not an honest man, but he's a joyous one. And he gives joy to others'" (340–41).

Finally, then, the Fabian characterization assumes coherence. Originally an American idealist, he was disillusioned by the selfishness and brutality of World War II. Living in a world of moral chaos, he decided simply to enjoy himself. Fabian is, in fact, virtually a personification of the lost generation—having tried idealism and feeling betrayed, he has adopted hedonism as a safer philosophy. Thus, his obsession with educating Douglas Grimes originates in his seeing the innocent American as a virtual reincarnation of his own youth. When Fabian does die, Grimes realizes that, by the terms of the contract they signed in Europe, the elegant con man has left him "free and absurdly wealthy" (344). The novel's last twist comes when a mysterious man appears and demands the original one hundred thousand dollars. Grimes has, of course, long expected this and hands over the money with no argument. Shaw said, in the 1980 interview, that Grimes's willingness to return the money to a stranger who never identifies himself is the crucial joke that makes the entire novel work.[24] It is more than a simple joke, however. One of the mysterious figure's comments emphasizes the social satire which underlies all of *Nightwork*: " 'It might ease the pain of having to return the money to know that it saved several distinguished people . . . *very* distinguished people from considerable embarrassment' " (342).

Despite its serious undercurrents, *Nightwork* is, as intended, essentially a light-hearted, entertaining novel. Everything turns out perfectly for Douglas Grimes—largely through accident, he gets the beautiful girl and more money than he had ever imagined having. Irwin Shaw knows that things do not ordinarily turn out so happily; but *Nightwork* was written largely as a fantasy, and it is an entertaining one. It seems unnecessary to argue that a fantasy does not define a writer as "semiserious."

The Top of the Hill (1979)

In the 1980 interview, Shaw concisely described his then most recent novel, *The Top of the Hill,* as unifying two central thematic strands: a rather basic Freudianism and a revulsion against spiritually suffocating white-collar work.[25] The novel does smoothly integrate these two themes, but it lacks the density of feeling and characterization found in the best Shaw. For once, the commonplace critical attack that Shaw's work suffers from his apparently effortless style is valid; *The Top of the Hill* too often seems superficial in theme and characterization.

Still the novel's main themes are clearly developed and interrelated. The basic Freudian concepts underlying the novel are the Oedipus complex and the death wish. The main character, Michael Storrs, is introduced as a man who perpetually risks his life and has virtually destroyed his marriage. Storrs is obsessed with taking unnecessary risks in inherently dangerous sports. Through a series of flashbacks, Shaw informs the reader about the development of Storrs's obsession with death.

When Michael was five, his father, a bank executive, was killed in a senseless barroom brawl. His mother, "a fragile, overeducated, incompetent beauty of twenty-eight," thereafter vowed that "the accidents of life" would never touch her son. In fact, she attempted to shield him from reality and caused him to suffer a miserable childhood and adolescence.[26] Not surprisingly, Michael grew up hating his mother and, as soon as he was free of her direct control, began to defy her by risking his life in dangerous sports and by being sexually promiscuous. Even after the mother's death and his subsequent marriage to Tracy Lawrence, a beautiful woman whom he truly loves, he is unable to stop his psychological rebellion.

In addition, he is a promising managerial consultant and hates the spiritual suffocation and heartlessness inherent in his work: "'We are the church militant of efficiency...'" (29). His distaste for his work has started to produce mental lapses and "increasing difficulty in breathing" (73). An effective symbol of Michael's sense of being suffocated by his work is his office window, which cannot be opened. Thus, the dangerous sports represent to him "...the illusion of escape...of conquering danger...." This illusion is all that allows him to tolerate his job. When Tracy becomes insistent that he stop risking his life, he makes a genuine attempt to do so, but feels himself becoming sexually impotent. Obviously, Michael's subconscious has linked his hatred for his mother and for his work (49).

Tracy leaves him; and, in an effectively symbolic scene, Michael attempts, on his thirty-fifth birthday, to break his office window by hurling a soda bottle at it. The bottle shatters, but the window is left unmarked. Knowing that he must do something drastic literally to save his life, he leaves his job and returns to the small town in Vermont where, after graduating from college, he had spent "the calmest and healthiest period of his life" as a ski instructor (120–21).

The bulk of *The Top of the Hill,* concerning Michael's finding salvation in Vermont, is too pat and oversimplified. Still, its stylistic cleanness makes for entertaining reading, and it has some memorable touches. The characterization of Heggener, the dying native of Austria, now devoted to life and to America, is the most effective aspect of the novel.

Conclusion

These seven novels do not represent the same level of artistic achievement as Shaw's brilliant short stories. Nearly all of them are, however, entertaining fiction obviously written by a skilled professional storyteller. Cumulatively, they convey Shaw's central vision of the need to discover "harbors" in a chaotic, accident-dominated universe. Moreover, the best of the seven, *Two Weeks in Another Town, Evening in Byzantium,* and *Voices of a Summer Day,* are important, and much-underrated, novels.

Chapter Six

The Jordache Saga: Investigation of a Peculiarly American Hypocrisy

With the two novels which constitute the Jordache saga, *Rich Man, Poor Man* (1970) and *Beggarman, Thief* (1977), Shaw attained the greatest popular success of his career. *Rich Man, Poor Man* was made into an immensely successful ABC television "mini-series," and *Beggarman, Thief* was adapted into a TV special. Neither adaptation by the mass media fully pleased Shaw; and, in an author's note for *Beggarman, Thief,* he specifies that "the new book is a sequel to the *printed* version of *Rich Man, Poor Man,* not the televised one. . . ."[1] Although *Beggarman, Thief* often reads like a work consciously aimed at a mass audience, the main thematic concerns underlying virtually all of Shaw's fiction are central to both Jordache books. Class conflict is crucial to *Rich Man, Poor Man;* and accidents and luck (good and bad) control the lives of the central characters in each work.

The two novels constitute a saga of three generations of one American family, with emphasis upon the second generation. For the first time since *The Young Lions,* Shaw utilizes a broad historical panorama as a background to illuminate the actions of the central characters. *Rich Man, Poor Man* opens in 1945, and most of the major events which have since shaped American history receive emphasis in the saga. The actions which initially determine the destinies of all three members of the second generation of the family occur on VE Day; the McCarthy hysteria of the 1950s momentarily poses an insoluble moral and practical dilemma for Rudolph Jordache; and he is partially destroyed by the 1960s student rebellion against the Vietnamese war. The corruption of the Nixon years and the international terrorism of the 1970s constitute the background of *Beggarman, Thief*. This historical underpinning is utilized by Shaw to convey the idea that the Jordache story is a peculiarly American one.

As in *Nightwork* and many of his short stories, Shaw is interested in investigating the effects of money upon human character. The Jordache saga communicates the idea that, partially because of historical American ideals, such effects are more dramatically obvious in the United States than anywhere else in the world. As a frontier society, America has traditionally emphasized the importance of social mobility, rising in status and power. Axel and Mary Jordache are immigrants locked into an embittering poverty. On the surface, their three children, Rudolph, Gretchen, and Thomas, seem to realize the American dream of financial success and social mobility. Rudolph, especially reminiscent of the Benjamin Franklin ideal, rises to great wealth and comes close to political power. Gretchen becomes a motion-picture director whose first film is shown at the festival in Cannes. Ultimately, Thomas owns his own excursion boat on the French Mediterranean.

Yet all three fall short of a success which carries with it total personal gratification. In part, this failure is due to the accidents and bad luck which plague so many Shaw characters. More basically, it results from a recurrent difficulty in finding or expressing love. This difficulty is depicted as having uniquely American origins. Beginning with Mary Jordache, the family, for three generations, has a tendency to define love as synonymous with, and limited to, sex. Sex, in turn, is seen as a destructive force antithetical to American middle- and upper-class respectability. Money is, of course, the means to such respectability. Shaw is presenting an essentially Freudian vision of an American inability to view sex as a nondestructive force or as something unrelated to social and economic power. This problem is complicated even further for Gretchen Jordache by an early realization that her sexuality represents potential escape from poverty.

Those members of the Jordache family like Mary and her son Rudolph, devoted to the American success ethic, attempt to deny the power of sex. Thomas Jordache and his nephew, Billy Abbott, who are always in rebellion against their family, rush to embrace sexuality apart from any affection or emotional commitment. Inevitably, given her brutal initiation into a sexual life, Gretchen is constantly torn between the conflicting needs to embrace and to deny her sexual being. Consequently, all these characters are, in some way, at war with the Dionysian aspects of their inner selves. This internal warfare is made all the more destructive by its being interrelated with the real, and the symbolic, power of money.

Mary Pease Jordache is the personification of the crippling effects of attempting to deny the Dionysian in oneself. Illegitimate at birth, she grows up in a Catholic orphanage in Buffalo, New York, where she is given the name Mary Pease. Shaw seems to be punning ironically with her orphanage name, since peace is precisely what she does not find until shortly before her death. In the orphanage, she idolizes the nuns and longs to become one. Instead, she marries Axel Jordache, an emigrant from Germany who works as a deck hand on steamboats.

Her courtship with Axel Jordache proved to be the most misleading experience of her life. Throughout it, he was unfailingly polite and respectful, always clean, and thoroughly receptive to the demands she made before agreeing to marriage. Above all, she felt it esssential that they move away from Buffalo, where people knew their backgrounds, and that he not continue working as an unskilled laborer. Axel had some money saved with which he agreed to buy a bakery in Port Royal, New York. Mary, then, felt that she had escaped everything—especially her past as an illegitimate child and a future among the lower classes.

Immediately upon her marriage, her illusions of escape crumbled. Axel approached sex brutally; and, when his brutality so terrified her that she retreated into grim passivity, he became enraged. Thus, sex became a form of warfare between them. After her one-week honeymoon, Mary wrote the first of a long series of suicide notes. In addition, Axel revealed himself to be a miser and fanatical enemy of the church. The neighborhood in which the bakery was located, once respectable and clean, crumbled into disrepute. Mary found herself even further removed from the respectability for which she had longed, with the added torment of a hideous sexual relationship.

Her resulting bitterness and frustration are inevitably passed along to her children. She constantly lectures her daughter Gretchen: "With marriage... decay set in immediately. Corruption lay in the touch of a man."[2] After she discovers that Gretchen is having an affair, she makes another halfhearted suicide attempt and writes a note for her daughter to find proclaiming that the family is suffering from " 'the curse of sex' " (103). Thus, she relates all the other suffering of her life (the poverty, the filth, the isolation from respectable, middle-class people) to her illegitimacy and her nightly "Calvary" with Axel. Her son Rudolph is the sole source of redemption she sees from the nightmare of her existence; she believes that Gretchen has merely fulfilled an old prophecy by turning to "decay" and "corruption," and she views her other son, Thomas, simply as a reincarnation of the bestial Axel.

There is much effective irony in Mary's pronouncement of the family's "curse of sex." It is a valid prophecy, although not for the reasons she means. In no small part because of her, her children are doomed to a lifelong struggle for sexual health. Moreover, Rudolph does indeed rescue her from filth and poverty. Still, even though Rudolph as a man becomes all that she has wanted him to be and suffers much inconvenience caring for her, she is not able to feel close to him after he is successful. It is only when Thomas, who has apparently fulfilled her expectations for him as well, returns after several years for a reconciliation that she begins to find peace. On her deathbed, she forgives Axel and Gretchen, thus finally accepting her sensuality and denying "the curse of sex."

Axel Jordache, described by his brother as "not a civilized man," is one of Shaw's most memorable and complex characters. As a member of the German army, he was physically wounded in World War I. Much more disastrous, however, was the psychological damage which the war inflicted upon him. Always bitter, Axel became, because of the lasting vision of humanity he derived from the war, a total nihilist. Ever since, his life has been devoted to mocking the values which man places in abstract entities. The hideousness of his experience convinced him that faith in religions or nations was ludicrous, since hypocrisy is the dominant characteristic of mankind.

In 1945, he enjoys VE Day not because the United States has won, but because Germany has lost: "Jordache was a patriot of no country, but he reserved his hatred for the land in which he was born.... He hoped he'd be around twenty-seven years from now, when Germany would lose another war" (97). Contemptuous toward his native land, he came to America, like most immigrants, in search of a more rewarding existence. Almost immediately, he found himself virtually slaving in a bakery which is perpetually on the verge of failure and married to an equally embittered woman with whom he is totally unable to communicate. Increasingly, brutality becomes his instinctive response to everything.

Still, there are traces of decency in Axel Jordache which the horrors of his experience have not quite destroyed. This not quite extinct gentleness is symbolized by a boat which he buys in order to rebuild: "Some river memory of youth and health from his boyhood on the Rhine was behind the purchase..." (69). Like his wife, he sees in Rudolph the family's last chance to realize something of the dream for which he came to America. In a moving last scene with his son, Axel tells Rudolph that the building which houses the bakery has been condemned in the name of urban renewal ("'In Cologne they knock the building down with bombs. In America they do it with money'" [253]); and he describes how he had robbed and murdered a drunken Englishman to get the money to come to America. He then gives his son some fatherly advice ("'Go for the money,...'" and ignore "'Other Values'" [255]). Finally, he apologizes for his inability to leave Rudolph anything and elaborates his theory of the family curse, in which he links violence with sex.

After this scene, the father prepares to die. He leaves one random poisoned roll in a fresh batch ("My message to the world, he thought." [257]), then climbs into his boat and begins to row toward New York City. The next day, the overturned boat is found, but not Axel's body. The very magnitude of the man's bitterness has made him into an almost supernatural force, a symbolic statement reinforced by the missing body and the fact that his wife refuses to believe he is dead. Unlike Mary, Axel does not repeatedly threaten suicide; he simply acts one night, with his only warning being the poisoned roll.

On and just after VE Day, a series of events unfold which indicate that Gretchen, Rudolph, and Thomas Jordache do suffer from a "curse" of sex and violence. Nineteen-year-old Gretchen is the catalyst for these crucial events. Of an inherently romantic temperament and driven by the need to escape her environment, Gretchen is a virgin, both fascinated by and afraid of sex. While doing volunteer work at a military hospital, she has established a friendly, if superficial, relationship with Arnold Simms, a recuperating black soldier. Abruptly, Simms offers her eight hundred dollars to spend a day at an isolated cabin with himself and another black soldier.

Simms's advance causes Gretchen much mental anguish. As by sex in general, she is both fascinated and repulsed by the idea of a rendezvous with the two soldiers. In addition, Gretchen reacts to their blackness precisely in the way such writers as James Baldwin and Eldridge Cleaver have said most white Americans do—she associates their race with unbridled sexuality. Further complicating her response, she views the eight hundred dollars as representing escape from the ugliness and poverty of her life.

Thus, she boards a bus, telling herself that she intends only to spy on Simms and his friend at the remote cabin as they await her arrival. The Shaw concern with accidents dramatically enters the novel at this point. While stranded on a remote country road and attempting to decide what she really does want to do, Gretchen is offered a ride by Theodore Boylan, the owner of the factory at which she works and which dominates Port Royal's economy. Boylan is essentially a more refined embodiment of Axel Jordache's nihilism; wealthy and sophisticated, he believes in nothing but sensual gratification. He practices his own kind of cruelty as well.

Gretchen spends the rest of the day and all night with him, during which she describes the Simms incident; upon arriving at work the following Monday, she finds waiting for her eight hundred dollars in an envelope. Thereafter, Gretchen becomes Boylan's mistress, even though she cares nothing for him and recognizes his need to humiliate her; he is, for her, simply "the male principle, an abstract, unconnected priapus, for which she had been waiting, unknowing, all her life" (85). The most dramatic example of his need to humiliate her occurs when Boylan takes her to a New York City brothel where they can see a young black man and a white prostitute making love.

Still, if only because of her youth and beauty, Boylan needs her more than she needs him and, on VE Day, asks her to marry him. He finds her waiting at a bus stop; and, as much as she hates him, she knows that she is only prevented from accepting his proposal by the arrival of her bus. Boylan gets revenge for her refusal, accidental though it is, by having her fired from her job at the factory. Now she must leave Port Royal and begins formulating specific plans to escape to New York City.

She has two dramatic confrontations before she escapes, however. Her mother curses her and calls her a " 'harlot.' " More importantly, she learns that Rudolph knows about her affair with Boylan and tries to explain to her brother why it happened: she asserts that she did not like Boylan, but " 'I liked *it*. . . . ' " She further warns Rudolph to escape from home, before he is " 'crippled' " (133–35). Gretchen will still face many difficult moments before attaining peace, but that such attainment is ultimately possible is foreshadowed by her awareness that life at home is crippling her psychologically.

Rudolph has learned about Gretchen and Boylan from his younger brother, Thomas. Sixteen in 1945, Thomas initially seems to have inherited only his father's worst characteristics. The reader first sees him provoking a fight with a soldier in a movie theater. He shares his father's contempt for abstract values and ideals: "The war bored him. He didn't mind the fighting, it was the crap about sacrifice and ideals and our brave boys all the time that made him sick" (19). During the fight, he is described in language that recalls Nietzsche's "blond beasts": "something unnatural and dangerous" (22). In contrasting him with Rudolph, Shaw again makes one think of Nietzsche. Thomas sleeps only in his shorts, while Rudolph wears pajamas, and Rudolph tells his brother that he smells " 'like a wild animal' " (24).

Ironically, Thomas is the personification of a potentially healthy Dionysian principle; in the Jordache family, only he has the capacity to attain a saving totality of self. For years, however, he responds to the view of him that his family, and apparently everyone else, shares in a quite natural manner: "Well, if that's what they thought of him, that's what he was going to be—a wild animal" (24). Thomas is never shown anything but brutality and rejection by his parents; like his father, he starts his sexual education with prostitutes; and he can hardly help but resent Rudolph, whom the entire family views as the decent child. Further, he understands the social stigma attached to his family and constantly lashes out against the world.

Recognizing Thomas's Dionysian power, Gretchen and Rudolph, not surprisingly, fear him. In 1955, the two see Thomas again after a ten-year separation. He is now a professional boxer and is fighting a bout with Virgil Walters, a black middleweight. Rudolph persuades Gretchen to go to the fight, and she is shocked and repulsed by it. Later, however, she is erotically stimulated by images of the black and white bodies in brutal physical combat. As adults, Gretchen and Rudolph both struggle to comprehend precisely what Thomas has represented.

In *Beggarman, Thief,* the two come closest to a viable understanding of their brother as they attempt to describe him to Wesley Jordache, Thomas's son. Gretchen confesses that she was " 'a snob' " and " 'thought of Tom as a dangerous peasant. . . . [who] seemed to come from another world. An awful world' " (137). Rudolph is best able to put his brother into a meaningful perspective: " 'What [Gretchen] was afraid of was that what she saw in him she saw in herself, and recoiled from it. . . . ' " Thomas seemingly personified complete and unashamed abandonment to the Dionysian, an abandonment to which Gretchen herself succumbs, but never without shame. Rudolph continues his analysis by asserting: " 'I believed that your father was born with an *affinity* for destruction, an affinity that gave him great pleasure. Destruction of all kinds. Including self-destruction' " (175).

Thomas does originally act in a self-destructive manner, but this is primarily because of his angry decision to fulfill the family's view of him. Ironically, he is finally destroyed by accident and, indirectly, as a result of Rudolph's inadequacy.

There is also considerable irony in Gretchen's view of him as a "'peasant'" during the events of *Rich Man, Poor Man,* since it is her affair with Boylan which results in the first climactic events in Thomas's life. With a companion, Thomas spies on Gretchen in Boylan's house and is overcome by "a dumb rage, a sense of being violated, of being a witness to an unspeakable obscenity..." (82). His reaction to Gretchen's affair with Boylan is the key to much about Tom. Lurking beneath his violence and self-destructiveness is a longing for peace, but he feels his family's social ostracism and understands how Boylan and Gretchen are using each other. In retaliation, he helps burn a cross on Boylan's property on VE Day, which results in a destructive fire.

Upon discovering what his son has done, Axel hits Tom as hard as he can with his clenched fist and orders him to leave town. Before he begins his permanent exile, Thomas makes certain that Rudolph knows about Boylan and Gretchen; thus, "his rebellion was pure and complete" (129). Still, after several years and much travel, he will find, for a short time, the peace he longs for.

Irony is a recurrent force in the history of the Jordache family, and nowhere is it more present than in Rudolph's shock upon learning of Gretchen's relationship with Theodore Boylan. Boylan, because of Gretchen, will be the first of several mentors who make possible Rudolph's realization of the respectability and power of wealth.

Not quite seventeen years old when the novel opens, he is clearly different from the rest of his family. In contrast to his father and to Thomas, he views the war romantically and longs to participate in it. He is already preparing somehow to earn the respectability denied his parents. Well aware that he embodies his parents' hopes and dreams, he is careful to avoid trouble. Still, he is nearing late adolescence, and his sexuality has begun to awaken. His romanticism causes him to become obsessed with his high-school French teacher. A virgin, Rudolph, one day in class, falls into an imaginative daydream and draws the teacher nude. When he is discovered, he is only saved from trouble by his father, who brutally humiliates the teacher. Still a determined romantic, he plays the *"Marseillaise"* for the teacher on VE Day, while Thomas is setting fire to the cross.

After Thomas and Gretchen both leave town, Rudolph is sought out by Theodore Boylan. Despite his knowledge, and resentment, of the man, he allows Boylan to befriend him ("He was practical at moments that demanded honor" [149]). Initially, Boylan's only interest in him is as a possible source of Gretchen's New York City address. Rudolph is aware of this, too, and decides to allow himself to be "bribed." Awed by Boylan's material possessions, he vows to live someday in an equally spectacular manner ("This was America." [194]).

At some indiscernible point, Boylan becomes interested in Rudolph for himself. Although still pressing for Gretchen's address, he decides to conduct a kind of experiment with the boy from the slums and pay for his education. One can hardly miss the irony that Rudolph allows himself to be bought by Boylan more completely than Gretchen had. Fully realizing the drudgery of his parents' lives, the son vows to escape a similar fate by whatever means necessary.

Years later, Gretchen accurately tells Rudolph that she has "'carried the luck of the whole family.'" She explains that their lives, as well as Thomas's, were irrevocably launched in certain directions when Boylan picked her up as she stood inwardly debating Arnold Simms's proposition. Rudolph has only been saved from real suffering thus far by "luck," she adds (557–58).

Rudolph Jordache

For a long time, luck does seem to be Rudolph's ally. It ultimately turns against him, however, and it is probable that he experiences less real happiness in his lifetime than either Gretchen or Thomas. In a much more subtle way than his father or Thomas, Rudolph is one of Shaw's most effective characterizations. Somewhat reminiscent of the husband Oliver in *Lucy Crown*, he is a decent, even generous, man who is nevertheless doomed never to be fully understood by himself or others. Inability to come to terms with his own sexuality is a key to most of his disappointment. As is evident in the incident with his French teacher, Rudolph tends always to idealize sex: "It was going to be perfect or it wasn't going to happen" (251).

Seriously interested in a girl named Julie, he loses her because of his need for a perfect sexual consummation. As discussed, Shaw's characters are plagued by moral accidents; thus, it is not surprising that, after a fight with Julie, Rudolph loses his virginity to a corrupt woman who brags afterward about her experiences of sexual perversity. Escaping, Rudolph attempts to call Julie, but one of Shaw's accidents intrudes and he is unable to get her on the phone.

Thereafter, Rudolph decides to suppress sex and concentrate all his energy upon attaining material success. Theodore Boylan has paid for Rudolph's education; but, upon graduation in 1950, the young man has already started to cut himself loose from Boylan's control. Boylan had wished him to go to an Ivy League university to study law; instead, Rudolph insisted upon attending Whitby, an obscure upstate New York college. After graduation, he further angers his mentor by accepting permanent employment in Calderwood's, a Whitby department store where he has worked part-time while attending school. Rudolph knows too well why Boylan first became interested in him and is determined to gain independence from such a morally ambiguous legacy. Sensing that he is losing his protégé, Boylan makes a bitter, and ultimately prophetic, toast after Rudolph's graduation: " 'To the future,... That dangerous tense' " (296).

Rudolph has found a new mentor in Johnny Heath, a young stockbroker. Heath can teach him about such intricacies of American capitalism as tax shelters and mergers. Thus, Rudolph feels confident of realizing all his goals: "to be rich and free and beloved" (278). Although he struggles very hard for the other two, wealth is all Rudolph finally attains. Free of Boylan, he is never able to transcend the crippling legacy of his parents, especially in the realm of sexuality. His struggles to be beloved reach the extreme of being the person to whom everyone always turns during times of trouble, but he can win no one's deepest affection. Rudolph knows that he fears and despises weakness in himself and others; what he realizes only after much pain is that he most fears that side of himself he has attempted to repress. Ultimately, the weakness which results from his own incompleteness partially ruins him and literally destroys Thomas. Because he has rejected self-integration, Rudolph, who is always willing to give any and everything, finally can never give himself.

Still, for a long time Rudolph is able to balance his needs to be wealthy and beloved. From the moment he becomes a full-time employee of Calderwood's, he consciously adopts a code derived from Benjamin Franklin. He dresses informally and rides a motorcycle to work (one remembers Franklin pushing wheelbarrows through the streets of Boston to attract the attention of local businessmen); he works out in order to keep in excellent physical condition; and he ignores all sexual invitations from the store's female employees. (From Franklin's *Autobiography*: "Rarely use venery but for health or offspring.") Not surprisingly, he is soon viewed by Mr. Calderwood, the owner, as being indispensable to his store and as a surrogate son.

Potential conflicts between his ambitions to be wealthy and beloved for a time automatically resolve themselves. When a favorite professor from Whitby becomes a victim of 1950s McCarthyism, he asks Rudolph for help. Despite his misgivings about possible scandal, Rudolph agrees to help, but is exultant when the man resigns before his scheduled hearing. Later, Gretchen, who has married an alcoholic actor named Willie Abbott, is unable to obtain a divorce. She asks Rudolph to hire a private detective to spy on Abbott; sickened by such a request, Rudolph agrees out of his need to be "beloved." Luck plays a role again, however, when he decides not to give Gretchen the results of investigation only after failing to get her on the phone. Partially horrified with himself, he mentally analyzes Gretchen as being "sick with the sickness of the age. Everything was based on sex. The pursuit of the sacred orgasm" (402). Gretchen has a quite different, if equally unflattering, evaluation of her brother: " 'Work now, live later. He's demented' " (438).

Rudolph's devotion to the work ethic continues to pay off in material ways. Mr. Calderwood allows him a free hand at running the business, and soon he and Johnny Heath have built a financial empire. The climax of Rudolph's success and the beginning of his downfall occur simultaneously. At the opening of a shopping center which he and Heath have planned, he meets, and falls in love with, a young female photographer, Jean Prescott.

Jean causes Rudolph to abandon *almost* entirely his carefully cultivated restraint—he tells her that he will be "'partially broken'" if she refuses to marry him. She is a woman of mystery who tells Rudolph nothing about her family or her past. All that is really clear about her initially is that she is beautiful and ambitious (she forces Rudolph to agree that she will continue her profession in New York City after their marriage).

On their French Mediterranean honeymoon, Rudolph believes that he has realized his childhood dream of an idyllic love affair. He even allows his habitual devotion to "responsibility" to slip by, refusing to rush home when he learns that his mother is dying. His "luck" appears still to be intact when Rudolph discovers that Jean is the heiress to one of the largest pharmaceutical fortunes in America. Still, there are hints of an ultimate disaster—Jean, who has always projected an inner instability, begins to show signs of alcoholism.

Ignoring these signals of trouble, Rudolph feels, in Europe, that it is time to begin a new phase of his life. He is no longer content simply making money ("'My acquisitive instinct has been deadened by acquisition.'"), and he wants to discover some higher meaning for his life ("I don't want to turn into a Teddy Boylan" [572–73]). Rudolph's sense of responsibility is still present; now, however, he desires to extend it beyond his family to society in general.

Back in Whitby, he attempts to realize this goal by working actively as a member of the University Board of Directors; allied with a new, liberal president, he battles successfully against right-wing board members, with his biggest triumph being the reinstatement of the professor driven away during the McCarthy period. In 1964, Jean gives birth to a daughter, Enid Cunningham Jordache. Now a family man with a local reputation as a self-made millionaire and backer of liberal causes, Rudolph is approached to enter politics as a "Kennedy-type Republican." He does and becomes mayor of Whitby. His dream of finding a higher meaning in life seems to be on the verge of realization when he receives national recognition as a progressive young Republican.

Rudolph's luck abruptly turns bad, however. In her second pregnancy, Jean suffers a miscarriage, and, subsequently, gives up her photography and retreats socially. Gretchen witnesses a particularly ugly scene in which Jean destroys her expensive photography equipment and describes herself as an "'appendage.'" Afterward, she attempts to warn Rudolph that Jean is an alcoholic; but her brother ignores her: "'This isn't Hollywood'" (662–66).

Ironically, Rudolph, the liberal university board member, is further destroyed by the student rebellion of the 1960s. Distracted by a friend's business duplicity and a call from Gretchen pleading with him to keep her son Billy out of Vietnam, he allows the Whitby newspaper, which he owns, to run an editorial supporting a voluntary ROTC and permits a campus marijuana raid. Returning from Dallas, where he has been attempting to salvage the financial wreckage caused by his friend, he discovers that the student demonstration has climaxed in front of his house, where Jean has appeared, drunken and nude, at the front door.

Rushing to the university administration building, he finds the students barricaded inside, holding aloft a blown-up photograph of his nude wife. Outraged, he orders a tear-gas attack during which a student is blinded. All of this makes the national news and Rudolph Jordache's political career is over. Later, he tells Thomas: "'I had a little bad luck'" (697). His luck is to get worse, however. He takes Jean to Europe to get away from the scandal; and, along with Gretchen, they stay on Thomas's Mediterranean pleasure boat. It is clear that Thomas, alone of the family, has now found peace; but Jean's alcoholism soon shatters that. She escapes the boat and goes to a notoriously unsafe waterfront bar where she is almost raped by a sadistic pimp named Danovic. Thomas rescues her; but, later, Danovic murders him out of revenge. This incident ends *Rich Man, Poor Man*; and, throughout *Beggarman, Thief,* Rudolph is a badly shaken man trying to find answers to how and why his luck suddenly turned so drastically and attempting to atone for Thomas's death by once again assuming responsibility for his family.

More importantly, he admits to himself some responsibility for what his wife has become. He has not slept in the same room with her since her miscarriage over a year ago: "Sometimes, he thought, you must remember you are a man. Bare, forked animal. Even he" (41). Later, when Jean proposes a divorce, he surrenders to despair and agrees: "Somewhere along the years there must have been a moment when she could have been saved. He had been too busy, too preoccupied, to recognize the moment..." (95). Ironically, after this painful agreement, the two share an idyllic night in bed. Rudolph has come close to an admission that he has crippled himself by attempting to deny his sexuality for professional advancement. Perhaps the strongest irony of his life is that things fall apart for him only after he has tired of financial success.

Still, Rudolph is a decent man; and he continues to assume responsibility for his family, especially for his nephews, Wesley Jordache and Billy Abbott. He even dreams of buying a ranch in Nevada and bringing Wesley and Billy there to live. Bad luck continues to hound him, however. Before he can consummate the deal on the Nevada ranch, he is robbed and severely beaten, necessitating a series of operations. He has already purchased Thomas's pleasure boat in order to save it for Wesley (contributing to the saga's irony is the fact that Thomas would never have owned the boat except for Rudolph's planning and financial astuteness). Wesley does not know any of this, but, although unable to feel close to Rudolph, he senses his uncle's decency ("...there's just a wall between what he is and what he sounds like. Wesley wished he could like Uncle Rudolph more than he did" [208]).

Certainly, Billy Abbott and Wesley Jordache provide Rudolph with ample opportunity to examine his sense of responsibility. Billy, in military service but stationed safely in Europe through Rudolph's influence, becomes dangerously involved with a small band of terrorists. Wesley vows to kill Danovic in order to revenge his father. Rudolph is especially concerned about the latter: "You suffered according to your capacity to suffer and there was something about the boy that made you feel his capacity was dangerously great" (320).

Wesley's determination for revenge finally forces Rudolph into a desperate choice: the uncle attempts to hire an assassin to kill Danovic so that Wesley will not destroy his own life. Rudolph, who has lived his life according to a rigid moral code, cannot ethically reconcile what he is doing: "all his life he had believed in goodness and morality and he was now committing an evil act.... Morality can be a trap, he thought, just like a lot of other noble words" (381–82). The tragedy set in motion by his wife's drunkenness has forced Rudolph to see that ethical values are not as clearly defined as he had always pretended to himself they were. Thus, he chooses family over a more abstract morality. It is no longer possible for him to assume responsibility for abstract society, but he still can attempt to protect those closest to him. Irony continues to dominate Rudolph—his decency and sense of responsibility lead him to arranging a murder. The reincarnation of Benjamin Franklin hires a "hit man."

Rudolph is saved, however, from his evil act when his luck once again turns good. He ultimately learns that Danovic was already dead some six months before Wesley returned to Europe for revenge. Finally, Rudolph comes to some degree of peace. He is last seen doing "unpaid but seemingly important work for the Democratic Party" (429). In an anonymous way, he has returned to his ambition to benefit society. It is Rudolph himself who, in *Beggarman, Thief,* best sums up the limitations of his life. Recalling his father's bitter poverty, he says, " 'I recoiled in my own way. Toward money, respectability...' " (175). He need only add that such reactions involved denial of the totality of his self.

Gretchen Jordache

The struggle with the Dionysian is most dramatic in the characterization of Gretchen Jordache. From Theodore Boylan, she learns that she enjoys sex; but, given her background, such enjoyment could not be free of guilt. Moreover, Boylan has taught her that her body represents escape from poverty. In New York City, reality initially confirms Boylan's lesson. Her first acting part, described in *Rich Man, Poor Man,* is a nonspeaking role in which she simply walks across the stage in a bathing suit. According to the director, the part symbolizes "'The Mystery of Woman'" (159). Shaw is obviously poking fun at the superficiality of the New York theater, but he is making the serious point that Gretchen is again told that her body constitutes her worth.

Partially in reaction against this societal view of her, she falls in love with Willie Abbott, a witty, cynical war veteran. Willie works as a radio critic, while planning to write a play. Initially, his intellectuality seems to offer Gretchen an escape from society's view of her as "The Mystery of Woman"; thus, she can sleep with him without guilt or disgust. She discovers, however, after marrying him, that Willie has little real talent for, and less dedication to, writing. His witty cynicism is a mask for his weakness and insecurity.

Gretchen quits the theater after the birth of her son, Billy. Still, there is no stability in her marriage or her life; and she and Willie both turn despairingly to other sexual partners. Her reaction to this new disappointment is complex; she becomes an active participant in the world of intellect by writing stinging criticism of the mass media and, indirectly, of American society, while still seeking spiritual meaning in promiscuous sex. Finally, she tires of "the endless party" of New York City and marriage to Abbott and demands a divorce.

After divorcing Abbott, she moves to Los Angeles and, for a short time, finds inner peace through marriage to a brilliant, caring stage and film director, Colin Burke. In contrast to Willie Abbott, Burke embodies real creativity, as well as a capacity for personal devotion. Shaw foreshadows the fact that Gretchen's peace is to be shattered when he emphasizes that Burke is a bad, careless driver. In the most literal sense, accident inflicts virtually unbearable pain upon Gretchen when Burke is killed in a car wreck. After Burke's death, which occurs late in *Rich Man, Poor Man,* "a quick music that had been special to her ever since she was a young girl" goes out of Gretchen's voice (464).

She forces herself consciously to plan her life as a widow and makes one decision which is to have ironic repercussions: "Do not build your life on your son. It is the most certain way to lose him" (502). Billy Abbott deeply admired Colin Burke and loves Willie Abbott and, with the irrationality of childhood, blames Gretchen for the loss of both of them. In *Beggarman, Thief,* his rebellion against his mother comes close to destroying him.

Ultimately, Gretchen realizes that she must create a new life for herself by herself and that the past must be buried. After one false step, she is largely successful in making a fresh start. A symbolic moment in her recovery comes when she sees Theodore Boylan at her mother's funeral, in the first of the Jordache books, and feels no "distaste or hatred or wish for revenge" (554). Viewing Boylan calmly is an important first step in viewing her past calmly. Taking an action that parallels Rudolph's, she decides to attend UCLA in order to become a lay analyst, hoping to be of use to society.

This ambition ends in disaster when she attempts to seduce a black graduate student from Ghana. Brutally, the African assaults her sexually and then tells her that he understands the condescension implicit in her association of sexual prowess with the black male. Alone, Gretchen thinks to herself: "Arnold Simms, ... I have paid for you" (581). Recognizing that she still, in part, associates the Dionysian with the forbidden, she renounces her dreams of aiding society.

Belatedly, she recognizes that her salvation lies in Colin Burke's legacy of creativity and in recapturing the love of her son. *Beggarman, Thief* recounts her struggles to direct a film which no male director will touch. The film is successfully shown at the Cannes Festival. Moreover, she makes peace with Billy Abbott. Still, one cannot be certain of the degree of Gretchen's salvation. She marries a kind and devoted man, but one given to fits of drunkenness; Colin Burke, she decides, was the sole exception to "the relation between talent and liquor in the arts in America" (321). Whatever her final fate, Gretchen has come a long way toward psychic health since the day she got in Theodore Boylan's car and irrevocably altered the lives of herself and her brothers.

Thomas Jordache

For most readers of the first volume of the Jordache saga, Thomas is the truly memorable character. His inner passion, which causes him to be repeatedly described as "a wild animal," gives him a unique dramatic power. After his exile from Port Royal, Thomas's life is a long, desperate search for a saving gentleness which will humanize his passionate intensity. From Port Royal, he is sent to live with an uncaring aunt and uncle in Elysium, Ohio. There he learns from Clothilde, a Canadian house servant, that sex can be gentle and even idyllic. Clothilde shows Thomas the first love he has ever known, calling him " 'Saint Sebastian. Without the arrows' " (175). The nickname so intrigues Thomas that he enters a library for the first time to discover the identity of Saint Sebastian; he learns first that Sebastian was " 'a Christian martyr' " and then that " 'he is a favorite subject of sacred art, being most generally represented undraped. . . ' " (180).

The identification of Thomas with St. Sebastian is symbolically important on several levels. He is repeatedly martyred in a figurative sense and ultimately in a literal one. Most importantly, he has, from the beginning, personified a Dionysian power necessary for human totality and, thus, worthy of veneration. The symbolic overtones of Elysium, however, are, with the significant exception of the meeting with Clothilde, ironic. Thomas is figuratively martyred there in two ways.

First, his uncle, who has been forcing Clothilde to have sex with him, destroys Thomas's relationship with the servant. Second, he is blackmailed as the seducer of two socially prominent, but sexually promiscuous, teen-aged twins who both become pregnant. Thomas has slept with both of them, but so have several other young men in the town. Their father charges Thomas with statutory rape on the correct assumption that, as an outsider, he is the most vulnerable to being blackmailed. During Thomas's stay in jail, Shaw introduces a wonderfully eccentric character named Dave, " 'a mountain man,' " who has been arrested for illegal hunting. The scene is Shaw at his best. Dave recalls Cooper's Natty Bumppo, the personification of the American frontier spirit imprisoned after the frontier has disappeared. He is also an unheeded prophet of the sickness of America. Proclaiming that "'hypocrisy is the canker in the soul of the America people,'" he points out the contradiction between America's devotion to wholesale killing in war and its habit of writing laws which prohibit a man like him from hunting: "'I'm an American out in the American forest livin' off American deer. . . .'" He further emphasizes to Thomas that he has been convicted of statutory rape because he is socially vulnerable (238–40).

Axel Jordache is forced to come to Elysium to free Thomas from jail by paying the father of the twins five thousand dollars. He makes it clear to Thomas that he is only acting for Rudolph, so that the decent son will not have a brother with a prison record. Ironies proliferate at this point. The money was intended for Rudolph's college education, and its loss destroys the embittered father's last hope for the salvation of the family. Further, it necessitates Rudolph's relying on Theodore Boylan, his sister's seducer, for his education.

Of course, the incident adds to Thomas's already strong hatred of the rich and, in the boy's mind, confirms Dave's theory of American hypocrisy. Whatever else Thomas may be at this point, he is not hypocritical and he vows someday to repay his brother for the loss of his education. Four years later, he gets his chance in a manner which also allows him to retaliate against the upper classes. Working in an exclusive athletic club, he discovers a wealthy young kleptomaniac in the act of theft and blackmails him for five thousand dollars. In one of the saga's most effective and moving scenes, Thomas returns to Port Royal in an attempt to repay his family, only to discover that his father is dead, everyone else has moved away, and even the bakery no longer exists.

Six more years pass before Thomas enters *Rich Man, Poor Man* again. It is 1955 when Rudolph and Gretchen discover by accident that he is a boxer and go to see him fight. Besides disgust at his profession, they are shocked to learn that, two years earlier, he had married a crude, shrewish woman whom he had gotten pregnant. This reunion scene provides further clues of Thomas's potential for gentleness, however. He is devoted to his son and, after the bout, goes to his defeated black opponent's dressing room to offer him congratulations for a good fight and to make sure that he has not been hurt. Later, he is unable to sleep because once again his brother and sister have made him feel inferior. He also reflects that only Clothilde has ever treated him differently.

Thomas's obsessiveness is demonstrated by the fact that he is still holding the five thousand dollars. He seeks out Rudolph and forces his brother to take the money; however, when Rudolph presses for a total reconciliation and even offers his brother a job in his corporation, Thomas contemptuously refuses. Without telling him, Rudolph invests the money in the corporation in Thomas's name.

Part of Thomas's bitterness toward his family is alleviated in a surprising manner—he abruptly receives a letter from his mother asking for a reconciliation. When he visits her, she seems to have become an entirely different person. Totally dependent upon Rudolph for support, she nevertheless tells Thomas that she feels closer to him: "'We're the same kind of people. We're simple. Not like your sister and your brother'" (419). Thomas is pleased with the reunion: "there was one less person in the world that he had to hate" (420).

There is still a lot of hatred and self-destructiveness left in him, however. When the reader next sees him, in 1960, his career and his marriage have deteriorated. After his victory over Virgil Walters, the black fighter, he had had a real chance at the world middleweight championship and had gone to Europe to box. After one impressive victory in Europe, he had ruined himself in an orgy of sex, alcohol, and food on the French Riviera and was knocked out in his next fight. In 1960, he is reduced to working as a sparring partner for a "serious fighter" named Quayles. He destroys even this fragile connection with his former profession by first sleeping with Quayles's wife and then injuring the fighter in a hotel-room brawl. Forced to flee from organized crime, which has invested in Quayles, he becomes a sailor aboard a ship named the *Elga Anderson*.

The *Elga Anderson* represents the turning point in Thomas's life. He becomes friends with another sailor, Dwyer, who inspires him with the ambition of someday captaining his own craft, and he discovers that, like his father, he loves the sea ("He felt that he had found his place on the planet..." [597]). Perhaps of most importance, he is forced to fight a ship bully, Falconetti, who especially loves to harass Renway, a black sailor. After attempting to avoid Falconetti for some time, Thomas is virtually forced to fight him and, of course, beats him badly. After the fight, he feels "exultation" and begins a systematic humiliation of his opponent until the man commits suicide.

The Falconetti incident recalls the reader's initial view of Thomas as a boy, picking a fight with a soldier in the movie theater. Again, he fights like "a wild animal" and exults in victory. This time there are crucial differences, however. Initially, he attempted to avoid confrontation and finally challenged Falconetti, in part, to protect Renway. Moreover, he is badly shaken by the suicide which resulted from his sadistic humiliation of Falconetti. For the first time, Thomas sees clearly the necessity of restraining his rage and violence: "He yearned for peace" (543).

He is next reunited with Rudolph and Gretchen at his mother's funeral. There, he begins to make peace. He confesses to Gretchen that he had burned the cross years ago out of rage over her affair with Boylan:

> [Gretchen:] "Tom...you're not like that *any more*, are you?"
> [Thomas:] "I hope I'm not...." (556)

Ironically, though he is not yet ready to make peace with Rudolph, he learns that his brother had invested the five thousand dollars for him and that it is now worth sixty thousand. Abruptly, he calls Dwyer and tells him to begin looking for a pleasure boat for sale.

Five years later, the reader sees Thomas as the owner of a Mediterranean cruising yacht named the *Clothilde*. He is close to the peace for which he yearned. He no longer fights and is, in fact, a consistent peacemaker in Mediterranean bars. Most surprisingly, he discovers that he no longer needs sex as desperately as he always has. Only two things mar his happiness: he is still haunted by Falconetti's death; and he misses his son, Wesley, whom he had to leave with Teresa after the Quayles episode. Despite these problems, his happiness is augmented when he hires Kate, an Englishwoman, as the *Clothilde*'s cook. With Kate, he finds again the gentle love he had known so long ago with Clothilde: " 'Kate, every time I make love to you I forget one more bad thing in my life' " (634). Kate, in fact, becomes the virtual reincarnation of Clothilde. Thomas's Dionysian passion is no longer a destructive force; rather, it now allows him, as Gretchen did with Colin Burke, to discover a deep and meaningful love.

While he can do nothing about the memory of Falconetti, he does, with the help of Rudolph, find his son. Rudolph hires a lawyer who discovers that Teresa has twice been convicted of prostitution. Thus, it is easy for Thomas to get legal custody of his son. He finds Wesley in a military school where the boy has a reputation for savage fighting and brings him to Europe and the *Clothilde*. Thomas gives the boy firm, but loving, care, to which Wesley immediately responds. Wesley accepts without argument his father's order that he will have no more fights.

In 1968, Thomas marries Kate, who is already pregnant; and his happiness is as total as it can ever be. He invites Rudolph and Jean, as well as Gretchen, to the wedding and appears to move " '... in an atmosphere of love' " (704). Accident strikes quickly, however. The *Clothilde* is momentarily stalled, and Jean escapes for her climactic meeting with the pimp, Danovic. A final irony of Thomas's life is that when he rescues Jean, he stops short of killing Danovic because of the memory of Falconetti and is afterward proud of his retreat.

Thomas's dying words are, " 'No more ... ' "; they can be seen as his final repudiation of the violence which has so long tormented him. His ashes are fittingly dropped into the sea, the place where he found peace on this planet. One also remembers that his father disappeared after his small boat overturned. Unlike that of Axel Jordache, however, Thomas's death is regretted by several people. Gretchen says: " 'Tom ... the one of us who finally made a life' "; and Rudolph painfully adds: " 'Dead for one of us who didn't ... ' " (722). In *Beggarman, Thief,* Gretchen continues to analyze the meaning of her dead brother's life and death: *"It has to happen. ... All that violence could not have a nonviolent end. True son of his father, the blond stranger in the family ...*" (11–12). Shaw proposes a determinist view of Thomas, just as he does of Rudolph.

Thomas, the personification of Dionysian passion (again, one senses echoes of Nietzsche's "blond beasts"), achieves a healing totality of self, but too late to enjoy it for long. For most of his life, socioeconomic factors beyond his control set him at war with himself and with the world. Just as he reaches a truce in this war, accident enters and destroys him.

Billy Abbott and Wesley Jordache

Compared to *Rich Man, Poor Man, Beggarman, Thief* is the weaker novel; and much of the weakness of *Beggarman, Thief* comes from its concentration upon Billy Abbott. As established initially in *Rich Man, Poor Man,* his characterization is psychologically consistent and plausible. From the time of his parents' divorce, he is sent away to schools in which he feels alienated. He is a boy, and then a young man, desperately in search of a father figure. Even though he recognizes his weaknesses, he loves his father and feels that his mother is responsible for the divorce. He idolizes Colin Burke and, after the director is killed in the car wreck, Billy is shattered by grief. When the boy learns later that Gretchen is sleeping with other men, he understandably, but irrationally, blames her for Burke's death. At one point, he asserts that he has respect for Albert Camus and no one else.

As the characterization is continued in *Beggarman, Thief*, it becomes clear that his cynicism is a mask for a self-pity much like his father's. Part of this novel is narrated through a notebook Billy keeps; and his self-pitying cynicism, while psychologically valid, becomes tedious over the course of a long novel.

Wesley Jordache, who shares the narrative focus of *Beggarman, Thief* with Billy Abbott, is a much more intriguing character. Very much his father's son, Wesley shares Thomas's passionate intensity which has been diverted from self-destructiveness only by his father's belated care of him. After accident, through Jean and Rudolph, destroys his father, Wesley's intensity, in combination with societal factors, almost destroys him again. Ironically, he is ultimately saved by a series of fortuitous accidents.

Beggarman, Thief has been criticized as a melodramatic novel. Shaw pointed out in 1980 that the novel's underlying structural irony is the fact that while violence seems imminent throughout, the only violent scene occurs when a supposedly expert terrorist accidentally kills himself.[3] Still, the novel has a melodramatic feel, in part because of implausibilities in plotting and thematic digression. In addition, Billy Abbott's self-pity robs it of much dramatic power.

Conclusion

There is some irony in Shaw's achieving his greatest popular success with "the Jordache saga" since the two novels do not represent his best work. Too much of *Beggarman, Thief* seems written at an artistic level noticeably lower than what one expects from Shaw. It inevitably forces one to consider Fiedler's charge of "half-art." *Beggarman, Thief,* however, is only half of one extended story; and *Rich Man, Poor Man* is obviously more serious in intent. Moreover, the same quite serious thematic concerns underlie both novels. The complete saga presents a vision of an America which is less than it should be because of what Old Dave, the imprisoned hunter, describes as a "hypocrisy" lurking in the very heart of the nation.

Certainly, much of the artistic and popular success of both novels lies in their depictions of vivid, memorable characters—Thomas, Axel, Wesley, and Teresa Jordache. Rudolph is perhaps the most subtly successful characterization in the two books, since he must simultaneously embody the destructive symptoms of America's crippling hypocrisy and emerge finally as a sympathetic character. No little skill was required to make such a characterization artistically plausible. *Rich Man, Poor Man* lacks the total structural control of *Two Weeks in Another Town, Evening in Byzantium,* and *Voices of a Summer Day;* but it is a memorable and entertaining novel.

One last point must be made about the Jordache books. Since Shaw makes it quite clear that three generations of the family suffer because of the bitter poverty of Axel and Mary Jordache, the common critical complaint that Shaw has abandoned the proletariat hardly seems justified.

Chapter Seven
A Thoroughly Professional Writer

Any critical assessment of the career of a living writer, especially one as prolific as Irwin Shaw, must be tentative. Nevertheless, it can be said that Shaw's present standing as a best-selling novelist obscures the diversity of his literary achievement. Academic critics have largely ignored his work for more than a decade. This neglect is especially ironic in view of the fact that the initial acceptance of his work came largely from critics rather than the general public. Shaw's career can, in fact, be divided into three distinct stages.

Shaw has said that he was initially recognized as a "cult figure."[1] In the last half of the 1930s, *Bury the Dead* and *The Gentle People* established him as a leading figure in the new militant theater. He and Clifford Odets were commonly linked together as the important young revolutionary playwrights. This assessment, however, was misleading in two important ways. First, Shaw's significant contribution to the theater was in innovative technique rather than political content. *Bury the Dead* and *The Gentle People* are not thesis plays in the sense that *Waiting for Lefty* is. In fact, Shaw's most doctrinaire, and least experimental, play, *The Assassin,* was unjustly denounced by the critics. As a result, he largely abandoned the theater after 1945. Second, despite being blacklisted, Shaw was never a doctrinaire Marxist. *The Assassin,* in fact, satirizes dogmatic Marxists. As *The Gentle People* should have made abundantly clear, Shaw's faith was always a highly personal, and quite romantic, belief in the inherent goodness and courage of the common man, especially the ordinary American. Such a faith could never be translated into a strict political dogma. Shaw is comparable to other American writers such as John Steinbeck and James Jones in his largely romantic, and essentially nonpolitical, faith in the common man. Like Steinbeck and Jones, he has always been a leftist who rejected any strict political dogma.

This rejection of doctrinaire politics was obvious in the excellent short stories he began publishing in the late 1930s. A story such as "Second Mortgage" effectively protests the economic exploitation of the masses, but does not endorse any specific political solution for this injustice. "Main Currents of American Thought" focuses on the problems of the artist trapped in an economically unjust society. His best-known prewar stories, "The Girls in Their Summer Dresses" and "The Eighty-Yard Run," depict the spiritual emptiness of the middle and upper classes.

The first stage of Shaw's career ended with the publication of his first novel, *The Young Lions*, in 1948. Prior to 1948, he had been critically recognized in two distinct ways: as a politically revolutionary playwright and as a master of the technique of short fiction. The second critical assessment was much more accurate than the first, and Shaw has continued to enhance his reputation as a master of the short story.

With *The Young Lions*, Shaw enjoyed his first major commercial success and entered the second stage of his career. Since the novel was critically well received, its appearance can be said to represent the peak of Shaw's acceptance on both the critical and the popular levels. *The Young Lions* is still regarded as one of the major American World War II novels. It is, in fact, the only American novel that attempts a panoramic view of the war in Europe. The fact that much of the best American fiction about the Second World War is set in the Pacific enhances the importance of Shaw's focus on the European theater.

Like *The Gentle People, The Young Lions* thematically emphasizes a faith in the American common man. Michael Whitacre is the most reluctant of heroes; but, through the inspiration of Noah Ackerman, he does realize courage and dignity. Alarmed by the excesses of McCarthyism, Shaw followed *The Young Lions* with his only overt thesis novel, *The Troubled Air*. Again, underlying faith in an American decency which would transcend the ugliness of the times pervades the novel. While not minimizing the damage it was inflicting, Shaw clearly regarded McCarthyism as an historical aberration. As in *The Assassin,* he reserves some of his sharpest satire for the Marxist who seeks to exploit for purely selfish ends the hysteria induced by the far right.

Shortly after writing *The Troubled Air,* Shaw began his voluntary exile in France. He also began to write a different kind of fiction. In such novels as *Lucy Crown, Two Weeks in Another Town,* and *Evening in Byzantium,* his thematic emphasis shifted to a vision of a morally chaotic world in which accidents are the only rule. Initially, one feels that the old Shaw faith in American decency has disappeared. His main characters in these novels are generally wealthy, and often even powerful, individuals; and Paris, Rome, and Cannes replace New York as the setting. Nevertheless, a closer examination reveals that Shaw's belief in American decency has not disappeared, but has undergone a transformation.

While the main characters in these novels are wealthy individuals living predominantly in Europe, they are still Americans who have arrived at critical moments in their lives. Certain events have caused them to look back at the moral accidents which have victimized them and by which they have victimized others. The struggle is then to save their souls. They attain salvation essentially by admitting their past errors and vowing to live up to the decency they know lies within them. Thus, while Shaw's vision of external reality becomes increasingly pessimistic in *Lucy Crown* and the succeeding novels, his faith in the latent capacity for decency of the individual American remains intact.

The novels Shaw has published since *The Young Lions* and *The Troubled Air* have generally been commercially successful. It is this body of his work, however, which has met with either hostility or neglect from academic critics. The hostility culminated in Leslie Fiedler's charge that Shaw writes a superficial "half-art," a judgment which the neglect of his work by academic critics might seem to support. In fact, one could easily plot a graph demonstrating that Shaw's critical reputation has decreased in almost an exact correspondence to his commercial success.

As previously discussed, the "half-art" charge primarily reveals a failure on the part of academic critics to comprehend and accept the directions in which Shaw's fiction has moved since *The Young*

Lions and *The Troubled Air*. One suspects that an important element in this academic critical hostility to Shaw's last seven novels is their commercial success. The idea that a commercially successful novelist can rarely be an artistically good one seems to be widely held in academia. Moreover, Shaw's emphasis upon the problems of wealthy and powerful Americans living temporarily in romantic European settings probably contributes to the "half-art" assessment as well. Such books may initially seem irrelevant to the lives of most Americans. A careful reading reveals, however, that Shaw is as much a moral writer in these novels as he was in *The Gentle People*. Wealthy individuals can undergo spiritual crises; and, by placing his Americans in Europe, Shaw is simply following a very old and honorable American literary tradition—that tradition exemplified by Hawthorne's *The Marble Faun,* the best work of Henry James, and F. Scott Fitzgerald's *Tender Is the Night*.

In the attack on Shaw by Leslie Fiedler in particular, one detects personal, and unjustified, resentment. Fiedler seems most offended by the fact that Shaw is not in his recent work the kind of writer Fiedler believed him once to be, but which, in fact, he never truly was. On the basis of *Bury the Dead,* Fiedler, like many other critics, labeled Shaw as a militant, overtly political writer, and thus has viewed his recent novels focusing on wealthy Americans abroad as a kind of artistic betrayal. In fact, Shaw's social protest was never equivalent to doctrinaire political concerns and was, from the first, secondary to aesthetic innovation and form. In all his work, Shaw is an intensely moral writer, sometimes focusing upon the relationship of groups of individuals to the dominant society and sometimes upon the relationship of isolated individuals to their own souls. Social protest is certainly a factor in much of his work, but never in the way that it is in an overtly Marxist writer.

There are other, more valid reasons for the academic critics' negative reaction to these seven novels. In them, Shaw continues to write in the great tradition of realistic fiction which can be traced back to Flaubert and James. For more than a decade now, academic literary criticism has been much more concerned with technical innovation than with content in American fiction. Terms such as "metafiction," "surfiction," "postmodern fiction," and so on have arisen to describe the writings of John Barth, Thomas Pynchon, Richard Brautigan, and Donald Barthelme, to name a few. What is important in the work of these writers is rarely the story they tell, but the radical innovations which they utilize in order *not* to tell it.[2] Irwin Shaw remains preeminently a storyteller; and his commitment to the Flaubert-James realistic tradition makes him seem outdated to many academic critics.

Shaw is much less innovative in the novel than in the other literary genres in which he has worked. The unique mingling of fantasy and realism found in the plays *Bury the Dead, The Gentle People,* and *Sons and Soldiers* does occasionally reappear in his short stories, but never in his novels. Still, important critical voices are beginning to be heard arguing the seemingly obvious point that metafiction or postmodern fiction is not the only valid fiction. Malcolm Cowley, in *—And I Worked at the Writer's Trade,* argues that, since storytelling has an ancient and honorable history, it would be unwise to dismiss it as outmoded and irrelevant.

A more important consideration in discussing Shaw's last seven novels is the fact that four of them—*Lucy Crown*, the Jordache books, and *The Top of the Hill*—are flawed works. Shaw's failure to realize these novels fully seems to arise directly out of his vision of "accidents" as the dominant influence upon human beings. His career seems to prove that the short story is a much more natural vehicle than the novel for depicting a chaotic, accident-ridden world. It must be said, however, that *Two Weeks in Another Town, Evening in Byzantium,* and *Voices of a Summer Day* are much better novels than generally recognized. They are, in fact, structurally superior to *The Young Lions.*

With *Rich Man, Poor Man* in 1970, Shaw entered the third stage of his career. The Jordache saga, and the television adaptations, made him not just a successful commercial writer, but an enormously successful one. In fact, the tremendous popularity of these books does make it difficult to judge them by normal critical standards. Certain elements in their mass appeal are obvious. The public has always responded to memorable characters in fiction; and Axel and Mary Jordache and their sons, Thomas and Rudolph, are quite memorable. Thomas Jordache, especially, is one of those rare characters in fiction who seem to take on a life that transcends the book in which he appears. In addition, the story of the Jordache family represents several variations upon the American success story; and there is no more appealing national myth. Finally, *Rich Man, Poor Man* does have the kind of raw power that only expert literary craftsmanship can create.

Bread Upon the Waters (1981)

Since the completion of this study, two related events have occurred that may signal a new stage in Irwin Shaw's long career. His eleventh novel, *Bread Upon the Waters*, appeared in August 1981 and immediately sparked a literary controversy. In the same month the controversy gained momentum because of a featured *Saturday Review* article by Ross Wetzsteon calling, in the specific context of *Bread Upon the Waters,* for a reappraisal of Shaw's work throughout his life. The new novel, Wetzsteon argues, clarifies several long-standing misconceptions about Shaw's fiction—most importantly, the fact that, instead of having sold out after *The Young Lions,* Shaw has remained a writer of rigorous moral fables. Wetzsteon is one of the first published critics to see that Shaw's devotion to "*stories*" and his preoccupation with glamorous settings in many of his novels have allowed critics to overlook the real heart of his fiction:

> But, all the time, in every novel, sometimes embedded in the narrative structure itself, sometimes barely glimpsed through the smoke of post-coital cigarettes, we can see that the key to his novels is moral choice. Yes, in Irwin Shaw's novels, one has to make moral choices even in Cannes![3]

If *Bread Upon the Waters* does produce the most serious and extensive investigation of Shaw's work in more than thirty years, it will be somewhat surprising. On the surface, the novel seems not unlike its author's other recent novels: the prose is smooth and controlled and the plot has its share of chic settings. In the very first chapter, a social accident occurs, which has the almost immediate effect of completely changing the protagonist's life. But these facts are the surface; they only represent Shaw's real concerns.

What he is truly concerned with is quality—the quality of a man's life and work and the quality of our civilization. Shaw's protagonist is Allen Strand, a history teacher in a New York City public school. Strand is an old-fashioned kind of man devoted to old-fashioned values, and he feels everywhere about him signs of a civilization on the brink of collapse. He enjoys the old movies at the Museum of Modern Art, especially Westerns and Buster Keaton comedies. Early in the novel he considers going to the museum to see *Fort Apache*: "It was a delicious retelling of a naive and heroic American myth, an antidote to doubt."[4] Strand has other, more substantial antidotes to doubt, however. He is deeply devoted to his family and to his profession.

His devotion to family is not shaken by the real generation gap that sometimes separates him from his three children or by a symbolic one that occasionally isolates him from his wife. His commitment to teaching has survived years of public school bureaucracy, often indifferent and sometimes overtly hostile students, and a culture that undergoes such rapid transformations that one must struggle simply to keep up with its modes of communication. Strand is, in fact, a great deal like his creator, who describes himself as "'in ways . . . always . . . conservative—believing in honesty, courage, fidelity.'"[5]

The bulk of the novel describes the ways in which two forces do temporarily shake Strand's devotion to his old-fashioned values. In the first chapter, his daughter saves a man from being mugged in Central Park and then brings him to the Strand home to wait for a doctor. The man turns out to be the first of the forces which almost overwhelm Strand; he is Russell Hazen, a famous multimillionaire and philanthropist who virtually takes over the Strand family. The personification of the dark side of the American dream, Hazen is one of Shaw's most intriguing characters. His family life is as nightmarish as Allen Strand's is superficially ideal, and his legendary achievements in business and law have made him cynical about, and contemptuous of, the ethical reality of American society. Hazen is a man looking, one last time, for something in which to believe; and, without asking them, he adopts the Strands as his substitute family.

Allen Strand and Russell Hazen are, in fact, two sides of the same dream. Still, they are two sides which, Shaw seems to say, never confront each other except through the most extreme of accidents. Strand is the American idealist largely shielded from reality by his position in academia; Hazen is the American power broker embittered by his firsthand knowledge of the corruption of others and, most importantly, of himself. Shaw understands very well how strongly a Strand may be tempted by a Hazen. Weekend trips to the Hamptons, vacations in Paris, plastic surgery and a college education in an expensive western school for one of Strand's daughters, incredibly advantageous career breakthroughs for Strand's wife and son—Hazen arranges all this and more. Initially, Strand is grateful, of course, for all these favors. Moreover, he is truly caught off guard, since he is honestly unable to imagine what he might have that Hazen could ever want or need.

What he has is a wife and family; but Strand, an innocent, fails to see Hazen's sexual interest in his wife until very late in the novel and, by the time he realizes the moral damage the philanthropist has done his children, it is almost too late to help them.

Hazen's bounty does not shake Strand's idealistic dedication to his profession in any truly fundamental way until the second force allies itself with the millionaire. At Hazen's Long Island home, Strand suffers a heart attack that leaves him near death. Death, or rather the fear of it, finally convinces the history teacher to place himself almost totally in the hands of his philanthropist friend. Hazen obtains for him a teaching job in Dunberry, a quiet small-town Connecticut prep school; and he is thus able to escape the challenges and dangers of New York City. Hazen and Strand together make a crucial mistake, however. Since Hazen can apparently arrange anything, he is able to pressure the exclusive New England school into enrolling Strand's most promising, and most angry, ghetto student, Jesus Romero. The millionaire and the history teacher both have ideas about saving the brilliant and alienated boy. The novel's central irony, however, is that Romero is finally doomed, but not before he saves Strand.

The boy from the streets of New York is never able to overcome the snobbery of Dunberry and finally explodes in a manner that results in his expulsion and arrest. Earlier, he has told his teacher some things that Strand inwardly knows are true:

"This place is staffed by time-servers, Mr. Strand. And I don't think you're a time-server...."

"The other teachers are grazing animals, Mr. Strand. They graze in peace on grass...."

"You hunt on cement, Mr. Strand.... That's why you understood me. Or at least half-understood me. Everybody else here looks at me as if I belong in a zoo." (345)

When Hazen commits suicide near the end of the novel, after irrevocably destroying his reputation on national television, Strand is forced to act upon the things Jesus Romero has lectured him about. The millionaire's self-destruction makes him confront the fact that he cannot hide from death in small-town Connecticut; that, in fact, hiding in Connecticut or anywhere else is a form of death. He decides to return to New York City and all the uncertainty and changes of its public school system:

I did not enter the profession merely to be comfortable and events have led me to forget that. For a time. For a time. That time is now over. (437–38)

At this point, the family to which Strand was so devoted has been irrevocably estranged from each other by Russell Hazen's generosity. Strand is not even certain that he can save his marriage—his wife was never sexually seduced by the millionaire, but Hazen did provide her with a Parisian art career, which Strand knows he has no right to ask her to give up. The history teacher now fully comprehends that any attempt to save his life by living it in an unnatural sanctuary is the most certain way to lose it. All he is certain of saving by returning to the New York City school system is his soul. Yet, Allen Strand has finally learned that such salvation is the only kind there is.

Bread Upon the Waters is a novel full of apocalyptic passages. In it, Shaw expresses more fully than he has before his concern about the future of our civilization. His fear is not of atomic bombs and missiles; he fears, instead, the total decline of "honesty, courage, fidelity" and all the old-fashioned, "conservative" virtues. He believes factors are at work to destroy such values in our society—the worship of money and the power to manipulate other people's lives which it inevitably brings; a cynicism so pervasive that it infects everything it touches. Still, as Wetzsteon clearly points out, all this is nothing very different from what Irwin Shaw has always believed.

Finally, *Bread Upon the Waters* is a new and different kind of Shaw novel in mood and structure much more than in content. It is easily his most meditative novel; and, after the first chapter, it is not dominated by accidents. It is something of a return to the cause-and-effect structure of *Voices of a Summer Day,* with a reflective, meditative mood replacing the lyricism of the earlier novel. What is most important to emphasize is the resolution the novel posits for its frequent moments of cosmic despair—Allen Strand, an obscure history teacher, returns to the "concrete" of New York City hoping to be able to reclaim his old job. Shaw's answer is the same as it has always been—the good "gentle people" will struggle to do their jobs and perhaps society will be saved. If *Bread Upon the Waters* does result in a reappraisal of Shaw's fiction, one hopes that there will be a concurrent realization that Allen Strand is nothing more, and nothing less, than one of the most fully realized of the "gentle people."

In reviewing Shaw's career, it seems obvious that he will ultimately be seen as a significant figure in American literary history. His work in drama, although controversial, was of historic importance in revolutionizing the American theater. *The Gentle People, Bury the Dead,* and, to a lesser degree, *The Assassin* will survive as powerful plays. *The Young Lions* will last as one of the most important American World War II novels; and *Two Weeks in Another Town, Evening in Byzantium,* and *Voices of a Summer Day* will inevitably receive critical reappraisal as intelligent, powerful, and well-written novels. *Bread Upon the Waters* and the three succeeding novels he has contracted to write by 1985 will undoubtedly add much to the historical evaluation of Shaw's work; he has spoken of these books with a particular determination and reflectiveness, as though he intends more than ever to give in them the best of his craft and his living.[6]

Most of all, Shaw will be remembered for his short stories. Several of them rank among the masterpieces of that genre in America. During all three stages of his career, Shaw has continued to write superb short fiction. "God Was Here But He Left Early" and "Where All Things Wise and Fair Descend" constitute achievements as impressive in their own way as "The Girls in Their Summer Dresses," "The Eighty-Yard Run," and "Main Currents of American Thought." While virtually everyone agrees that Shaw is a master of the craft of storytelling, his contributions to the development of the modern short story have yet to be properly understood and evaluated. If Shaw had produced nothing but the body of work collected in *Short Stories: Five Decades,* he would be a writer of lasting importance. The volume constitutes perhaps the best evidence that Irwin Shaw has been, for nearly a half-century, a thoroughly professional writer.

Notes and References

Chapter One

1. Interview with Irwin Shaw, Southampton, New York, July 1980.
2. Ibid.
3. Stanley J. Kunitz and Howard Haycraft, eds., *Twentieth Century Authors* (New York, 1942), pp. 1270–71.
4. Interview with Irwin Shaw, July 1980.
5. Ibid.
6. *Literary Digest*, 2 May 1936, p. 19.
7. Ibid.
8. *Time,* 27 April 1936, p. 56.
9. Interview with Irwin Shaw, July 1980.
10. Ibid.
11. Willie Morris and Lucas Matthiessen, "Irwin Shaw: The Art of Fiction IV, continued," *Paris Review* 21 (Spring 1979): 248–62.
12. Ibid., pp. 259–61.
13. Interview with Irwin Shaw, July 1980.
14. Ibid.
15. Irwin Shaw and Ronald Searle, *Paris! Paris!* (New York, 1976, 1977), pp. 198–99.
16. Interview with Irwin Shaw, July 1980.
17. Ibid.
18. Morris and Matthiessen, "Irwin Shaw," p. 250.
19. Leslie A. Fiedler, "Irwin Shaw: Adultery, the Last Politics," *Commentary* 22 (July 1956): 71–74.
20. Lionel Trilling, "Some Are Gentle, Some Are Not," *Saturday Review*, 9 June 1951, pp. 8–9.
21. William Peden, "Best of Irwin Shaw," *Saturday Review*, 18 November 1950, pp. 27–28.
22. Morris and Matthiessen, "Irwin Shaw," p. 250.
23. Interview with Irwin Shaw, July 1980.
24. Trilling, "Some Are Gentle," p. 8.
25. Interview with Irwin Shaw, July 1980.
26. Ibid.

Chapter Two

1. Interview with Irwin Shaw, July 1980.
2. Ibid.
3. *Literary Digest*, 2 May 1936, p. 19.
4. *Theatre Arts* 20 (June 1936): 460.
5. Stark Young, *New Republic*, 13 May 1936, p. 21.
6. Joseph Wood Krutch, *Nation*, 6 May 1936, pp. 592–93.
7. *Time*, 27 April 1936, p. 56.
8. John Gassner, "Introduction," *20 Best Plays of the Modern American Theater, 1930–1939* (New York, 1939), pp. viii–ix.
9. Ibid., p. x.
10. Ibid., p. xx.
11. *Bury the Dead*, in *20 Best Plays of the Modern American Theater, 1930–1939*, ed. John Gassner (New York, 1939), p. 740. All subsequent references to this work will be cited in the text.
12. *Time,* 27 April 1936, p. 56.
13. George Jean Nathan, "Two Up, One Down," *Newsweek,* 16 January 1939, p. 26.
14. *Theatre Arts Monthly* 23 (March 1939): 170.
15. *Time,* 16 January 1939, p. 41.
16. Gassner, "Introduction," p. xxi.
17. "Prefatory Note," *The Gentle People* (New York, 1939). All subsequent references to this work will be cited in the text.
18. "Broadway in Review," *Theatre Arts* 29 (December 1945): 685.
19. Stark Young, "Assorted Murders," *New Republic*, 29 October 1945, p. 573.
20. *The Assassin* (New York, 1946), p. 28. All subsequent references to this work will be cited in the text.

Chapter Three

1. Irwin Shaw, "Introduction," *Short Stories: Five Decades* (New York, 1978), p. xii.
2. Ibid.
3. Ibid., p. xi.
4. *Short Stories: Five Decades,* pp. 62–68. *Short Stories: Five Decades* will be considered the standard collection of Irwin Shaw's short fiction, and all stories contained in it will subsequently be noted in the text with the abbreviation *SSFD*.

5. Cleanth Brooks and Robert Penn Warren, *Understanding Fiction,* 2d ed. (New York, 1958), pp. 89–90.

6. *Short Stories of Irwin Shaw* (New York, 1966), pp. 590–94. Stories contained in this collection and not in *Short Stories: Five Decades* will subsequently be noted in the text with the abbreviation *SSIS*.

7. Interview with Irwin Shaw, Wainscott, New York, August 1978.

8. *In the Company of Dolphins* (New York, 1964), p. 108.

9. Irwin Shaw and Ronald Searle, *Paris! Paris!* (New York, 1976, 1977), pp. 198–99.

Chapter Four

1. *Writers at Work: The Paris Review Interviews, 5th Series,* ed. George Plimpton (Middlesex, England, and New York: Penguin Books, 1981), p. 143.

2. John W. Aldridge, *After the Lost Generation* (New York, 1951), pp. 149–50.

3. Peter G. Jones, *War and the Novelist* (Columbia: University of Missouri Press, 1976), pp. 140–41.

4. *The Young Lions* (New York, 1948), p. 101. All subsequent references to this work will be cited in the text.

5. Aldridge, *After the Lost Generation,* pp. 149–53.

6. Jones, *War and the Novelist,* p. 143.

7. Interview with Irwin Shaw, August 1978.

8. Aldridge, *After the Lost Generation,* p. 153.

9. *Writers at Work,* p. 152.

10. Interview with Irwin Shaw, August 1978.

11. Ibid.

Chapter Five

1. Diana Trilling, "Fiction in Review," *Nation,* 9 October 1948, pp. 409–10.

2. Ihab Hassan, *Radical Innocence: The Contemporary American Novel* (Princeton, N.J.: Princeton University Press, 1961), p. 294.

3. Leslie Fiedler, "Saul Bellow," *Prairie Schooner*, Summer 1957, p. 107.

4. Leslie A. Fiedler, "Irwin Shaw: Adultery, the Last Politics," *Commentary* 22 (July 1956): 71–74.

5. Chester E. Eisinger, *Fiction of the Forties* (Chicago, 1963), p. 109.

6. Fiedler, "Irwin Shaw," p. 73.

7. William Startt, "Irwin Shaw: An Extended Talent," *Midwest Quarterly* 2 (Summer 1961): 325–37.

8. *Lucy Crown* (New York, 1960), pp. 316–17. All subsequent references to this work will be cited in the text.

9. *Two Weeks in Another Town* (New York, 1960), pp. 316–19. All subsequent references to this work will be cited in the text.

10. Interview with Irwin Shaw, July 1980.

11. Bergen Evans, "Irwin Shaw," *English Journal* 40 (November 1951): 485–91.

12. Interview with Irwin Shaw, July 1980.

13. *The Troubled Air* (New York: 1951), p. 66. All subsequent references to this work will be cited in the text.

14. Dorothy Commins, *What Is an Editor? Saxe Commins at Work* (Chicago, 1978), pp. 149–52.

15. Startt, "Irwin Shaw," pp. 331–32.

16. Interview with Irwin Shaw, July 1980.

17. Ibid.

18. *Evening in Byzantium* (New York, 1973), pp. 12–13. All subsequent references to this work will be cited in the text.

19. Interview with Irwin Shaw, July 1980.

20. *Voices of a Summer Day* (New York, 1965), p. 8. All subsequent references to this work will be cited in the text.

21. Interview with Irwin Shaw, July 1980.

22. *Nightwork* (New York, 1975), pp. 16–17. All subsequent references to this work will be cited in the text.

23. Interview with Irwin Shaw, July 1980.

24. Ibid.

25. Ibid.

26. *The Top of the Hill* (New York, 1979), pp. 12–14. All subsequent references to this work will be cited in the text.

Chapter Six

1. "Author's Note," *Beggarman, Thief* (New York, 1977). All subsequent references to this work will be cited in the text.

2. *Rich Man, Poor Man* (New York, 1970), p. 25. All subsequent references to this work will be cited in the text.

3. Interview with Irwin Shaw, July 1980.

Chapter Seven

1. Interview with Irwin Shaw, July 1980.

2. For a good discussion of the relationship of this group of writers to "modern American fiction," see James M. Mellard, *The Exploded Form: The Modernist Novel in America* (Urbana: University of Illinois Press, 1980).

3. Ross Wetzsteon, "Irwin Shaw: The Conflict between Big Bucks and Good Books," *Saturday Review,* August 1981, pp. 12–17.

4. *Bread Upon the Waters* (New York, 1981), p. 4. All subsequent references to this work will be cited in the text.

5. Wetzsteon, "Big Bucks and Good Books," p. 17.

6. Interview with Irwin Shaw, July 1980.

Selected Bibliography

PRIMARY SOURCES

1. Novels

Acceptable Losses. New York: Delacorte Press, 1982.

Beggarman, Thief. New York: Delacorte Press, 1977.

Bread Upon the Waters. New York: Delacorte Press, 1981.

Evening in Byzantium. New York: Delacorte Press, 1973.

Lucy Crown. New York: Random House, 1956.

Nightwork. New York: Delacorte Press, 1975.

Rich Man, Poor Man. New York: Delacorte Press, 1970.

The Top of the Hill. New York: Delacorte Press, 1979.

The Troubled Air. New York: Random House, 1951.

Two Weeks in Another Town. New York: Random House, 1960.

Voices of a Summer Day. New York: Dial Press, 1965.

The Young Lions. New York: Random House, 1948. Modern Library edition published in 1958.

2. Short-Story Collections

Act of Faith and Other Stories. New York: Random House, 1946.

God Was Here But He Left Early. New York: Anchor Books, Doubleday, 1973.

Love on a Dark Street. New York: Delacorte Press, 1965.

Mixed Company. New York: Random House, 1950.

Sailor off the Bremen and Other Stories. New York: Random House, 1939.

Selected Short Stories of Irwin Shaw. New York: Modern Library, Random House, 1961.

Short Stories: Five Decades. New York: Delacorte Press, 1978.

Short Stories of Irwin Shaw. New York: Random House, 1966.

Tip on a Dead Jockey and Other Stories. New York: Random House, 1957.

Welcome to the City and Other Stories. New York: Random House, 1942.

3. Published Plays

The Assassin. New York: Random House, 1946.

Bury the Dead. New York: Random House, 1939. Reprinted in John Gassner, ed. *20 Best Plays of the Modern American Theater, 1930–1939.* New York: Crown, 1939.

Children from Their Games. London: Samuel French, 1962.

The Gentle People. New York: Random House, 1939.

Sons and Soldiers. New York: Random House, 1944.

4. Unpublished Plays

"Patate" (Adaptation of play by Marcel Archard). 1958.

"Quiet City." 1939.

"Retreat to Pleasure." 1940. With Peter Viertel.

"Siege." 1937.

"The Survivors." 1948. With Peter Viertel.

5. Nonfiction

In the Company of Dolphins. New York: Bernard Geis Associates, 1964.

Paris! Paris! New York: Harcourt Brace, Jovanovich, 1976, 1977. With Ronald Searle.

Report on Israel. New York: Simon and Schuster, 1950. With Robert Capa.

SECONDARY SOURCES

1. Biographical

Alpert, Hollis. "The Joys of Uncertainty." *Saturday Review*, December 1962, pp. 16–17. Account of Shaw's writing and producing of the film *In the French Style.*

Commins, Dorothy. *What Is an Editor? Saxe Commins at Work.* Chicago: University of Chicago Press, 1978. Biography of Shaw's Random House editor. Contains account of Shaw's problems in the writing of *Lucy Crown.*

Kunitz, Stanley J., and Haycraft, Howard, eds. *Twentieth Century Authors: A Biographical Dictionary.* New York: H. W. Wilson, 1942, pp. 1270–71. Valuable for information concerning Shaw's early work in the theater.

"Shaw Strikes Back." *Newsweek,* 5 November 1961, pp. 109–11. Account of Shaw's writing and producing of the film *In the French Style.* Contains interesting interview concerning the difficulties of the writer in Hollywood.

2. Criticism

Aldridge, John W. *After the Lost Generation.* New York: Noonday Press, 1951. Negative analysis of *The Young Lions,* particularly attacking the structure of the novel: "a system of carefully contained parallels, near-parallels, and pseudo parallels" which give only an "appearance of unity."

"The Assassin." *Theatre Arts* 29 (December 1945): 679, 684–85. One of few favorable and perceptive reviews of *The Assassin*: ". . . in spite of its shortcomings, it provided an evening of intelligent interest as well as theatric pleasures in acting, writing and mise-en-scène. This, in a period given over almost exclusively to mediocrity, was much to be thankful for."

Brooks, Cleanth, and Warren, Robert Penn. *Understanding Fiction: Second Edition.* New York: Appleton-Century-Crofts, 1959. Contains analysis of "The Girls in Their Summer Dresses": "This story is a very good example of the compact, well-made short story. . . . The conclusion is quick and sharp. The point is clear and carries with its little ironic turn, a serious idea—the failure of love through the failure to recognize the beloved as a person, as more than a convenience."

Eisinger, Chester E. *Fiction of the Forties.* Chicago: University of Chicago Press, 1963. Contains a largely negative assessment of Shaw which repeats the common charges of slickness and "superficiality" in his fiction. Still, Eisinger adds: "He is of inestimable value, without regard for the quality of his fiction, for the close way he works with the surface of his society and gives so much of the range of its manners. He does not penetrate to its heart, but he knows its surface tensions and the ready conversational currency it exchanges for ideas."

Evans, Bergen. "Irwin Shaw." *English Journal* 40 (November 1951): 485–91. Largely positive analysis of *The Young Lions*: "Whatever faults may be found with the book's 'message,' it remains a good, perhaps a great war book." Also remarks of Shaw's short stories that "where his pity overcomes his self-restraint and still evades his indignation, he has produced some of the best short stories in contemporary literature."

Fiedler, Leslie A. "Irwin Shaw: Adultery, the Last Politics." *Commentary* 22 (July 1956): 71–74. The most influential critical attack on Shaw, it contains the charge that he produces a "half-art": "[Shaw's books] remain still slickness and sentimentality, never reach the outrageous level of imagination and poetry. If mere 'decency' of intent could redeem banality, Shaw would be a first-rate writer rather than a symptom."

———. "Saul Bellow." *Prairie Schooner,* Summer 1957, pp. 103–10. The essay in which Fiedler classified Shaw as a "middle middle-brow" Jewish writer.

Gardiner, Harold C., S. J. *Fifty Years of the American Novel: A Christian Appraisal.* New York: Charles Scribner's Sons, 1951. Contains mixed analysis of *The Young Lions*: it is "the most ambitious and spacious of the [World War II] novels," but "the contrived over-all structure breaks down into a series of effective single episodes which do not have forward momentum."

Jones, Peter G. *War and the Novelist: Appraising the American War Novel.* Columbia: University of Missouri Press, 1976. Contains a highly favorable analysis of *The Young Lions*. Jones is one of the first critics to detect the novel's allegorical unity; he finds a subtle mythological substructure which creates "a tightly integrated book."

Krutch, Joseph Wood. "Over Most of These Stations." *Nation,* 15 May 1943, pp. 714–16. Negative review of *Sons and Soldiers* in which Krutch dismisses, in retrospect, *Bury the Dead* and *The Gentle People*. Interesting as an example of the critical failure to comprehend the element of fantasy in Shaw's early plays.

Peden, William. "Best of Irwin Shaw." *Saturday Review,* 18 November 1950, pp. 27–28. Highly favorable review of Shaw's short-story collection, *Mixed Company,* and of his overall achievement: "Like Dickens, Mr. Shaw has created, prodigally, a crowded gallery of memorable people. Like Dickens, too, he handles scenes superbly. . . ."

Saal, Herbert. "Disenchanted Men." *Saturday Review,* 3 August 1957, pp. 12–13. Negative review of short-story collection *Tip on a Dead Jockey;* but contains highly favorable comments about Shaw's earlier short fiction: "Did any writer of that prewar time have a better eye and ear for what went on around him? Shaw cared, and his characters cared about politics and injustice and loneliness and love and growing up and growing old. They (and clearly he) believed fiercely in what Faulkner was later to spell out: 'that man will not merely endure: he will prevail.' "

"Savage Sputtering against War." *Literary Digest,* 2 May 1936, p. 19. Not untypical review of *Bury the Dead,* describing it as a major revolutionary moment in the American theater. Contains this comment about Shaw: "He is being hailed as a new magician in the contemporary theater. A young, blistering dramatist with scourging things to say."

Startt, William. "Irwin Shaw: An Extended Talent." *Midwest Quarterly* 2 (Summer 1961):325–37. The most balanced and thorough essay yet published on Shaw. Argues that Shaw is a natural dramatist and short-story writer whose talent is sometimes strained by the demands of the novel, but that *Two Weeks in Another Town* is a serious, much underrated, novel.

Trilling, Diana. "Fiction in Review." *Nation*, 9 October 1948, pp. 409–10. Mixed review of *The Young Lions*, which Trilling, nevertheless, finds preferable to Shaw's "plays or his much-admired short stories."

Trilling, Lionel. "Some Are Gentle, Some Are Not." *Saturday Review*, 9 June 1951, pp. 8–9. Primarily a negative review of *The Troubled Air*. Most important, however, as an answer to the Aldridge-Fiedler school of critics who attack Shaw's sincerity: "... nothing Mr. Shaw might write could be wholly lacking in interest of one kind or another. For one thing, he always *does* observe and always *does* feel, and even when he is facile in observation and sentiment he is not insincere." Perceptively described Shaw as a "moral" spokesman for "the gentle people."

Wetzsteon, Ross. "Irwin Shaw: The Conflict between Big Bucks and Good Books." *Saturday Review*, August 1981, pp. 12–17. Review-essay focusing upon *Bread Upon the Waters*, but more significant for its call for a reassessment of Shaw's entire work. Emphasizes that Shaw has consistently been a writer of "moral fables" and that he has been critically underrated because of his devotion to telling "'*stories*.'"

Young, Stark. "Assorted Murders." *New Republic*, 29 October 1945, p. 573. Mixed review of *The Assassin*. Young still was one of the few critics to perceive Shaw's main intention of creating "an intelligent hero who can express himself and whose motives are both complex and intense."

———. "Current Slapping." *New Republic*, 8 April 1946, pp. 479–80. Refutation of Shaw's attack on the Broadway critics contained in the preface to the published version of *The Assassin*: "A great deal that Mr. Irwin Shaw says of the theatre situation, and of the critics, is certainly true.... But neither he himself in this Preface nor his works are convincing."

———. "The Great Doom's Image." *New Republic*, 13 May 1936, p. 21. Largely favorable review of *Bury the Dead*: "'Bury the Dead'"...

presents the finest image that has appeared in our theatre this year. . . . Not often in drama anywhere do we find so powerful an image as dominates the whole of 'Bury the Dead.' A myth is created, a veritable fable is established."

3. Interviews

Morris, Willie, and Matthiessen, Lucas. "Irwin Shaw: The Art of Fiction IV, continued." *Paris Review* 21 (Spring 1979):248-62.

Writers at Work: The Paris Review Interviews, 5th Series. Interviews by John Phillips and George Plimpton and by Willie Morris and Lucas Matthiessen. Middlesex, England, and New York: Penguin Books, 1981.

Index

FINKELSTEIN MEMORIAL LIBRARY